I0010367

Mastering Redmine
Second Edition

An expert's guide to open source project management with Redmine

Andriy Lesyuk

BIRMINGHAM - MUMBAI

Mastering Redmine
Second Edition

Copyright © 2016 Packt Publishing

All rights reserved. No part of this book may be reproduced, stored in a retrieval system, or transmitted in any form or by any means, without the prior written permission of the publisher, except in the case of brief quotations embedded in critical articles or reviews.

Every effort has been made in the preparation of this book to ensure the accuracy of the information presented. However, the information contained in this book is sold without warranty, either express or implied. Neither the author(s), nor Packt Publishing, and its dealers and distributors will be held liable for any damages caused or alleged to be caused directly or indirectly by this book.

Packt Publishing has endeavored to provide trademark information about all of the companies and products mentioned in this book by the appropriate use of capitals. However, Packt Publishing cannot guarantee the accuracy of this information.

First published: January 2013

Second edition: May 2016

Production reference: 1260516

Published by Packt Publishing Ltd.
Livery Place
35 Livery Street
Birmingham B3 2PB, UK.

ISBN 978-1-78588-130-5

www.packtpub.com

Credits

Author
Andriy Lesyuk

Reviewer
Ilya Lyamkin

Commissioning Editor
Amarabha Banerjee

Acquisition Editor
Prachi Bisht

Content Development Editor
Shweta Pant

Technical Editor
Utkarsha S. Kadam

Copy Editor
Vikrant Phadke

Project Coordinator
Kinjal Bari

Proofreader
Safis Editing

Indexer
Mariammal Chettiyar

Production Coordinator
Nilesh Mohite

Cover Work
Nilesh Mohite

About the Author

Andriy Lesyuk is an open source evangelist. He is an enthusiastic and passionate developer with more than 14 years of experience. He is skilled in Ruby, PHP, Perl, C, and more. His primary areas of interest are web development and Linux system development. Andriy is also the author of more than 20 open source plugins for Redmine. He lives and works in Ivano-Frankivsk, Ukraine. His website is `http://www.andriylesyuk.com`. He started his career as an engineer at the Ivano-Frankivsk National Technical University of Oil and Gas, where he later became the head of the Software and Networking Laboratory. For some time, he worked as a freelancer, developing custom Redmine plugins for companies worldwide, the most famous of which is oDesk. Later, Andriy joined the Kayako team, which develops the world's leading helpdesk solutions.

About the Reviewer

Ilya Lyamkin is a full-stack developer with a passion for JavaScript on the client and the server. He likes everything that has to do with web design and development and he feels creating something new and important.

During the last couple of years, Ilya has developed various web applications and helped to make the internal overtime management system at T-Systems RUS.

To get in touch with him, you can visit his website, `http://lyamkin.com`.

He is the founder of CVPicker (`https://cvpicker.ru`), a SaaS platform designed to simplify the process of hiring.

I am grateful to the author for patiently listening to my critique. Special thanks to my parents, without whom I would have never grown to love learning as much as I do.

Last but not least, I would like to thank my workfellows, Den Patin and Pavel Gordon, for their friendship and for facilitating the completion of my high workload.

www.PacktPub.com

eBooks, discount offers, and more

Did you know that Packt offers eBook versions of every book published, with PDF and ePub files available? You can upgrade to the eBook version at www.PacktPub.com and as a print book customer, you are entitled to a discount on the eBook copy. Get in touch with us at customercare@packtpub.com for more details.

At www.PacktPub.com, you can also read a collection of free technical articles, sign up for a range of free newsletters and receive exclusive discounts and offers on Packt books and eBooks.

https://www2.packtpub.com/books/subscription/packtlib

Do you need instant solutions to your IT questions? PacktLib is Packt's online digital book library. Here, you can search, access, and read Packt's entire library of books.

Why subscribe?

- Fully searchable across every book published by Packt
- Copy and paste, print, and bookmark content
- On demand and accessible via a web browser

Table of Contents

Preface

This book describes the functionality and capabilities of Redmine, reveals its secrets, and gives tips on how to use it effectively. Here, you will find all the information needed to install, configure, use, and master this application. As the book is intended to be a practical guide, it also pays special attention to practical examples of using Redmine.

Additionally, you will find mentions of some third-party plugins in chapters and sections where they are pertinent. We will also review five of them in *Chapter 10, Plugins and Themes*.

Redmine is a very powerful and an extremely flexible project management tool and issue tracker. As it comes with many great features for working with projects, it is also often used as an application for project hosting. It's free, open source, built on the popular Ruby on Rails framework, and has a strong community.

What this book covers

Chapter 1, Getting Familiar with Redmine, prepares us for the next chapters by briefly going through the concept of the Redmine interface and reviewing replaceable components of the application.

Chapter 2, Installing Redmine, includes detailed instructions on how to install Redmine in two different ways, each of which is preferable for different purposes. Additionally, it mentions some other ways to easily install Redmine.

Chapter 3, Configuring Redmine, reviews the configuration options, which are available on the **Settings** page in the **Administration** menu, and covers the advanced options that are concealed behind them. Also, this chapter contains a section that describes how to troubleshoot problems in the application.

Chapter 4, Issue Tracking, reviews what makes Redmine one of the best issue trackers, also paying heed to the configuration options that are related to issue tracking.

Chapter 5, Managing Projects, covers the major part of Redmine functionality, which is related to projects, and demonstrates why this is one of the best applications for project hosting.

Chapter 6, Text Formatting, is a comprehensive tutorial for the Redmine rich text formatting syntax, which is used all over Redmine. This chapter mainly describes Textile (one of the supported markup languages), at the same time mentioning analogs in Markdown.

Chapter 7, Access Control and Workflow, is aimed at enlightening the permission system and the issue life cycle by explaining what the role, tracker, and issue status are and how they are connected.

Chapter 8, Time Tracking, describes the time tracking capabilities of Redmine and shows how to work with time reports.

Chapter 9, Personalization, will help you make Redmine more comfortable for yourself and ensure that you'll be notified about events that are important or interesting for you. Additionally, this chapter describes how third-party user accounts can be used to access Redmine.

Chapter 10, Plugins and Themes, guides the readers to find plugins for a particular version of Redmine, covers installation of plugins and themes, and reviews some plugins and themes.

Chapter 11, Customizing Redmine, shows the power of custom fields and shows how to customize Redmine without breaking upgrade compatibility. In particular, this chapter explains how to create a simple theme and plugin.

Appendix, Quick Syntax Reference, contains a brief list of syntax rules that are supported by Redmine's Wiki syntax. This reference includes the syntax rules of Textile and Markdown.

What you need for this book

For this book, you need access to a Redmine installation (or you will need to install it as described in *Chapter 2, Installing Redmine*). It's better if you are an administrator of the installation.

This book describes Redmine 3.2.x. However, earlier versions should also be fine.

Who this book is for

This book is for anyone who already uses or plans to use Redmine. But its readers should consider that some of the discussed topics are specific to the software industry (Redmine can be used for other industries as well). As the book sometimes describes things that require privileged access, it will be especially useful for project managers and administrators. No prior knowledge of Redmine is required.

Conventions

In this book, you will find a number of text styles that distinguish between different kinds of information. Here are some examples of these styles and an explanation of their meaning.

Code words in text, folder names, filenames, file extensions, pathnames, dummy URLs, user input, and so on are shown as follows: ".rb is the extension for Ruby files."

A block of code is set as follows:

```
<VirtualHost *:80>
        RailsEnv production
        DocumentRoot /opt/redmine/redmine-3.2.0/public
        <Directory "/opt/redmine/redmine-3.2.0/public">
                Allow from all
                Require all granted
        </Directory>
</VirtualHost>
```

Any command-line input or output is written as follows:

```
$ sudo service apache2 reload
```

New terms and **important words** are shown in bold. Words that you see on the screen, for example, in menus or dialog boxes, appear in the text like this: "Then select the **Information** page from the sidebar."

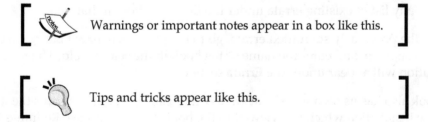

Warnings or important notes appear in a box like this.

Tips and tricks appear like this.

Reader feedback

Feedback from our readers is always welcome. Let us know what you think about this book—what you liked or disliked. Reader feedback is important for us as it helps us develop titles that you will really get the most out of.

To send us general feedback, simply e-mail feedback@packtpub.com, and mention the book's title in the subject of your message.

If there is a topic that you have expertise in and you are interested in either writing or contributing to a book, see our author guide at www.packtpub.com/authors.

Customer support

Now that you are the proud owner of a Packt book, we have a number of things to help you to get the most from your purchase.

Downloading the color images of this book

We also provide you with a PDF file that has color images of the screenshots/ diagrams used in this book. The color images will help you better understand the changes in the output. You can download this file from https://www.packtpub. com/sites/default/files/downloads/MasteringRedmine_ColorImages.pdf.

Errata

Although we have taken every care to ensure the accuracy of our content, mistakes do happen. If you find a mistake in one of our books—maybe a mistake in the text or the code—we would be grateful if you could report this to us. By doing so, you can save other readers from frustration and help us improve subsequent versions of this book. If you find any errata, please report them by visiting http://www.packtpub. com/submit-errata, selecting your book, clicking on the **Errata Submission Form** link, and entering the details of your errata. Once your errata are verified, your submission will be accepted and the errata will be uploaded to our website or added to any list of existing errata under the Errata section of that title.

To view the previously submitted errata, go to https://www.packtpub.com/books/ content/support and enter the name of the book in the search field. The required information will appear under the **Errata** section.

This book also has its own website at mastering-redmine.com that runs the Redmine installation which is reviewed in the book. So, you can use Redmine on this website to submit errata as well.

Piracy

Piracy of copyrighted material on the Internet is an ongoing problem across all media. At Packt, we take the protection of our copyright and licenses very seriously. If you come across any illegal copies of our works in any form on the Internet, please provide us with the location address or website name immediately so that we can pursue a remedy.

Please contact us at copyright@packtpub.com with a link to the suspected pirated material.

We appreciate your help in protecting our authors and our ability to bring you valuable content.

Questions

If you have a problem with any aspect of this book, you can contact us at questions@packtpub.com, and we will do our best to address the problem.

Discussions

You can also discuss this book on its website using the message board that can be found at mastering-redmine.com/projects/book/boards.

1
Getting Familiar with Redmine

When we are about to try out a new web application, we often look for experts who are familiar with it to ask what they would recommend for use, for example, which database backend, platform, and so on. That's actually what this chapter will also do. It will let you know which options are available and help you understand which of them fit your needs better than others.

The power of Redmine is in its components. Some of them affect performance, while others influence functionality. Such components are the options that are discussed in this chapter. I'm quite sure that even experienced users will discover new options here and may decide to switch to or utilize them. In this chapter, you will also find a quick tour through the Redmine interface. It's going to be short as I believe this interface is easy to learn. Anyway, you'll be able to play with the interface more in the next chapters, where we'll discuss how to install and use Redmine.

In this chapter, we will cover the following topics:

- What is Redmine?
- Walking through the Redmine interface
- MySQL, PostgreSQL, SQLite, or Microsoft SQL Server
- Textile or Markdown
- Selecting a **Source Control Management (SCM)**
- Selecting a web server and an application server
- Redmine versions
- Forks

What is Redmine?

If you search for a free project management tool, most likely you will find Redmine. This is an open source Ruby on Rails web application. It can be considered to be the de facto flagship of project management solutions in the open source world. It supports all that you need for effective project management: scheduling, calendars, Gantt charts, roadmaps, version management, document management, news, files, directories, activity views, member roles, permission management based on roles, and so on. With its third-party plugins, you can also get invoice management, Scrum backlogs, Kanban boards, burn down charts, and much more. But it's not just a matter of project management.

It's hard to conclude whether Redmine is more of a project management tool or an issue tracker. Ideally, a good issue tracker must come with some project management features. And in Redmine, these two components are combined flawlessly. However, what makes it a perfect issue tracking application is the fully configurable workflow, which lets you set permissions to change issue statuses and field values for each role-tracker pair individually (here, **tracker** is an issue type in Redmine terms). As an issue tracker, Redmine also supports essential issue tracking features such as priorities, subtasks, subscribing, commenting, custom fields, filters, and more.

Anyone who has worked in a team will understand the importance of project documentation. For this purpose, many teams even establish dedicated Wiki sites and Redmine ships with its own per-project Wiki system. This system supports a special markup language and source code syntax highlighting. However, the staggering thing is that the same Wiki syntax is supported throughout Redmine—in issue descriptions, comments, news, and so on. Additionally, this syntax allows us to create cross links to other issues and projects.

Redmine can also serve as a support system. Thus, it comes with a simple bulletin board module, which allows you to have as many forums in a project as you need. Then, each forum can have any number of threads. And finally, forums and threads can be **watched**.

To host your projects, in addition to the aforementioned features, you would probably want Redmine to be able to integrate with version control systems. Such a feature is also available. Thus, the special module allows Redmine to be used as a source code browser. But, this module also integrates flawlessly into other Redmine components such as the issue tracker and Wiki. For example, an issue can be associated with code revisions, a Wiki page can link to a revision, a commit, a source file, and so on. With some additional plugins, Redmine can even be turned into a repository manager. The list of supported version control systems is also impressive: Subversion (SVN), Git, CVS, Mercurial, Bazaar, and Darcs.

All of these allow Redmine to be used as a project hosting platform by many individuals and organizations. And by the way, it's not limited to a single project—it is multiproject, and each project can have any number of subprojects to any nesting level. Many companies also utilize Redmine's collaborative capabilities for forge or labs sites. Moreover, its usage is not limited to software development. Other companies use Redmine for customer support, order fulfillment, task management, document management, and more.

I cannot describe Redmine without mentioning the people who created this fabulous software. As soon as you open Redmine, at the bottom of each page (near the copyright section), you can see the name of its primary author – Jean-Philippe Lang. A huge contribution to Redmine was also made by Toshi Maruyama and Eric Davis.

Why Redmine succeeds?

The previous section might have created the impression that Redmine is an all-in-one software application. To some extent, it is. It was the evolution of Redmine that made it look like this. It is extremely popular these days, and that's why it constantly gets new features. But what makes it so popular?

Having first seen Redmine, I got the impression that it was a very easy-to-use and friendly application. It is not overloaded with design and UI elements and everything seems to be in its place. This helps users get used to Redmine and like it at first sight. The very first time I saw Redmine, I also thought that perhaps it was too limited for my needs, mainly because it looked too simple. Eventually, it appeared that both of my assumptions were wrong: it's not easy-to-use software and it's not limited. The ease of the look and feel, however, does its job. So, if you need only the basic features, you are ready to use Redmine right after you have seen it for the first time. But when you need more advanced features, you need to spend some time to learn them. That's the main thing that makes Redmine so popular, I believe.

The right tools are built with the right technologies. What makes Redmine so "right" is Ruby and Rails. Ruby is known as, perhaps, the most modern metaprogramming and truly object-oriented language. This programming language is very flexible and is considered to allow building powerful applications fast and easily. The same can be said about Redmine. The same can be said about Ruby on Rails (or just Rails) as well. Rails is a web framework like Symfony and Zend Framework, but unlike others, it is the de facto standard for Ruby, the language it is written in. The names Ruby and Rails are so closely associated that many people believe they are the same language. You can treat Rails as a construction set for building web services such as Redmine. Also, Ruby on Rails became the source of inspiration for many other frameworks and libraries, such as CakePHP and Grails. Redmine is built on this technology and this is what makes it so good.

But what exactly is in Ruby on Rails that makes it good? Ruby (and therefore Ruby on Rails) supports metaprogramming. It's a technique that allows an application to modify its own code (that is, itself) at runtime. This means that there is almost nothing in Redmine that cannot be altered programmatically. Usually, the API of an application is limited to some functionality, but there are no such limitations in Ruby, thanks to metaprogramming. This makes the Redmine plugin API extremely flexible.

Thereby, we come to the next thing that makes Redmine so popular — its plugins. If you are familiar with Ruby and Ruby on Rails, you only need to learn little to start developing Redmine plugins. Taking into account the fact that Ruby on Rails is very popular nowadays, Redmine has a huge number of potential developers. Therefore, it has a large variety of plugins. Thus, with its plugins, you can even turn Redmine into a CRM or helpdesk. By the way, some of its plugins will be reviewed in *Chapter 10, Plugins and Themes*.

There is a recognized issue of incompatibility between some Redmine versions and some plugins. The Redmine plugin API and Rails API used to change from version to version without good backwards compatibility. This is especially critical as many plugins use metaprogramming to alter non-API (core) functionality (and, in fact, it's impossible to preserve full backwards compatibility in such cases). Thus, this issue can be seen in Redmine 3.0, which switches from Rails 3 to Rails 4. Hence, when selecting a plugin, you should always check whether it is compatible with the Redmine version you are using.

The last but not least important benefits are that Redmine is cross-platform, open source, and freely available. Open source code and the GPL license make any modification possible. Nothing limits you from making Redmine better fit your needs.

Walking through the Redmine interface

It's always better to meet rather than just hear about. I cannot imagine a person who is familiar with Redmine but who has never seen it. So, let's start by checking out the Redmine interface.

As mentioned earlier, Redmine has an easy-to-use and simple user interface. The following screenshot shows its **Home** page:

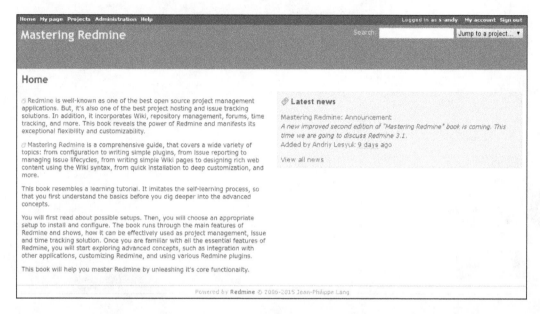

In the top-left corner of the page, we have the global menu (**Home**, **My page**, and so on). To the right-hand side of the global menu, we have the account menu (**Logged in as**). These menus are repeated on every page of Redmine. The blue area below these menus contains the site title. The content area contains the site introduction and recent news for all projects.

Generally, a page in Redmine can be either a global one (the previous screenshot) or a project one:

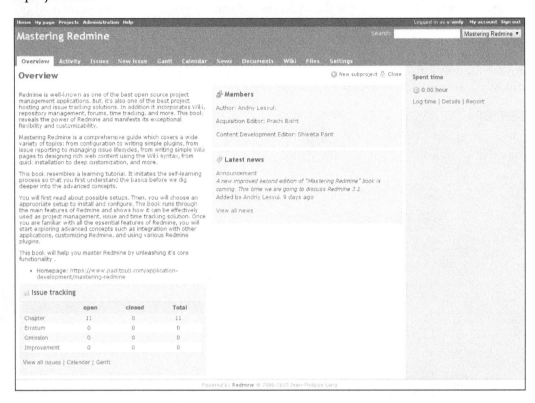

This is the start page of the project, which is also referenced as the project home page. Most of the time, when working with Redmine, you will be interacting with project pages. The blue top area on a project page contains the project title. The project menu is displayed in this area below the title. The project home page contains the description of the project, issues summary, members summary, and latest news of the project. Most project pages also include the sidebar with some contextual information, such as links, and sometimes forms.

As one of the primary features of Redmine is issue tracking, let's check out the issue list:

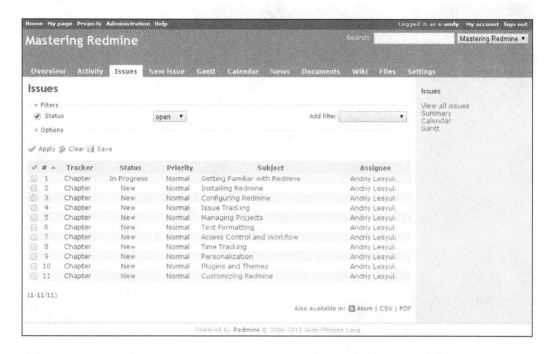

As you can see, the layout is quite simple and friendly. Collapsible boxes such as **Filters** and **Options** are used all over Redmine to hide rarely used elements. If table headers contain links, as in this case, they can be used to change the order of rows. Below the issue listing, you can see export links (near **Also available in:**). Such links are usually provided if the content can be exported to other formats.

The following screenshot illustrates the issue page:

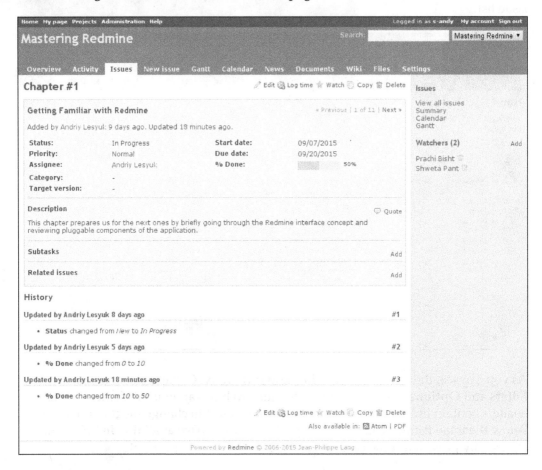

In the top-right corner of the content area of this page, you can see the contextual menu, which is also duplicated at the bottom of the page. Similar contextual menus are also used for many other Redmine objects such as projects, Wiki pages, and so on.

The issue page is an example of a Redmine page that contains multiple hidden forms. Thus, such a form can be activated if you click on the **Edit**, **Quote**, and **Add** links (all three links open the same form). Trash icons near **Watchers** are another common Redmine interface element that can be used to delete an object.

By the way, some hidden forms, such as the one that can be activated by clicking on the **Add** link to the right of the **Watchers** heading on the sidebar, are shown in a light box:

Another interface element that is used extensively in Redmine is the tabular menu. Such a menu can be found on, for example, the project's **Settings** page:

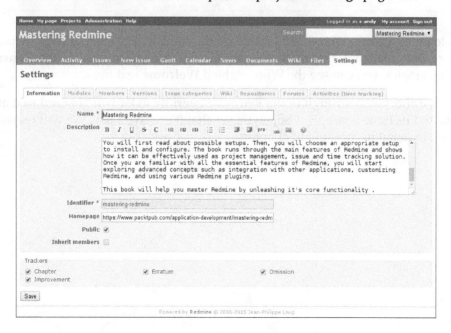

Here, you can see another interface element that is widely used in Redmine — the text area, which supports Wiki syntax. Such a text area usually comes with the text formatting toolbar.

The following screenshot illustrates the administration settings:

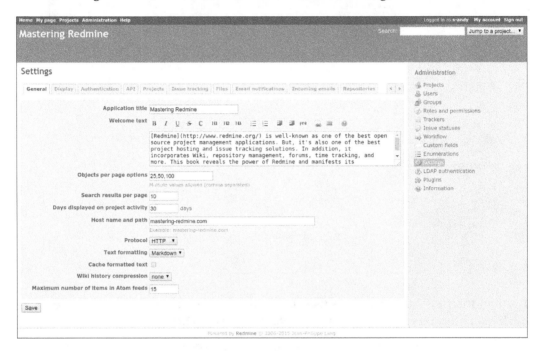

Links to administration pages are located on the sidebar. The current page, which is **Settings**, uses the tabular menu that we saw in the project settings. On the **General** tab of this menu, you can see the Wiki-enabled **Welcome text** field.

This was a short walkthrough of the Redmine interface to let you get used to it and understand its basic concepts. I hope you see that it is easy to use. We will review the interface in detail in subsequent chapters.

MySQL, PostgreSQL, SQLite or Microsoft SQL Server

Redmine can be used with MySQL, PostgreSQL, SQLite or Microsoft SQL Server database backends (the first three ones are actually natively supported by Ruby on Rails). But which one should you select for your Redmine installation? It's perhaps too important a question to be ignored in this book. No, I'm not going to praise some databases or criticize others—that's out of scope here. Instead, I'll cover things that you should consider when choosing a database backend.

Having worked with Redmine for quite a long time, I have noticed that most users use it with MySQL. Despite their reasons for choosing it, this means that Redmine has been better tested with this database backend. This argument becomes even more important if we consider that some plugins use SQL directly (that is, without the Rails SQL query builder).

But if you are seeking a reliable source on which database is faster with Redmine, you can check out the Redmine build logs at `http://www.redmine.org/builds/index.html`. These logs contain results of tests for different versions of Ruby and different database backends. Thus, at the time of writing this section, tests of the latest revisions, r14600, r14597, and r14596, in the latest stable branch 3.1-stable were running for the following time periods (only for ruby-1.9.3-p194):

	mysql	postgresql	sqlite3	sqlserver
r14600	901.068992 s	752.914607 s	698.311900 s	1356.417375 s
r14597	684.866031 s	815.066303 s	636.497712 s	1056.660942 s
r14596	733.023295 s	781.173148 s	726.835502 s	1019.416963 s
Average	772.986106 s	783.051353 s	687.215038 s	1144.165093 s

In the previous table, I used the data from the aforementioned logs. Certainly, by the time you read this section, there will be new data, but as practice shows, the results will most likely be the same. Anyway, you can check out new data or take more revisions into account to recheck the results.

So, according to this data, SQLite is the fastest, SQL Server is the slowest, and PostgreSQL is a little slower than MySQL.

But don't hurry to make a decision in favor of the fastest backend. Unfortunately, SQLite has scalability issues (you can't put it on a separate server) and will behave incorrectly in a multiuser environment. And I'm quite sure that you'll want to serve many users at a time.

You should also note that in addition to the comparative slowness, Microsoft SQL Server runs only on Windows, its full edition is not free, and the free one (Express) is limited. Also, support for this database backend was added especially to Redmine and is not native to Rails. This means that it was not tested as well as other alternatives. Anyway, if you already have SQL Server running in your corporate network, it can be a good idea to use it for Redmine.

Textile or Markdown?

Good readability helps improve perception. Rich formatting is very important for issue tracking software as it allows us to highlight more important things, in this way drawing special attention to them. In Redmine, rich formatting can be achieved using a lightweight markup language—Textile or Markdown—and is supported almost in every text area. Both of these markup languages use plain-text formatting syntax.

Textile has been used by Redmine as the default and the only available formatter for many years. It is greatly supported and perfectly tested. Any experienced Redmine user is familiar with Textile and many Redmine plugins extend its syntax. Particularly for these reasons, the majority of Redmine installations, including the official website Redmine.org, use this formatter. So, most Redmine users definitely use Textile.

However, I did not see Textile being used by any other application except Redmine. On the contrary, Markdown seems to have become the de facto standard for rich formatting that is based on plain text. Thus, it is used by GitHub (in fact, it was GitHub that made it so popular) and Stack Overflow. It can be said that most developers who use a markup language use Markdown.

This means that for a fresh installation, if your target audience have not gotten used to Textile yet, you should probably select **Markdown**. Also, currently Redmine does not come with any converter from Textile to Markdown and I'm not sure whether it ever will (as it's complicated). So, if you choose Textile for your fresh installation, you will probably be tied to it forever. On the other hand, 3.1 is actually the first Redmine version for which the Markdown formatter is not considered to be experimental any more (it was added in 2.5). This means that this formatter has just entered the intensive testing phase (you can still help with this though). Another possible reason for keeping Textile as your formatter is that many existing Redmine users, if any of them are going to use your installation, will probably expect Textile to be used. So, generally you are better off asking your users.

But let's not be too verbose and compare the basic rules of these formatters:

	Textile	Markdown
Bold text	`*Bold*`	`**Bold**`
Italic text	`_Italic_`	`*Italic*`
Underline text	`+Underline+`	*Not available*
Inline code	`@inline code@`	`` `inline code` ``

Pre-formatted text	`<pre>`
	
	`...`
	
	`<pre>`
		`~~~`
		
		`...`
		
		`~~~`

Syntax highlighting	`<pre><code class="ruby">`
	
	`...`
	
	`</code></pre>`
		`~~~ ruby`
		
		`...`
		
		`~~~`

Bullet list	`* Item 1` `* Item 2`	`* Item 1` `* Item 2`
Numbered list	`# Item 1` `# Item 2`	`1. Item 1` `2. Item 2`

Headings	`h1. Heading 1`
	`h2. Heading 2`
	`...`
	`h6. Heading 6`
		`# Heading 1`
		`## Heading 2`
		`...`
		`###### Heading 6`

Links	`"Anchor":http://link`	`[Anchor](http://link)`
Images	`!image_url(Title)!`	`![Title](image_url)`

Tables	`|_.Table|_.Heading|`
	`|Cell    |Cell      |`
		`|Table|Heading|`
		`|-----|-------|`
		`|Cell |Cell    |`

Still, which one is more powerful? Markdown is known to be more feature rich in general as, for example, it supports some HTML tags. However, its Redmine implementation is limited. Thus, no HTML tags are actually supported under Redmine. This can nonetheless change in the future, of course. On the contrary, the long usage history of Textile by Redmine has made it more powerful at the moment. See also *Chapter 6, Text Formatting*.

Selecting a Source Control Management (SCM)

Source Control Management (SCM) is better known as revision control management. Redmine currently supports the following revision control systems: Subversion (SVN), Git, Mercurial, Bazaar, Darcs, and CVS.

As it has been mentioned, Redmine can use SCMs not just as source code readers. It can also associate a revision with issues (and have revisions listed on issue pages). It can close an issue automatically and/or change its done ratio when an appropriate commit is made to the repository. It allows us to use the Wiki syntax in commit messages. It also allows us to refer to a revision, a commit, or a file from any Wiki-syntax-powered content, which can be a Wiki page, an issue description, a project description, a forum message, and so on. But all this makes Redmine an (advanced) source code browser, not an SCM manager (which can be done with plugins though). Then why is choosing the right SCM so important?

Most likely, you will want a deeper integration between Redmine and SCMs as soon as you know the options. Thus, it can be said that Redmine supports three levels of integration:

- Redmine as a source code browser
- Redmine as an SCM authenticator
- Redmine as an SCM manager

The basic code browser level requires corresponding SCM clients to be installed on the same server on which Redmine is running, so you may want to use only some of the supported SCMs. Also, the basic support is not equivalent for all SCMs. Thus, the revision graph (similar to the one on GitHub; see the following screenshot) is supported only for Git and Mercurial. Also, these two SCMs can be only local (repositories should be on the same server where Redmine is).

Revisions   Revision: master   OK

#			Date	Author	Comment
fb7abea9	●		03 May 2012 15:41	José Valim	Merge pull request #6139 from pwim/extract_options-actionpack use extract_options!
54174b5f	○	●	03 May 2012 15:26	José Valim	Merge pull request #6141 from mhfs/mailer_tweeks Minor ActionMailer tweaks
e821611c	○	○	03 May 2012 15:21	Paul McMahon	use extract_options!
5f2f9b57	○	○	03 May 2012 15:11	Marcelo Silveira	No need to force conversion to Symbol since case ensures it's already one.
3d021951	○	○	03 May 2012 15:10	Marcelo Silveira	No need to work around 1.8 warnings anymore.
ab7b5501	○	○	03 May 2012 14:59	Vijay Dev	Merge pull request #6137 from FLOChip/cache_documentation cache_store has an extra option of :null_store.
e608588d	○	○	03 May 2012 14:58	Oscar Del Ben	Update command line guide
5c0cbb3d	○	○	03 May 2012 11:50	José Valim	Merge pull request #6138 from bogdan/routes RouteSet: remove some code dups
7273adab	○	○	03 May 2012 11:28	Teng Siong Ong	cache_store has an extra option of :null_store.
c9e809c8	○	○	03 May 2012 11:20	Paul McMahon	I found it strange that this guide is redirecting questions to a specific person. Heiko Webers' (@hawe) last blog post is a year and a half old, so it's not obvious that he's still active with Rails security. If he is, feel free to revert.
3e541799	○	○	03 May 2012 10:53	Jon Leighton	Merge pull request #6134 from carlosantoniodasilva/ar-relation-kernel-private-methods Fix issue with private kernel methods and collection associations
5d26c8f0	○	○	03 May 2012 05:23	Carlos Antonio da Silva	Fix issue with private kernel methods and collection associations. Closes #2508 Change CollectionProxy#method_missing to use scoped.public_send, to avoid a problem described in issue #2508 when trying to use class methods with names like "open", that clash with private kernel methods....

Also, Redmine comes with `Redmine.pm`—a Perl module for the Apache web server that can be used to authenticate Subversion, Git, and Mercurial users against Redmine. If the `Redmine.pm` tool has been integrated, you can control who has access to the project's repository and what kind of access (read or write) they can have by simply managing project members (and roles). Something similar (with additional changes made to Redmine and/or the system) can also be achieved for Bazaar. However, Subversion and Git SCMs are best supported by the `Redmine.pm` tool and their support works out of the box. At the same time, you will most likely have problems configuring other SCMs to authenticate against Redmine.

The only missing functionality for Redmine to become a full-featured SCM manager is the ability to create repositories. But such functionality also comes with Redmine and is provided by the `reposman.rb` command-line tool. This tool supports Subversion, Darcs, Mercurial, Bazaar, and Git (that is, all except CVS). However, the problem with it is that to make it work, you need to create a cron job that will execute this tool periodically. Luckily, alternative solutions that do not have such problems are provided by third-party plugins such as SCM Creator and Redmine Git Hosting (see also *Chapter 10, Plugins and Themes*).

When choosing SCM, you should also consider your requirements, your experience, the preferences of your team or audience, ease of use, and so on. However, the best integrable SCMs seem to be Subversion and Git.

Selecting a web server and an application server

Redmine as a Ruby on Rails web application should be run under a web server. This can be an independent web server (such as Apache, Nginx, or Lighttpd) that runs Ruby on Rails using either Passenger or FastCGI, or a dedicated Ruby web server such as Puma, Unicorn, Rainbows!, or Thin.

A big option list, isn't it? And these are not even all the possible options. Redmine can also be used with JRuby under a Java virtual machine. It can be run under standalone Passenger, under Mongrel, WEBrick, and more. But the previously mentioned options were chosen by practical use, and therefore they are the most common. That's why we are reviewing only those options here.

These options can be divided into three categories:

- A dedicated Ruby web server
- A dedicated Ruby web server and, for example, Nginx as a load balancer
- A separate web server with a Ruby module

Ruby is often compared to PHP, but actually these technologies are very different. For PHP guys, which include me as well, the use of a web server written in Ruby to run a Ruby application sounds weird. But in fact, a Ruby application, like a Java one, runs under a virtual machine. Therefore, Apache, for example, needs to run a Ruby virtual machine in order to run a Ruby application. This way, eventually we get at least three processes: a web server, an application server, and the application itself. So, running a Ruby application under a Ruby server seems to be reasonable, because in this case, we get only two processes: an application server which serves as a web server as well and the application.

The lack of good multithreading support is a known problem of Ruby virtual machines, and this is the main reason people use a Ruby application server in conjunction with a web server to run Ruby applications in production. Thus, they launch many instances of a Ruby server and use some web servers as a load balancer to forward requests to these instances and as a web server to dispatch the static content (images, CSS files, and so on). The best combination for this category, according to many benchmark results, is Nginx plus Puma or Unicorn.

But in practice, for this configuration, people also often use a dedicated load balancer in addition to the web server. This can be either a special application, such as HAProxy, or a web server with support for reverse proxy mode. For Apache, such a mode is provided by the `mod_proxy` module. Nginx and Lighttpd have built-in proxies. In addition, some people use special software for monitoring of Puma/Unicorn instances, for example, Monit.

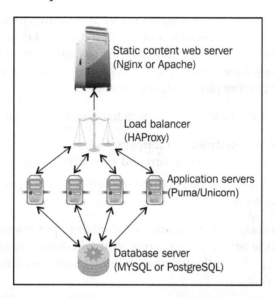

Certainly, the category just discussed is for advanced use and high-loaded services. The most commonly used, easiest to install, and best documented is the third category: a web server running a Ruby application using the **Passenger module** (also known as `mod_rails`) or the `FastCGI` module. The Passenger module is, in fact, another Ruby application server. It differs from Puma/Unicorn in that it runs as a module of a web server and not as a standalone application server (while the latter is possible). Unfortunately, the Passenger module has some limitations. It does not work under Windows and is not available for Lighttpd. For Lighttpd to run Ruby applications, people have to use FastCGI. Here, FastCGI is the name of the protocol that is used by web servers to communicate with Ruby virtual machines. Modules of the same name that implement this protocol exist for Lighttpd, Apache, and Nginx.

Generally, Passenger is more popular than FastCGI. Thus, it is used by the BitNami Redmine stack and TurnKey Redmine appliances (systems for easy Redmine deployment). It is suitable not only for small-sized and middle-sized websites, but also works great for high-loaded ones. Therefore, guys from the Ruby on Rails framework recommend using Passenger in favor of other options (check out `http://rubyonrails.org/deploy`).

When run under a web server, Passenger creates at least two processes: itself and an application instance. This can become a problem if it is used on a cheap OpenVZ-powered VPS hosting, where the amount of memory that is used by an application is very critical. This is where FastCGI helps. When run using FastCGI, Redmine occupies at least one process (an application instance).

If you still don't feel sure about which option to choose, let's summarize:

- If you plan to use Redmine for a heavy-loaded website, you should consider using Nginx with Puma/Unicorn and possibly HAProxy
- For all other cases, or if you are just unsure, go with Apache or Nginx and the Passenger module

While choosing, you should also consider your other requirements and services you plan to run on the same server. For example, you will definitely need Apache if you plan to use `Redmine.pm` for authentication of Subversion/Git users against Redmine, as it's an Apache module.

Redmine versions

At the time of writing these words, on the official Redmine website, you could find four different stable versions for download. They are a new release of 3.2, maintenance releases for 3.1 and 3.0, and another maintenance release for 2.6. This indicates that the installation of an application does not always mean the use of the most recent version.

But let's try to find out why the Redmine guys decided to release four versions of the application. Version 3.x uses Rails 4 and version 2.x uses Rails 3. For Ruby applications, a migration between major Rails versions, such as from 3 to 4, is a very serious step that often requires many changes to be made to the environment, custom tools, and so on. Major Rails versions are usually not compatible, so it's normal to give people some additional time for the migration. That's why we have 2.6 on the list. However, the Redmine developers also decided to give additional time for migration from Redmine 3.0 and 3.1 to 3.2. There were actually no special reasons for this, I believe.

By the way, the same that applies to Rails applies to Redmine. Major Redmine versions, such as, 1.x, 2.x, and 3.x, are known to be generally incompatible. That is, plugins must usually be modified a lot to work under the next major version. Therefore, their support for the new major version often comes with a big delay. On the contrary, minor versions, such as 3.0 and 3.1, are usually quite compatible, so plugins may run under the next minor version without any changes. And finally, tiny Redmine versions, such as 3.1.0 and 3.1.1, usually deliver fixes, which do not affect the working of plugins.

In most cases, people use the most recent version of an application, which is 3.2.x for Redmine at the moment. However, some Linux distributions or appliances may come with older versions. So should you stick to the distributed version or should you install the very recent one? Note that in the case of using distributions and appliances, switching to the most recent version usually involves performing manual migration and further manual maintenance. So, to be sure about what to choose, you should at least know what the difference between the versions in question is.

Therefore, let's shortly review the current stable versions of Redmine (the ones that are available at the time of writing this section):

- **3.2.x:**

  This version comes with the following new features:

  ° The Redmine interface becomes responsive; that is, Redmine can now be used on mobile devices.

  ° It's now possible to import issues from a CSV file.

  ° A new **Key/value** list custom field format is added.

  ° The issue list is now able to show totals for estimated and spent hours and numeric custom fields.

- **3.1.x:**

  This version comes with the following noticeable features:

  ° The Markdown formatter is no more considered experimental and has finally got its own help page.

  ° Subtasks can now be more independent and have their own dates, priorities, and done ratios that do not affect the parent issue.

  ° Security improvements: an option to expire passwords and password re-entry for some actions.

- **3.0.x:**

  This version upgrades Redmine to Rails 4.2.x. So, to migrate, users will need to update their custom Ruby tools, if any. Special attention should also be paid to find appropriate versions of third-party plugins, if any plugins are used.

  Additionally, this version comes with the following features:

  - Users can now have multiple emails.
  - Search functionality was improved. Thus, it's now possible to search in open issues.
  - Documents now have support for custom fields.

- **2.6.x:**

  This version includes the following new noticeable features:

  - Custom permissions can now be assigned to non-members and anonymous users of the project.
  - Improved PDF export.

Basically, due to the migration to Rails 4 — and, therefore, huge changes in API at the time of writing this book — not all Redmine plugins had been ported to Redmine 3.x.x yet. You should consider this while choosing the version for your installation if you use or plan to use any plugins.

Forks

In 2011, one of the most active Redmine developers, Eric Davis, with a group of other contributors from a company named Finnlabs, forked Redmine into ChiliProject. Unfortunately, this project was recently discontinued.

However, while working on ChiliProject, Finnlabs decided to make a custom version of this application. Eventually, having understood that ChiliProject was not good enough for them, they made their fork public and named it OpenProject. Right now, this fork is actively developed and already has quite a large community. Finnlabs also changed the style of the project — they made it more commercially oriented and created the OpenProject Foundation, which is funding it. These changes had a positive effect on the fork, which now looks quite cool and promising. However, it's obvious that the project is too young to replace Redmine. Also, it has not proven its durability yet (ChiliProject looked promising too).

 Check out OpenProject at `https://www.openproject.org/`.

Summary

The goal of this chapter was to familiarize you with Redmine and get you ready to dig deeper into this amazing web application. Therefore, we not only reviewed the advantages and the interface of Redmine, but also checked its installation components. We even discussed forks of Redmine, as I believe it's good to know about them if you are going to become a member of the Redmine community.

I have tried to share as much knowledge about the installation components of Redmine as possible so that you can understand them better, learn what options you have, and be able to choose the right one. Still, remember that usually the best option is the one that is used by most users. So, if you choose an uncommon option, you should be sure about your reasons for doing so.

The knowledge that you have gained by reading this chapter should come in handy in the next one, as you will need to decide which components to use for installation.

2
Installing Redmine

Now that we know what Redmine is and what it looks like, we can proceed to the next step in our relations with it, that is, getting Redmine up and running. So generally, this chapter is about setting up and maintaining Redmine, and it is intended mostly for administrators.

In this chapter, we are going to focus on two main options for installing Redmine. The first one is what I recommend (and what I actually use)—installing Redmine from a package on Debian or Ubuntu. The second one is the official option—installation of the recent version from sources. Certainly, we will also speak about the advantages and disadvantages of these options.

Many users used to claim that the Redmine installation is not an easy process, which is not true if we consider the installation of a package. But actually, its installation can be even easier. How? We will discuss this at the end of this chapter.

So, in this chapter, we will cover the following topics:

- Introduction to installation options
- Installing Redmine from a package
- Installing Redmine from sources
- Other installation options

Introduction to installation options

I have always believed that installation is not just a matter of getting an application to run. It's actually much more, as it involves making important decisions that can be hard to change in future, such as:

- What components and/or platform should be chosen to run the application (which is covered in the previous chapter)?
- What version should be used?
- What source should be used to install the application from?

Of course, the answers to these questions depend on the goals of using Redmine. This in turn raises other questions, such as the following:

- Will this be a production environment?
- Is this environment temporary or for development?
- Is there anyone who will maintain the installation?
- Should it be scalable and platform independent?

Many people go with the officially recommended installation procedure, which is in fact the most common one. But this procedure does not consider platform peculiarities (otherwise, there would be too many cases to document). So eventually, by following this procedure, you get an isolated subsystem that is not connected to the package management tools of the host system. Such a subsystem will require manual maintenance, can easily be broken by changes in the host system, can create obscure conflicts, and so on. This often ends up with this subsystem being, in fact, unmaintained, as administrators have some fear about touching it. In addition, the official installation procedure is the most complicated one.

Therefore, in this chapter, we will review not only the officially recommended procedure—which is actually a good choice in some cases—but also some alternative ones. All of these procedures differ in the source from which they get Redmine. So, they can be divided into three categories by the source type:

- Prepackaged Redmine
- Official Subversion/Git/Mercurial repository or tarball
- An appliance containing all that you need to run/install Redmine

The first category assumes that a Redmine package is available. Here, by "package" I mean a specially prepared software archive that contains not only Redmine itself but also instructions and possibly tools for installing it in the system. The best known package formats are RPM (for Red Hat-based Linux distributions) and DEB (for Debian-based Linux distributions). Certainly, such packages should be maintained and actively supported! Otherwise, there is no sense in using them.

To install Redmine as a package, you just need to answer a couple of questions, but this is not the only thing that makes packages so attractive. They are processed by the package manager, which also resolves conflicts and installs dependencies. Also, a package is usually associated with a repository where its dependencies and other system packages are stored, and that repository is updated periodically. So this means that the package manager will be able to update Redmine flawlessly when a new version arrives. Moreover, it won't allow the dependencies to get updated if this would break Redmine. Certainly, this makes its maintenance much easier.

Additionally, the packaged application is usually modified to conform to the standards of the operating system it is intended for. Thus, its configuration is located with other applications' configuration files (for example, in /etc/). The application itself is stored at the same location as other similar applications (for example, under /usr/share/). Its cache is stored under the system cache directory (for example, /var/cache/). Its logs are written to the system logs. And so on. This means that any administrator who is aware of the system standards — even if he/she is not aware of Redmine — will be able to understand the Redmine file structure and find or manage what he/she needs. Moreover, system tools (for example, log analyzers) will be able to pick up and process Redmine files if needed.

Unfortunately, Redmine is currently not available as a package for all Linux distributions. Thus, at the time of writing this section, Redmine packages are available (and well-supported) for Debian-based distributions such as Debian, Ubuntu and Mint, and some Red Hat based distributions, such as Fedora (through the RPM Sphere repository) and Mageia.

It may be that by the time you read this section, there will be Redmine packages for other Linux distributions as well. At least, you should try finding the one for your distribution, as this will make its maintenance much easier! When looking for a package, don't forget to check:

- Whether it's actively supported and well-tested
- Whether it's in an official repository
- The feedback on the repository, if it's not an official one
- The feedback on the package itself, and so on

Generally, I recommend that you use a package whenever possible, mainly due to the ease of maintenance. However, you should remember that packaged software usually comes with an outdated version. At the time of writing this section, the recent Redmine version is 3.2.x and the recent version of packaged Redmine in Debian stable distribution is an intermediate between 2.5.x and 3.0.x. In Ubuntu LTS, it was even older: 2.4.x. So, if you want to be up to date (just up to date and not secure, as Ubuntu/Debian guys follow security news and make updates when necessary), you should go with the recent official version. However, in this case, be sure to allocate resources needed to maintain your Redmine installation and to document changes made to the system (do mention that you installed Redmine without using the system package manager). Also remember that plugins are most likely not going to be available right away for the recent version of Redmine.

But don't hurry to leave this section and move on to the (appropriate) next one, as there is even an easier way.

You can use special appliances that contain Redmine along with everything that you need to run it: a web server and an application server (for example, Apache plus Passenger), a database server (for example, MySQL), Ruby, Rails, and so on.

Some appliances also come with the entire operating system (usually Linux) and can easily be deployed on a server or a cloud. The advantage of using such appliances is that you preserve the possibility of upgrading the application (as well as the rest of the system). However, these kinds of appliances can't be used to deploy Redmine on an existing server.

There are also appliances that don't include the operating system and are to be installed on existing servers. Their advantage (compared to normal installation) is that you don't need to spend time configuring the application, as this is done by the installer (which may ask you a couple of questions). However, after using such appliances, the installed application will be separate from the rest of the system, what means that you may experience issues while upgrading it. Moreover, an upgrade of the operating system may accidentally break your application. Therefore, these kinds of appliances are recommended only for development and testing.

Migrating to Redmine

The official Redmine documentation includes instructions for migration from Trac and Mantis. The community also provides migration tools for JIRA, Bugzilla, and more. Check out http://www.redmine.org/projects/redmine/wiki/RedmineMigrate for recent instructions.

Now, let's have Redmine installed in two different ways. For all installations, we will use Apache, Passenger and MySQL, that is, the most common components. However, if you've chosen different components after reading *Chapter 1, Getting Familiar with Redmine,* and have decided to go with a more advanced option, then you will need to find a tutorial elsewhere (for example, http://www.redmine.org/). Unfortunately, this book can't cover all the options.

Installing Redmine from a package

To install Redmine from a package, we will use Debian jessie 8.2. Usually, I would recommend that you use Ubuntu server **Long Term Support** (**LTS**) instead. I would did this because it's more popular and has a larger community, but the Redmine version that comes with Ubuntu LTS is too outdated to be reviewed in this book (it's currently 2.4). However, Ubuntu LTS is largely based on the Debian stable repository, so the installation procedure should be the same for both systems (to make sure that it will be, I'm also going to use Ubuntu-style commands). Also, this in turn means that the very next Ubuntu LTS version is going to come with the version of Redmine that is currently shipped with Debian stable distribution. So, it can be said that we are going to use the future version of Ubuntu Server. Additionally, I personally prefer Debian stable over Ubuntu as the former is an older Linux distribution, is the original one, and has a more professional community.

> Note that the version of the Redmine package in the Debian stable repository is stated to be 3.0~20140825, but when installed, Redmine itself shows 2.5.2.devel. In fact, it's not really 2.5 as it, for example, runs on Rails 4, but it's not completely 3.0 either. As I have mentioned, it's an intermediate between 2.5 and 3.0 (with respect to functionality, it's perhaps closer to 2.5). The displayed version is 2.5.2.devel as the Debian guys took a code snapshot of the 3.0.0 branch, in which the version had not been fixed yet (that's why it's suffixed with .devel).

I assume that you have already installed Debian 8.2 (or a more recent version, or Ubuntu Server LTS). If not, please do it! Also, assuming that you have a clean installation and will need to install Apache, MySQL and so on—that is, everything needed to run Redmine. But don't worry if some of these applications are already installed. It will still be safe to execute the specified commands, as the Debian package manager is smart enough to skip such packages.

Installing Redmine and MySQL server

So let's execute the following command from the console:

```
$ sudo apt-get install redmine redmine-mysql mysql-server
```

Instead of `redmine-mysql` and `mysql-server`, you can use `redmine-pgsql` and `postgresql` or `redmine-sqlite` and `sqlite3`. But remember that neither PostgreSQL nor SQLite3 is reviewed in this section.

This command will install Redmine and MySQL as well as many dependency packages, including Ruby on Rails. Before doing this, the `apt-get` package manager will ask you to confirm, as follows:

```
s-andy@debian:~$ sudo apt-get install redmine redmine-mysql mysql-server
Reading package lists... Done
Building dependency tree
Reading state information... Done
The following extra packages will be installed:
  binutils build-essential bundler cpp cpp-4.9 dbconfig-common dpkg-dev fakeroot fonts-droid g++ g++-4.9 gcc gcc-4.9 ghostscript gsfonts
  imagemagick-common javascript-common libaio1 libalgorithm-diff-perl libalgorithm-diff-xs-perl libalgorithm-merge-perl libasan0 libasan1 libatomic1
  libc-ares2 libc-dev-bin libc6-dev libcilkrts5 libcloog-isl4 libcupsfilters1 libcupsimage2 libcurl3 libdbd-mysql-perl libdbi-perl libdpkg-perl
  libev4 libfakeroot libfcgi-ruby1.9.1 libfcgi0ldbl libfftw3-double3 libfile-fcntllock-perl libgcc-4.8-dev libgcc-4.9-dev libgmp-dev libgmpxx4ldbl
  libgomp1 libgs9 libgs9-common libhtml-template-perl libjs-0.35 libisl10 libitm1 libjbig2dec0 libjs-coffeescript libjs-jquery libjs-jquery-ui
  libjs-prototype libjs-scriptaculous libjsoncpp0 liblqr-1-0 liblsan0 libltdl7 libmagickcore-6.q16-2 libmpc3 libmpfr4 libmysqlclient18 libquadmath0
  libruby2.1 libstdc++-4.8-dev libstdc++-4.9-dev libterm-readkey-perl libtsan0 libubsan0 libv8-3.14.5 libyaml-0-2 linux-libc-dev make manpages-dev
  mysql-client-5.5 mysql-common mysql-server-5.5 mysql-server-core-5.5 nodejs poppler-data rake redmine redmine-mysql ruby ruby-actionmailer ruby-actionpack
  ruby-actionpack-action-caching ruby-actionview ruby-activemodel ruby-activerecord ruby-activesupport ruby-arel ruby-atomic ruby-awesome-nested-set
  ruby-blankslate ruby-builder ruby-coderay ruby-coffee-rails ruby-coffee-script ruby-coffee-script-source ruby-dev ruby-erubis
  ruby-eventmachine ruby-execjs ruby-fcgi ruby-ffi ruby-hike ruby-hmac ruby-i18n ruby-jbuilder ruby-jquery-rails ruby-json ruby-listen ruby-mail
  ruby-mime-types ruby-minitest ruby-multi-json ruby-mysql2 ruby-net-http-persistent ruby-net-ldap ruby-oj ruby-openid ruby-passenger ruby-polyglot
  ruby-protected-attributes ruby-rack ruby-rack-openid ruby-rack-test ruby-rails ruby-rails-observers ruby-railties ruby-rb-inotify ruby-redcarpet
  ruby-request-store ruby-rmagick ruby-sass ruby-sass-rails ruby-sdoc ruby-spring ruby-sprockets ruby-sprockets-rails ruby-sqlite3 ruby-thor
  ruby-thread-safe ruby-tilt ruby-timers ruby-treetop ruby-turbolinks ruby-tzinfo ruby-uglifier ruby-yajl ruby2.1 ruby2.1-dev rubygems-integration
  zip
Suggested packages:
  binutils-doc cpp-doc gcc-4.9-locales virtual-mysql-client mysql-client postgresql-client debian-keyring g++-multilib g++-4.9-multilib gcc-4.9-doc
  libstdc++6-4.9-dbg gcc-multilib autoconf automake libtool flex bison gdb gcc-doc gcc-4.9-multilib libgcc1-dbg libgomp1-dbg libitm1-dbg
  libatomic1-dbg libasan1-dbg liblsan0-dbg libtsan0-dbg libubsan0-dbg libcilkrts5-dbg libquadmath0-dbg ghostscript-x apache2 lighttpd httpd
  glibc-doc libclone-perl libmldbm-perl libnet-daemon-perl libsql-statement-perl libfftw3-bin libfftw3-dev libgmp10-doc libmpfr-dev
  libipc-sharedcache-perl coffeescript libjs-jquery-ui-docs libmagickcore-6.q16-2-extra libstdc++-4.8-doc libstdc++-4.9-doc make-doc tinyca
  poppler-utils fonts-japanese-mincho fonts-ipafont-mincho fonts-japanese-gothic fonts-ipafont-gothic fonts-arphic-ukai fonts-arphic-uming
  fonts-nanum bzr cvs darcs git mercurial subversion ri ruby-builder-doc rails ruby-passenger-doc ruby-compass treetop doc-base
The following NEW packages will be installed:
  binutils build-essential bundler cpp cpp-4.9 dbconfig-common dpkg-dev fakeroot fonts-droid g++ g++-4.9 gcc gcc-4.9 ghostscript gsfonts
  imagemagick-common javascript-common libaio1 libalgorithm-diff-perl libalgorithm-diff-xs-perl libalgorithm-merge-perl libasan0 libasan1 libatomic1
  libc-ares2 libc-dev-bin libc6-dev libcilkrts5 libcloog-isl4 libcupsfilters1 libcupsimage2 libcurl3 libdbd-mysql-perl libdbi-perl libdpkg-perl
  libev4 libfakeroot libfcgi-ruby1.9.1 libfcgi0ldbl libfftw3-double3 libfile-fcntllock-perl libgcc-4.8-dev libgcc-4.9-dev libgmp-dev libgmpxx4ldbl
  libgomp1 libgs9 libgs9-common libhtml-template-perl libjs-0.35 libisl10 libitm1 libjbig2dec0 libjs-coffeescript libjs-jquery libjs-jquery-ui
  libjs-prototype libjs-scriptaculous libjsoncpp0 liblqr-1-0 liblsan0 libltdl7 libmagickcore-6.q16-2 libmpc3 libmpfr4 libmysqlclient18 libquadmath0
  libruby2.1 libstdc++-4.8-dev libstdc++-4.9-dev libterm-readkey-perl libtsan0 libubsan0 libv8-3.14.5 libyaml-0-2 linux-libc-dev make manpages-dev
  mysql-client-5.5 mysql-common mysql-server mysql-server-5.5 nodejs poppler-data rake redmine redmine-mysql ruby
  ruby-actionmailer ruby-actionpack ruby-actionpack-action-caching ruby-actionview ruby-activemodel ruby-activerecord ruby-activesupport ruby-arel
  ruby-atomic ruby-awesome-nested-set ruby-blankslate ruby-builder ruby-coderay ruby-coffee-rails ruby-coffee-script
  ruby-coffee-script-source ruby-dev ruby-erubis ruby-eventmachine ruby-execjs ruby-fcgi ruby-ffi ruby-hike ruby-hmac ruby-i18n ruby-jbuilder
  ruby-jquery-rails ruby-json ruby-listen ruby-mail ruby-mime-types ruby-minitest ruby-multi-json ruby-mysql2 ruby-net-http-persistent ruby-net-ldap
  ruby-oj ruby-openid ruby-passenger ruby-polyglot ruby-protected-attributes ruby-rack ruby-rack-openid ruby-rack-test ruby-rails
  ruby-rails-observers ruby-railties ruby-rb-inotify ruby-redcarpet ruby-request-store ruby-rmagick ruby-sass ruby-sass-rails ruby-sdoc ruby-spring
  ruby-sprockets ruby-sprockets-rails ruby-sqlite3 ruby-thor ruby-thread-safe ruby-tilt ruby-timers ruby-treetop ruby-turbolinks ruby-tzinfo
  ruby-uglifier ruby-yajl ruby2.1 ruby2.1-dev rubygems-integration zip
0 upgraded, 161 newly installed, 0 to remove and 0 not upgraded.
Need to get 95.0 MB of archives.
After this operation, 308 MB of additional disk space will be used.
Do you want to continue? [Y/n] y
```

Here, type `y` and then press *Enter*. This will make it download all the packages and start the installation process.

Configuring the MySQL server package

After unpacking the packages, apt-get will configure them. When it gets to the MySQL server, you will see the following dialog:

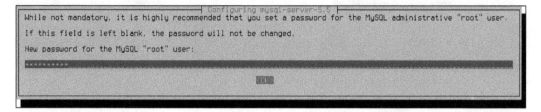

This dialog asks you to enter a new password for the MySQL superuser. In other words, this is the password that you will use to administer your MySQL server. The same password is to be used later to set up the Redmine database.

After you have entered the password, press *Tab* to move the cursor to the **Ok** button and then press *Enter*. Afterwards, you will need to repeat these steps in the password confirmation dialog.

Now it will take some time to configure other packages.

Configuring the Redmine package

The Debian/Ubuntu Redmine package supports multiple instances of this application. Thus, several instances can be used to run Redmine in production and development modes at the same time and on the same server (for example, on different ports). The configurator of the package, however, can help you to configure only a single default instance (if you want to configure more instances, you will need to do this manually).

After MySQL, it will not take long for apt-get to start configuring Redmine. When it does, the following dialog will be shown:

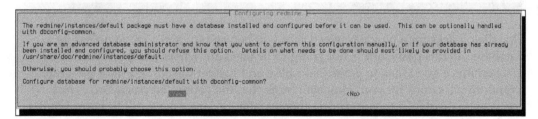

Here, the configurator offers assistance in creating and configuring the database for Redmine. Unless you wish to do this manually, just press *Enter*.

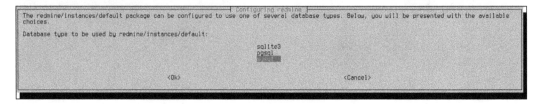

The next dialog that opens immediately asks you to select the database back-end. It lists all the supported (Linux) backends, as it is going to configure the database client for Redmine (the database server can potentially run on another machine).

As we have decided to use MySQL, we just press *Enter* here. And now comes the dialog that has already been mentioned:

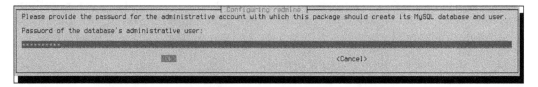

This window asks for the MySQL superuser password that you specified before. It is going to be used to create, configure, and populate the Redmine database.

So, we specify the password, press *Tab* to move to the **Ok** button, and press *Enter*.

Next, the final screen of the Redmine database configuration shows up:

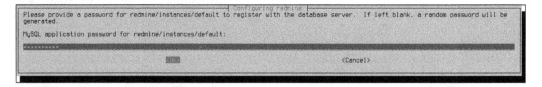

This dialog asks for a new password that will be used by Redmine to access its database. As this password is not going to be used anywhere except in Redmine, it is perhaps a good idea to press *Enter* here and just let the configurator generate a random password for you. However, note that the generated password is not going to be displayed to you during this installation process (it will be stored in the configuration file).

You may also need to specify this password in the Apache configuration files for advanced SCM integration. If you need it, you can find it in /etc/redmine/default/database.yml.

Thereafter, the package manager will configure the rest of the packages and return to the shell prompt.

That's it! Redmine has been installed and configured and it is actually ready to be run. But the system is not yet ready to run it.

Installing Apache and Passenger

To run Redmine, the system needs a web server. We are going to use Apache for this web server. Besides a web server, as you should remember from *Chapter 1, Getting Familiar with Redmine,* we need something to run Ruby applications on. This is going to be the Passenger module for Apache.

So let's install them:

```
$ sudo apt-get install apache2 libapache2-mod-passenger
```

As before, you will be asked to type y and press *Enter*. After this, the package manager will download the specified packages and their dependencies, install them, and start the Apache web server.

```
Setting up apache2-bin (2.4.10-10+deb8u3) ...
Setting up apache2-utils (2.4.10-10+deb8u3) ...
Setting up apache2-data (2.4.10-10+deb8u3) ...
Setting up apache2 (2.4.10-10+deb8u3) ...
Enabling module mpm_event.
Enabling module authz_core.
Enabling module authz_host.
Enabling module authn_core.
Enabling module auth_basic.
Enabling module access_compat.
Enabling module authn_file.
Enabling module authz_user.
Enabling module alias.
Enabling module dir.
Enabling module autoindex.
Enabling module env.
Enabling module mime.
Enabling module negotiation.
Enabling module setenvif.
Enabling module filter.
Enabling module deflate.
Enabling module status.
Enabling conf charset.
Enabling conf localized-error-pages.
Enabling conf other-vhosts-access-log.
Enabling conf security.
Enabling conf serve-cgi-bin.
Enabling site 000-default.
Setting up libapache2-mod-passenger (4.0.53-1) ...
apache2_invoke: Enable module passenger
Setting up ssl-cert (1.0.35) ...
Processing triggers for libc-bin (2.19-18+deb8u1) ...
Processing triggers for systemd (215-17+deb8u2) ...
s-andy@debian:~$ ▌
```

Now, if you request the index page of the newly installed web server using the URL http://127.0.0.1, for example (only from the same computer), you should see something like this:

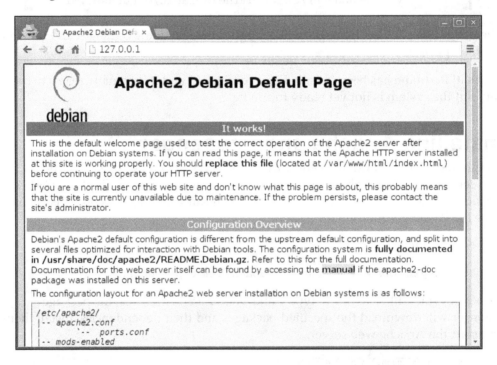

This is the default welcome page of the Apache web server on Debian.

Connecting Redmine and Apache

But wait. Where is Redmine? At the moment, it is not connected to Apache. Unfortunately, despite the power of the Debian package management, this part should be configured manually. Luckily, it's not complicated. The Debian Redmine package comes with sample configuration files for Redmine under the /usr/share/doc/redmine/examples directory. In this directory, you can find sample configurations for Apache and FastCGI or Passenger, Lighttpd, Nginx, and Thin. There, you can see two sample files for Apache and Passenger: apache2-passenger-alias.conf and apache2-passenger-host.conf. The former should be used if you want to run Redmine under an additional URL path, for example, www.yourdomain.com/redmine. The latter is to be used if you want to run Redmine under a subdomain or as the main website on your domain.

It is assumed that you have installed a clean Debian/Ubuntu (as I did), especially for Redmine; that is, you want to use the server only for Redmine or for Redmine as the primary application. So let's copy `apache2-passenger-host.conf` to `/etc/apache2/sites-available` (the path for site configurations on Debian/Ubuntu):

```
$ sudo cp /usr/share/doc/redmine/examples/apache2-passenger-host.conf
/etc/apache2/sites-available/
```

As it is clear from its name, this directory stores the configuration files of the available sites. For enabled sites, there is another directory — `/etc/apache2/sites-enabled/`. So, we need to move our new configuration into the latter. Let's do this in the correct Debian/Ubuntu way:

```
$ sudo a2ensite apache2-passenger-host
```

The `e2ensite` script is used to create symbolic links in `/etc/apache2/sites-enabled/` that point to configuration files from `/etc/apache2/sites-available/`. A similar script, `e2dissite`, can be used to disable configuration files (that is, to remove symbolic links). And we need to execute the latter script to disable the default welcome page that comes with Apache in Debian/Ubuntu:

```
$ sudo a2dissite 000-default
```

Next, reload Apache to apply the new configuration:

```
$ sudo service apache2 reload
```

Now, if we load the site, we get the following:

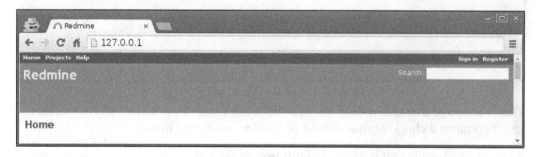

Congratulations! You have successfully installed Redmine. But still, there are a few things we need to do before we take a break for coffee and go ahead.

Verifying and completing the installation

Now we need to check whether the installation is correct. To do this, click on the **Sign in** link in the top-right corner and log in to your Redmine account. Use admin both as the login and the password.

After you have signed in, click on the newly appeared **Administration** item in the top dark blue menu bar. Then select the **Information** page from the sidebar. You will see something like this:

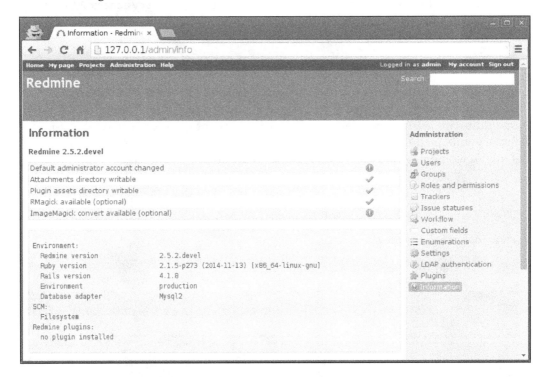

This is the page that one should always check after installing Redmine! As you can see, it contains a checklist that should be used to verify the installation.

As everyone knows that both the default username and password for Redmine are admin, you should change the password (at least) as soon as possible. To do this right now (what is recommended), go to the **Users** section of the **Administration** area, select the admin user, enter a new password in the **Password** and **Confirmation** fields of the **Authentication** box, and click on **Save**. This will make the corresponding item on the checklist green.

However, the checklist also shows that we have a problem with the ImageMagick `convert` tool. Actually, the problem is that it is not installed.

 RMagick is a Ruby interface for the ImageMagick/ GraphicsMagick image processing library. This library is used by Redmine to export a Gantt chart and to embed images in PDF files. It can also be expected to be installed by some third-party plugins. The convert tool is used to generate thumbnails for image attachments.

However, instead of the standard ImageMagick library, we will use its fork called GraphicsMagick, which is known to support more image formats (but it is also known for processing PSD files slower). So, to install GraphicsMagick, execute the following command (if you want the standard tool, specify `imagemagick` instead):

```
$ sudo apt-get install graphicsmagick-imagemagick-compat
```

Now, reload Apache to let Redmine see the changes:

```
$ sudo service apache2 reload
```

After this, you should see a green check mark to the right of ImageMagick convert **available**.

The only thing left to fix now is the administrator account. What should be done and how, will be reviewed at the beginning of the next chapter.

Upgrading the Redmine package

When you are using a Redmine package, the system package manager is going to upgrade it automatically along with the rest of the system. Such system upgrades can be triggered by the following commands:

```
$ sudo aptitude update
```

```
$ sudo aptitude safe-upgrade
```

However, you should not expect it to upgrade Redmine to a major or even a minor version (for which the first two digits differ; for example, 3.1.x and 3.2.x are different minor versions). Usually for a particular version of Debian/Ubuntu, the package manager can upgrade Redmine only to the next tiny version (that is, a version in which only the last digit differs, for example, 3.0.0 to 3.0.1). And you can expect a major or minor version upgrade only with the upgrade of the entire system to the next major release of the system. Certainly, this means that if you install Redmine 2.5/3.0 on Debian stable, you will end up sticking to this version for some time.

Anyway! Usually when you upgrade Debian/Ubuntu to the next major version, the upgrade of Redmine goes very flawlessly. So, you do not need to pay any special attention to it (as the package manager does everything needed automatically), unless you use plugins! Most plugins are not available as packages for Debian/Ubuntu (as well as other Linux distributions) and can be installed only manually. Such manual installations often become a huge problem when you upgrade the system to the next major release. Therefore, it is recommended to find updates for plugins first and only then upgrade the system. Certainly, this can delay the upgrade of the system (for example, you may need to wait for plugin code to be updated for the corresponding version of Redmine).

Installing Redmine from sources

This is the most complicated but the officially recommended installation option. It is also the best documented one. Certainly, these instructions can change for future versions of Redmine, so if you are going to install a version newer than 3.2, you should also check out the official installation tutorial, which is available at `http://www.redmine.org/projects/redmine/wiki/RedmineInstall`.

> I guess you are going to use SSH to install Redmine on a remote server? If so, consider using the `screen` tool. The network connection can potentially be dropped during the installation process, what can damages the incomplete installation. The `screen` tool can help here by creating a virtual terminal that will continue its work even if the connection gets lost. To install this tool, use `sudo apt-get install screen`. To create a terminal screen, just execute `screen`. Finally, to reattach the terminal, execute `screen -r`.

This time, I will use a clean Ubuntu Server 14.04 LTS, but Debian stable distribution should also be fine. If your Ubuntu/Debian server is not yet ready, prepare it now.

Downloading and installing Redmine

First of all, we need to decide where to store Redmine files. Let's use `/opt/redmine` (this path is fine for FHS, short for Filesystem Hierarchy Standard):

```
$ sudo mkdir -p /opt/redmine
```

This command will create the `/opt/redmine` directory. Now, let's go to it:

```
$ cd /opt/redmine
```

Next, we need to get the latest version of Redmine in the `tar.gz` archive from `http://www.redmine.org/projects/redmine/wiki/Download`. At the time of writing this chapter, it was 3.2.0. So get it:

```
$ sudo wget http://www.redmine.org/releases/redmine-3.2.0.tar.gz
```

Now unpack the archive into the current directory (which should be `/opt/redmine`):

```
$ sudo tar xvf redmine-3.2.0.tar.gz
```

This command will unpack everything into the `redmine-3.2.0` subdirectory. We move there:

```
$ cd redmine-3.2.0
```

Configuring the database

Before we proceed, we should fill in the database details in Redmine configuration files (because they will be needed to run Bundler in the *Installing dependencies* section). To help here, Redmine comes with a sample database configuration in the `config/database.yml.example` file. Let's rename it to `config/database.yml`:

```
$ sudo mv config/database.yml.example config/database.yml
```

Now, open the `config/database.yml` file in your favorite editor and modify it so that it looks like this:

```
production:
  adapter: mysql2
  database: redmine
  host: localhost
  username: redmine
  password: your_password_here
  encoding: utf8
```

Thus, to make the file look like this, I removed the `development` and `test` sections, changed the `username` from `root` to `redmine`, and set the password. You need to replace `your_password_here` with your own one.

> You can generate a random password with the `makepasswd` tool (it needs to be installed first using `sudo apt-get install makepasswd`), as follows:
> ```
> $ makepasswd --chars=32
> ```

Installing Ruby and Bundler

Redmine comes with Bundler support. Bundler is a Ruby gem dependency manager, that is, in some ways, similar to the Debian/Ubuntu package manager used in the previous section. In other words, Bundler simplifies the deployment process by ensuring that all dependencies are installed.

However, Bundler is not yet available in our clean system. Moreover, neither gem nor Ruby is available. So, we need to install them first:

```
$ sudo apt-get install ruby
```

When you are asked for confirmation, type y and press *Enter*. This command will install Ruby and all its dependencies, including the gem tool.

Now we can install Bundler. To do this, we will use the gem tool as follows:

```
$ sudo gem install bundler
```

```
s-andy@mastering-redmine:/opt/redmine/redmine-3.2.0$ sudo gem install bundler
Fetching: bundler-1.11.2.gem (100%)
Successfully installed bundler-1.11.2
1 gem installed
Installing ri documentation for bundler-1.11.2...
Installing RDoc documentation for bundler-1.11.2...
s-andy@mastering-redmine:/opt/redmine/redmine-3.2.0$ ▪
```

Resolving Bundler errors

Bundler can automatically resolve only gem dependencies. This means that when it's not able to find a Ruby library (which is called gem), it tries to fetch it from https://rubygems.org/. But some gems use native system libraries, and therefore they must be built before being installed. Moreover, in order to build such gems, Bundler needs the appropriate system libraries to be already available. Otherwise, it won't be able to install them and will give errors.

In this section, I will let you know which libraries to install to make Bundler run flawlessly, but future versions of Redmine (3.2.0+) may require some other system libraries. So, before you run Bundler, let me show you how to resolve possible Bundler errors. Again, as you are unlikely to get any such error this time, you can skip this subsection and move on to the *Installing dependencies* subsection.

If you are still here, let's review a sample Bundler error:

```
Installing request_store 1.0.5
Installing rmagick 2.15.4 with native extensions

Gem::Installer::ExtensionBuildError: ERROR: Failed to build gem native extension.

        /usr/bin/ruby1.9.1 extconf.rb
/usr/lib/ruby/1.9.1/rubygems/custom_require.rb:36:in `require': cannot load such file -- mkmf (LoadError)
        from /usr/lib/ruby/1.9.1/rubygems/custom_require.rb:36:in `require'
        from extconf.rb:4:in `<main>'

Gem files will remain installed in /tmp/bundler20160306-2434-13uao0hrmagick-2.15.4/gems/rmagick-2.15.4 for inspection.
Results logged to /tmp/bundler20160306-2434-13uao0hrmagick-2.15.4/gems/rmagick-2.15.4/ext/RMagick/gem_make.out
An error occurred while installing json (1.8.3), and Bundler cannot continue.
Make sure that `gem install json -v '1.8.3'` succeeds before bundling.
s-andy@mastering-redmine:/opt/redmine/redmine-3.2.0$ █
```

As it can be seen from the preceding screenshot, Bundler has failed to build the
`rmagick` gem. Consider this message:

require': cannot load such file -- mkmf (LoadError)

It tells us that Bundler failed to find the `mkmf.rb` file (`.rb` is the extension for Ruby
files). The most common reason for such an error is that the corresponding library
is missing. Also note that Bundler usually needs not only libraries but also their
development files. Thus, the `mkmf.rb` file comes with `ruby1.9.1-dev`—the package
that contains the development files for Ruby 1.9.1.

If Bundler gives a filename that it was not able to find, like in this case, on Debian/
Ubuntu you can use the `apt-file` tool to locate it in non-installed packages. To
install `apt-file` and initialize its database, use these commands:

$ sudo apt-get install apt-file

$ apt-file update

Afterwards, to search for a file, just specify it as an argument for the apt-file's `search`
command. For example, to find the package that contains the `Magick-config` file,
you should execute this:

$ apt-file search Magick-config

Installing dependencies

As we do not need Bundler to come to a halt with errors, let's install in one run all
the system dependencies, the lack can cause them:

**$ sudo apt-get install ruby1.9.1-dev make zlib1g-dev libmysqlclient-dev
libmagickcore-dev libmagickwand-dev**

This command will install the development files for Ruby, the MySQL client, and the ImageMagick libraries, as well as the libraries themselves and all their dependencies.

 If you do not need the support of RMagick, omit the `libmagickcore-dev` and `libmagickwand-dev` packages here.

Now let Bundler install the gem dependencies:

```
$ bundle install --without development test
```

This command will make Bundler install gems in system directories. To do this, it will use `sudo`, so it may ask for the password of your user account.

 You can skip the installation of RMagick here by adding the `rmagick` keyword to the `--without` option.

If the installation of the dependencies was successful, you should see something like the following:

```
Installing sprockets-rails 3.0.4
Installing jquery-rails 3.1.4
Installing roadie-rails 1.1.0
Installing rails 4.2.5
Bundle complete! 28 Gemfile dependencies, 53 gems now installed.
Gems in the groups development, test, postgresql and sqlite were not installed.
Use `bundle show [gemname]` to see where a bundled gem is installed.
s-andy@mastering-redmine:/opt/redmine/redmine-3.2.0$ █
```

Installing the MySQL server, Apache, and Passenger

As we plan to use the MySQL server and the Apache web server with the Passenger module and our system is clean, we need to install all of them as well. Generally, the procedure of their installation is identical to what was described in the previous section (*Installing Redmine from a package*):

```
$ sudo apt-get install mysql-server mysql-client apache2 libapache2-mod-passenger
```

Here, we will skip all the details related to their installation, as they have been reviewed before. Thus, you can check them out in the *Configuring the MySQL server package* and *Installing Apache and Passenger* subsections of the *Installing Redmine from a package* section.

Setting up the database

Now that we are ready to go further, let's create the database for Redmine. We'll do this in the console MySQL client, so run it:

```
$ mysql -u root -p
```

The client will ask for the password of the MySQL server's superuser (root), which you have specified during the installation of the MySQL server.

Execute the following SQL queries in the console of the MySQL client:

```
CREATE DATABASE redmine CHARACTER SET UTF8;
CREATE USER 'redmine'@'localhost' IDENTIFIED BY 'your_password_here';
GRANT ALL PRIVILEGES ON redmine.* TO 'redmine'@'localhost';
```

Don't forget to replace your_password_here with the password that you specified in the config/database.yml file while you were configuring the database for Redmine.

Once you've finished, type quit and press *Enter* to exit the client.

Finalizing the Redmine installation

At this moment, only a few things are left to do to prepare Redmine for running. We need to create a secret token for the Redmine session store:

```
$ bundle exec rake generate_secret_token
```

Next, we need to create the structure (tables, indexes, and so on) of the Redmine database:

```
$ RAILS_ENV=production bundle exec rake db:migrate
```

Be ready – this command will produce a lot of output.

Finally, we need to insert initial data (such as trackers, the administrator account, and so on) into the database:

```
$ RAILS_ENV=production bundle exec rake redmine:load_default_data
```

This command will ask you to select a language in which the role names, the tracker names, the issue statuses and priorities, and so on should be added. You should think carefully about what to answer (for example, are you sure that you want the tracker names to be non-English?).

Configuring Apache

So by now, Redmine has been installed and configured, but we can't access it. To be able to do this, we need to configure Apache. Then let's move on to Apache's configuration directory:

```
$ cd /etc/apache2
```

Now, create the `redmine.conf` file in the `sites-available` subdirectory with the following content (do this under `root`):

```
<VirtualHost *:80>
        RailsEnv production
        DocumentRoot /opt/redmine/redmine-3.2.0/public
        <Directory "/opt/redmine/redmine-3.2.0/public">
                Allow from all
                Require all granted
        </Directory>
</VirtualHost>
```

This is the configuration of the virtual host that will run Redmine. However, this is not the only virtual host that we currently have.

> Please note that Redmine, which is installed and configured this way, is going to run from your user account. If you prefer to use another user, `www-data`, for example, you need to add `PassengerDefaultUser www-data` to your virtual host configuration, and change the owner of the `redmine-3.2.0` directory by executing `chown www-data:www-data /opt/redmine/redmine-3.2.0 -R`.

In Debian/Ubuntu, Apache comes with a default page, which must be disabled to let Redmine run (otherwise, we will be getting that page instead of Redmine). This can be done by running the following command:

```
$ sudo a2dissite 000-default
```

In fact, as mentioned in the previous section, this command removes a symbolic link to the `sites-available/000-default.conf` file from the `sites-enabled` directory. And, as you must have probably guessed, we need to do the opposite for our `redmine.conf` file. This can be done by executing the line shown here:

```
$ sudo a2ensite redmine
```

Ready to try? Then reload Apache:

```
$ sudo service apache2 reload
```

Now, if you open a browser and point it to the IP or hostname of your server, you should get the following result:

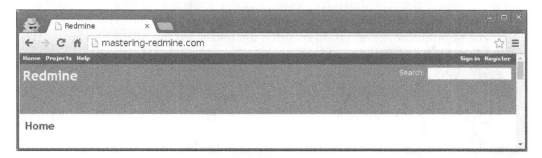

You can now log in to your new Redmine installation using admin as both the login and password.

Verifying and completing the installation

There is a page in Redmine that should always be checked after launching this application for the first time. This page is **Information**, and it can be found in the **Administration** menu.

The **Information** page was described in detail in the *Verifying and completing the installation* subsection of the previous section. So, please go there and check these details. Thus, you should change the password of the admin user as soon as possible. Also, you may want to install the ImageMagick convert tool.

Upgrading Redmine

As we have installed Redmine separately from the rest of the system (in other words, the system package manager won't able to see or recognize it), we will need to handle all its updates manually and on our own. The Redmine guys periodically issue maintenance releases aimed at fixing serious bugs. So by leaving the installation unmaintained, we risk having many issues, including but not limited to security and upgrade issues.

Also note that you will have to upgrade your Redmine installation to the next major or minor version when the Redmine guys stop maintaining the version that you are currently using. (For a package, this is not the case, as package maintainers usually handle security fixes and support the package as long as the corresponding release of the system is supported.) If you don't do this, you won't even know when a new serious bug is found in the version you use.

In other words, you need to keep a track of the new versions of Redmine to be sure that you upgrade as soon as a fix is available. But how do you know when a new Redmine version is released? To check this, you can subscribe to Redmine news using the ATOM feed at `http://www.redmine.org/projects/redmine/news.atom`. The appropriate news should mention the reason for the release—whether it is a security fix or it just contains new features.

> To read ATOM feeds, you can use Safari, Internet Explorer, Chrome (through a plugin), Mozilla Thunderbird, and so on.

Certainly, before performing an upgrade, you should always check the official Redmine upgrade documentation, which is available at `http://www.redmine.org/projects/redmine/wiki/RedmineUpgrade`. Nevertheless, we are going to discuss this procedure shortly here as well (focusing on the particulars of our installation).

> It's always a good idea to take a backup before upgrading. Thus, to back up the Redmine database, execute this command:
>
> `$mysqldump -u root -p redmine > /path/redmine.dump`
>
> It will ask for the MySQL superuser's password. Don't forget to replace `/path/redmine.dump` with your path.

As for the installation, we first need to download the recent version of Redmine. This can be done from the following URL (get the release in the `tar.gz` format): `http://www.redmine.org/projects/redmine/wiki/Download`. Unpack the archive into the `/opt/redmine` directory, where we already have `redmine-3.2.0`.

Now, we need to copy some configuration and other files from the old version of Redmine to the new one. In particular, we need `config/database.yml`, `config/configuration.yml` and everything inside the `files` directory.

Also, as for the installation, we will use Bundler to install all the Ruby dependencies. The command is the same:

```
$ bundle install --without development test
```

If anything goes wrong (say, any building errors), you know how to fix it (check out *Resolving Bundler errors* subsection).

Now copy the themes and plugins from the old version to the new one, but do this only if you are sure that each of them does support the new version of Redmine. If you are not sure, stop the upgrade procedure and go check if they do (see also *Chapter 10, Plugins and Themes*)! So, copy those themes and plugins that are known to work under the new version from the `public/themes` and `plugins` directories correspondingly, and install new versions of the plugins old versions of which do not work under the new version.

New versions of Redmine as well as those of plugins often come with changes to the database. So, it's important to execute the following commands:

```
$ RAILS_ENV=production bundle exec rake db:migrate
$ RAILS_ENV=production bundle exec rake redmine:plugins:migrate
```

These will update the database structure and will make any other fixes to the database, if needed.

As we have installed the new version in a separate directory under `/opt/redmine`, we need to update Apache to use this directory. So, open the `/etc/apache2/sites-available/redmine.conf` file in your favorite editor and replace `redmine-3.2.0` with the appropriate name of the new directory. Next, restart Apache:

```
$ sudo service apache2 reload
```

As I have mentioned before, I can't guarantee that the described upgrade procedure is proper (because at the time of writing this subsection subsection, there were no new versions to upgrade to). So, if you have upgraded Redmine using these instructions — and only them — and it runs fine, you are lucky. Never do it this way again! The goal of this subsection was to give you an idea of what an upgrade of Redmine sources looks like. More complicated and riskier than an upgrade of a Redmine package, isn't it?

Afterwards, if everything works fine, you can remove the old version of Redmine (at least, you might want to remove its `files` directory, which often occupies a lot of disk space).

Other installation options

Redmine is getting more and more popular and is therefore becoming a tool on which companies want to build their businesses. So, this certainly helps to obtain more and more options for easy installation of Redmine. I guess no one can now say that it's hard to establish a Redmine server.

Hosting Redmine

The easiest way to establish a Redmine website is perhaps by using a dedicated Redmine hosting provider. The problem with this option, however, is that you are limited in the customization of your Redmine instance (for example, you won't be able to install custom plugins). Also, you will have to deal with the customizations of the hosting provider (which you may like though).

One of the oldest and best known Redmine hosting providers (on which even some of its core contributors now work) is `https://plan.io/`. Their customized Redmine comes with the agile board, contacts, the CRM and helpdesk functionality (plugins of `http://www.redminecrm.com/`), news renamed to blogs, team chat, and more. Of course, it's not free, but the company offers a free 30-day trial at `https://plan.io/`.

Another hosting provider became known due to their interesting plugins that can be used for pure Redmine as well (but they are limited and their full versions are not free). It's EasyRedmine. Their Redmine version is highly customized and may come with many different amazing plugins, including plugins of `http://www.redminecrm.com/` and of their own. EasyRedmine can also be downloaded and installed on your server, but it's expensive. Luckily, you can try it for 14 days before buying. Their website is at `https://www.easyredmine.com/`.

There are also other dedicated Redmine hosting providers, such as `http://hostedredmine.com/`, which offers free hosting; `http://www.saas-secure.com/index.html`, which offers a limited free hosting service in addition to the paid one; and more.

Redmine server hosting

When I was going to create a DigitalOcean (VPS provider) Droplet with Ubuntu 14.04 LTS for a Redmine installation from sources, I found that the list of pre-installed applications contains **Redmine**, as shown here:

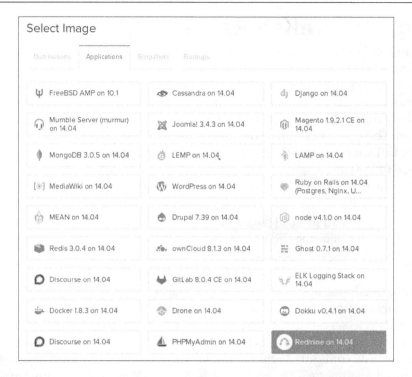

You just click on it (give it a name) and wait a little for the cloud hosting provider to establish a new server with Redmine that just runs. What can be simpler than this?

> To create a Redmine Droplet on DigitalOcean, you can use this link: `https://cloud.digitalocean.com/droplets/new?image=redmine`

However, don't think that I am claiming that this is a unique feature of DigitalOcean. It's quite possible that some other hosting providers offer similar Redmine server images. Just check out your favorite provider for such an option.

The DigitalOcean pre-installed Redmine server image currently uses Ubuntu 14.04 LTS. At the time of writing this subsection, the version of installed Redmine is 3.0.3, what means that the installation was done from sources and that they update the image periodically. Like us, DigitalOcean used the MySQL server and the Passenger module. Unlike us, however, they used Nginx. The installed Redmine does not ship with any plugins but includes the Subversion integration.

Using the TurnKey Redmine appliance

As the name suggests, the TurnKey Linux Redmine appliance comes as ready-to-use Linux images that can run under VirtualBox, VMWare, LXC, and Docker or can be deployed on a VPS (OpenVZ, Xen or OpenStack) or Amazon EC2 cloud. It is also available as a live CD ISO image, what means that you can first try and then install it. TurnKey Linux is based on Debian, so after deploying or installing it, you in fact get Debian. Therefore, you can update and install additional packages or security fixes from Debian repositories. However, it is not recommended to upgrade such an installation to the next major version of Debian. To migrate to a newer version of the appliance, TurnKey recommends that you use their special tool called TKLBAM.

> To download the appliance or deploy it on a VPS, use the following URL:
>
> `http://www.turnkeylinux.org/redmine`.

The TurnKey Redmine appliance currently comes with Redmine 3.0.3, which was installed manually, and therefore it is not connected to the system package manager. It uses the MySQL server, the Apache web server, the Passenger module, and Ruby Enterprise. The appliance comes with Subversion, Git, Bazaar, and Mercurial servers, which are already configured and integrated with Redmine. Email integration is also preconfigured and the mail transfer agent is Postfix. Besides, the system runs the SSH server, Webmin, and Webshell.

A special mention should also be made of TurnKey Hub. Like DigitalOcean, it allows you to quickly deploy the Redmine image on the Amazon EC2 cloud.

Using the Bitnami Redmine Stack

While the basic idea of the TurnKey Linux appliance is to ease the deployment of a new server, the basic idea of the Bitnami stack is to ease the deployment of an application. The Bitnami stack contains everything needed to run the application and, unlike TurnKey, supports Windows and Mac. In addition, you can download an Ubuntu-based virtual machine with the Bitnami Redmine stack intended for VirtualBox or VMware; or you can easily deploy the Stack on Amazon EC2, Google Cloud Platform, Microsoft Azure, VMware vCloud Air, or DigitalOcean. When deployed on the cloud, the Bitnami stack uses different host OSes for different cloud providers, thus for DigitalOcean, it uses Debian 8.1.

By the way, the deployment of a new Bitnami Redmine server on DigitalOcean is almost as easy as the deployment of the DigitalOcean's own Redmine image. But this feature is available only from the following Bitnami page: `https://bitnami.com/stack/redmine/cloud`. This page can also be used for deployment on other cloud providers.

The problem with Bitnami is that it is separate from the rest of the system, and therefore, you face all the maintenance issues mentioned earlier. Despite what you might expect, upgrading the Bitnami stack is not an easy task (Bitnami even recommends that you simply reinstall it). However, one good thing is that you can deploy other Bitnami stacks on the same server; for example, you can deploy the WordPress stack on the server that is already running Redmine. Another good thing is that the Bitnami stack always comes with the most recent version of Redmine.

Taking the preceding paragraphs into account, I can conclude that the Bitnami Redmine Stack is good for development and testing and it should not be chosen for production. Of course, it's only my opinion, and you should come up with yours considering all the said factors.

 To download the Bitnami Redmine Stack, go to this URL: `http://bitnami.org/stack/redmine`.

The Bitnami Redmine installer comes with Redmine 3.2.0 and everything you need to run it. Thus, it includes Apache, MySQL, Rails, Ruby, Passenger for Linux and Mac, and Thin for Windows. The installed Redmine ships with Subversion, Git, and CVS integration.

The Bitnami Redmine installation does not include any plugins, but Bitnami also offers the Redmine + Agile stack, which additionally includes the Agile plugin of RedmineCRM.com.

Using Docker

The Docker image is much like the Bitnami stack—it's a kind of a container that includes the application, everything needed to run it, and their dependencies. Like Bitnami stacks, multiple Docker images can be deployed to a single host system. But unlike Bitnami stacks, a Docker image is not self-contained. Thus, it requires Docker to be already available on the system to which the application is deployed.

Docker provides a registry of available applications, called Docker Hub, which lists more than 120 Redmine images. This registry includes an official Redmine image, but the most popular one is Sameer Naik's `sameersbn/redmine`. Both images should be used in conjunction with MySQL or PostgreSQL Docker images.

> **Links to the images**
>
> The official image is `https://hub.docker.com/_/redmine/` and Sameer Naik's image is `https://hub.docker.com/r/sameersbn/redmine/`.

While Docker is a Linux-based tool, it can also be run on Windows and Mac using a special tiny VirtualBox machine known as the Docker Machine. Certainly, this kind of setup is not to be used in production.

As you may have probably noticed, Docker is quite popular nowadays. Thus, it is available as an application on DigitalOcean and is supported by TurnKey and Bitnami (some appliances and stacks can be deployed on it). So, it's not a problem to deploy Redmine on a server through a Docker image.

Summary

Different users have different goals. Some users aim to have a stable installation without the need to pay much attention to it. Some users prefer to be up to date and have the latest features. Other users just want to give it a try. And so on. That's why we reviewed all the aforementioned options for a Redmine installation. Thus, there is no need to spend much time setting up Redmine from sources if you just want to play with it. So having read this chapter, you now have an idea on which option is best for you, and you should be able to install Redmine quickly and easily.

Probably, you have finished reading this chapter with a newly installed Redmine. If so, you should take time out to play with it. In fact, that would be good because when you get back to this book, you will understand what is written in the upcoming chapters better.

Note, however, that the just installed Redmine is too clean. Before using it, you should spend some time on its configuration, and that's what we are going to do in the next chapter. But don't expect to see only the basic configuration there. The next chapter should be interesting not only for those who will configure Redmine, but also for everyone else, as they will see what powerful things can be done in Redmine.

3
Configuring Redmine

When talking about the web interface (that is, not system files), all of the global configuration of Redmine can be done on the **Settings** page of the **Administration** menu. This is actually the page that this chapter is based on (it has many tabs; the other administration pages will be reviewed in the appropriate chapters later). Some settings on this page, however, depend on special system files or third-party tools that need to be installed. And these are the other things that we will discuss.

You might expect to see detailed explanations of all the administration settings here, but instead, we will only review a few of them in detail, as I believe that the others do not need to be explained or can easily be tested. So generally, we will focus on hard-to-understand settings and those settings that need to be configured additionally in some special way or have some obscurities.

So, why should you read this chapter if you are not an administrator? Some features of Redmine are available only if they have been configured, so by reading this chapter, you will learn what extra features exist and get an idea of how to enable them.

In this chapter, we will cover the following topics:

- The first thing to fix
- The general settings
- Authentication
- Email integration
- Repository integration
- Troubleshooting

The first thing to fix

A fresh Redmine installation has only one user account, which has administrator privileges. You can see it in the following screenshot:

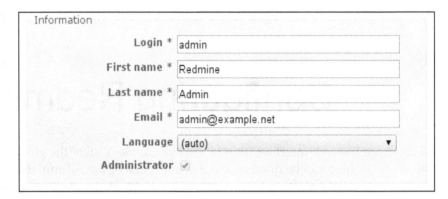

This account is exactly the same by default on *all* Redmine installations. That's why it is extremely important to change its credentials immediately after you complete the installation, especially for Redmine instances that can be accessed publicly.

The administrator credentials can be changed on the **Users** page of the **Administration** menu. To do this, click on the **admin** link. You will see this screen:

In this form, you should specify a new password in the **Password** and **Confirmation** fields (actually, you should have done this in the previous chapter). Also, it's recommended that you change the login to something different. Additionally, consider specifying your email instead of admin@example.net (at least), and changing the **First name** and **Last name**.

The general settings

Everything that is possible to configure at the global level (the opposite is the project level) can be found under the **Administration** link in the top-left menu. Of course, this link is available only for administrators.

If you click on the **Administration** link, you will get the list of available administration pages on the sidebar to the right. Most of them are for managing Redmine objects, such as projects and trackers. Such pages won't be reviewed in this chapter for the following three reasons: firstly, some of them are intelligible and need little explanation; secondly, many of them will be reviewed in later chapters; and thirdly, in this chapter, we will only be discussing general, system-wide configuration. Most of the settings that we are going to review are compiled on the **Settings** page, which is shown in the following screenshot:

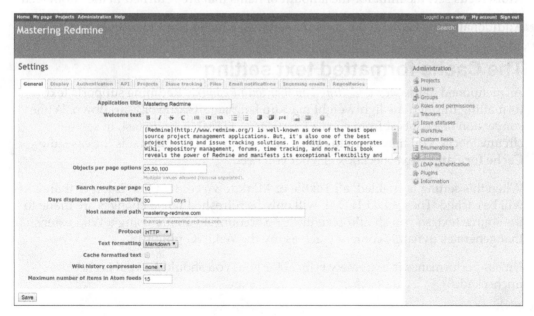

As all of these settings can't fit on a single page, Redmine organizes them into tabs.

 We will discuss the **Authentication**, **Email notifications**, **Incoming emails**, and **Repositories** tabs in the next sections. The **Projects** and **Issue tracking** tabs will be reviewed in the next two chapters.

The General tab

So let's start with the **General** tab, which can be seen in the previous screenshot. Settings in this tab control the general behavior of Redmine, thus **Application title** is the name of the website that is shown at the top of non-project pages, **Welcome text** is displayed on the start page of Redmine, **Objects per page options** specifies how many objects users will be able to see on a page, such settings as **Search results per page** and **Days displayed on project activity** allow you to control the number of objects that are shown on search results and activity pages correspondingly, the **Protocol** setting specifies the preferred protocol that will be used in links to the website, **Wiki history compression** controls whether the history of Wiki changes should be compressed to save space, and finally, **Maximum number of items in Atom feeds** sets the limit for the amount of items that are returned in the Atom feed.

Additionally, the **General** tab contains settings, which I want to discuss in detail.

The Cache formatted text setting

As mentioned in *Chapter 1, Getting Familiar with Redmine*, Redmine supports text formatting through the lightweight markup language Textile or Markdown. While conversion of a content from such a language to HTML is quite fast, in some circumstances, you may want to cache the resulting HTML. If that is the case, the **Cache formatted text** checkbox is what you need.

When this setting is enabled, all Textile or Markdown content that is larger than 2 KB will be cached. The cached HTML will only be refreshed when changes are made to the source text, so you should take this into account if you are using a Wiki extension that generates dynamic content (such as my the WikiNG plugin).

Unless performance is extremely critical for you, you should leave this checkbox unchecked.

Other settings tips

Here are some other tips for the **General** tab:

- The value of the **Host name and path** setting will be used to generate URLs in the email messages that will be sent to users, so it's important to specify a proper value here.

- For **Text formatting**, select the markup language that is best for you. The *Textile or Markdown?* section of *Chapter 1, Getting Familiar with Redmine*, can help you make a thoughtful decision. It's also possible to select none here, but I would not recommend doing this.

The Display tab

As it comes from the name, this tab contains settings related to the look and feel of Redmine. Its settings can be seen in the following screenshot:

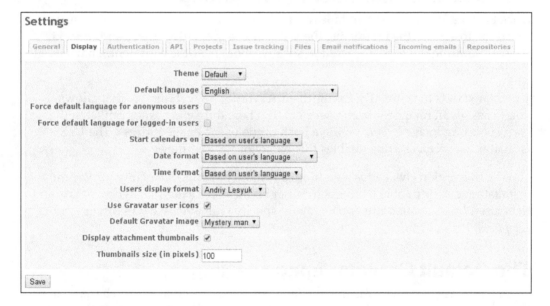

Using the **Theme** setting users can choose a theme for the Redmine interface (see also *Chapter 10, Plugins and Themes*). The **Default language** setting specifies which language will be used for the interface, if Redmine fails to determine the language of the user. Thus, for not logged-in users it will attempt to use the preferred language of the user's browser, what can be disabled by the **Force default language for anonymous users** setting, and for logged-in users it will use the language that is chosen by users in their profiles, what can be disabled by the **Force default language for logged-in users** setting. By default the user's language also affects the start day of the week, date, and time formats, what can also be changed by the **Start calendars on**, **Date format**, and **Time format** settings respectively. The display format of the user name is controlled by the **Users display format** setting. Finally, the **Thumbnails size (in pixels)** setting specifies the size of thumbnail images in pixels.

Now let's check what the rest of the settings mean.

The Use Gravatar user icons setting

Once I used a WordPress form to leave a comment on someone's blog. That form asked me to specify the first name, the last name, my email address, and the text. After submitting it, I was surprised to see my photo near the comment. That's what Gravatar does.

Gravatar stands for **Globally Recognized Avatar**. It's a web service that allows you to assign an image for each user's email. Then, third-party sites can fetch the corresponding image by supplying a hash of the user's email address. The **Use Gravatar user icons** setting enables this behavior for Redmine.

Having this option checked is a good idea (unless potential users of your Redmine installation can be unable to access Internet because, for example, Redmine is going to be used in an isolated intranet). How to specify Gravatars we will discuss in *Chapter 9, Personalization*.

The Default Gravatar image setting

What happens if a Gravatar is not available for the user's email? In such cases, the Gravatar service returns a default image, which depends on the **Default Gravatar image** setting.

The following table shows the six available themes of the default avatar image:

Theme	Sample image	Description
None		The default image, which is shown if no other theme is selected
Wavatars		A generated face with differing features and background
Identicons		A geometric pattern
Monster IDs		A generated monster image with different colors, face, and so on
Retro		A generated 8-bit, arcade-style pixelated face
Mystery man		A simple, cartoon-style silhouetted outline of a person

For all of these themes, except **Mystery man** and **none**, Gravatar generates an avatar image that is based on the hash of the user's email and is therefore unique to it.

The Redmine Local Avatars plugin

Consider installing the Redmine Local Avatars plugin by Andrew Chaika, Luca Pireddu, and Ricardo Santos, if you want users to upload their avatars directly onto Redmine:

`https://github.com/thorin/redmine_local_avatars`

This plugin will also let your users take their pictures with web cameras.

The Display attachment thumbnails setting

If the **Display attachment thumbnails** setting is enabled, all image attachments—no matter what object (for example, Wiki or issue) they are attached to—will be also seen under the attachment list as clickable thumbnails. If the user clicks on such a thumbnail, the full-size image will be opened.

The Redmine Lightbox 2 plugin

In pure Redmine, full-size images are opened in the same browser window. To open them in a lightbox, you can use the Lightbox 2 plugin that was created by Genki Zhang and Tobias Fischer:

`https://github.com/paginagmbh/redmine_lightbox2`

Note that in order for this setting to work, you must have the ImageMagick's convert tool installed (see the *Verifying and completing the installation* subsection of the *Installing Redmine from a package* section in *Chapter 2, Installing Redmine*).

The API tab

In addition to the web interface that is intended for human Redmine comes with a special **REST application programming interface** (**API**) that is intended for third-party applications. Thus, the Redmine REST API is used by Redmine Mylyn Connector for Eclipse and RedmineApp for iPhone. This interface can be enabled and configured under the **API** tab of the **Settings** page which is shown in the following screenshot:

Let's check what these settings mean:

- If you need to support integration of third-party tools, you should turn on the Redmine REST API using the **Enable REST web service** checkbox. But it is safe to keep this setting disabled, if you are not using any external Redmine tools.

- The Redmine API can also be used via JavaScript in the web browser, but not if the API client (that is, a website, that runs JavaScript) is on a different domain. In such cases to bypass the browser's same-origin policy the API client may use the technique called JSONP. As this technique is considered to be insecure it should be explicitly enabled using the **Enable JSONP support** setting, so in most cases you should leave this option disabled.

The Files tab

The **Files** tab contains settings related to file display and attachment as shown in the following screenshot:

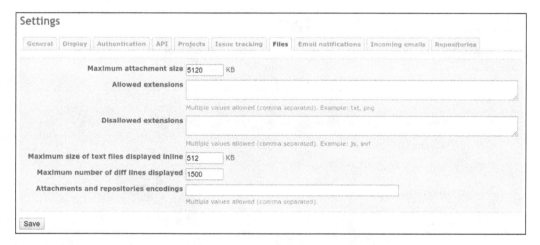

Here **Allowed extensions** and **Disallowed extensions** can be used to restrict file uploads by file extensions – thus you can use the former setting to only allow certain extensions or the latter one to forbid certain extensions. Such settings as **Maximum size of text files displayed inline** and **Maximum number of diff lines displayed** control the amount of the file content that can be displayed.

The rest of settings are used more often:

- You may need to change the **Maximum attachment size** setting to a larger value (it should be in KB). Thus, project files (releases) are attachments as well, so if you expect your users to upload large files, consider changing this setting to a bigger value.

- The value of the **Attachments and repositories encodings** option is used to convert commit messages to UTF-8.

Authentication

There are two pages in Redmine intended for configuring the authentication. The first one is the **Authentication** tab on the **Settings** page, and the second one is the special **LDAP Authentication** page, which can be found in the **Administration** menu. Let's discuss these pages in detail.

The Authentication tab

The next tab in the administration settings is **Authentication**. The following screenshot shows the various options available under this tab:

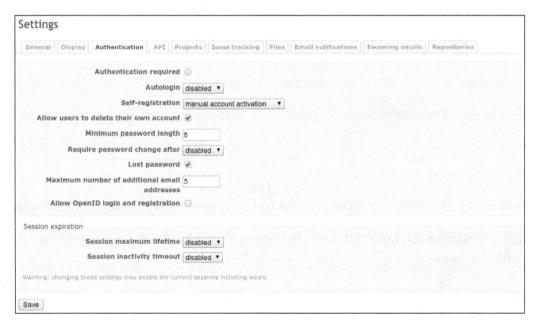

If the **Authentication required** setting is enabled, users won't be able to see the content of your Redmine without having logged in first. The **Autologin** setting can be used to let your users keep themselves logged in for some period of time using their browsers. The **Self-registration** setting controls how user accounts are activated (the **manual account activation** option means that users should be enabled by administrators). The **Allow users to delete their own account** setting controls whether users will be able to delete their accounts. The **Minimum password length** setting specifies the minimum size of the password in characters, and the **Require password change after** setting can be used to force users to change their passwords periodically. The **Lost password** setting controls whether users will be able to restore their passwords in cases when they, for example, have forgotten them. And finally the **Maximum number of additional email addresses** setting specifies the number of additional email addresses a user account may have.

After a user logs in Redmine opens a user session. The lifetime of such a session is controlled by the **Session maximum lifetime** setting (the value **disabled** means that the session hangs forever). Such a session can also be automatically terminated if the user was not active for some time, what is controlled by the **Session inactivity timeout** setting (the value **disabled** means that the session never expires).

Now, let's discuss a very special setting, which we skipped.

The Allow OpenID login and registration setting

If you are running a public website with open registration, you perhaps know (or you will know if you want your Redmine installation to be public and open for user registration) that users do not like to register on each new site. This is understandable, as they do not want to create another password to remember or share their existing password with a new and therefore untrusted website. Besides, it's also a matter of sharing the email address and—sometimes—remembering another login.

That's when OpenID comes in handy. OpenID is an open-standard authentication protocol in which authentication (password verification) is performed by the OpenID provider. This popular protocol is currently supported by many companies, such as Yahoo!, PayPal, AOL, LiveJournal, IBM, VeriSign, and WordPress. In other words, servers of such companies can act as OpenID providers, and therefore users can log in to Redmine using their accounts that they have on these companies' websites if the **Allow OpenID login and registration setting** is enabled.

Google used to support OpenID too, but they shut it down recently in favor of the OAuth2.0-based OpenID Connect authentication protocol. Despite the use of OpenID in its name, OpenID Connect is very different from OpenID.

So, if your Redmine installation is (or is going to be) public, consider enabling this setting. But note that to log in using this protocol, your users will need to specify **OpenID URL** (the URL of the OpenID provider) in addition to **Login** and **Password**, as can be seen on the following Redmine login form:

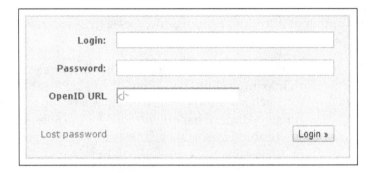

LDAP authentication

Just as OpenID is convenient for public sites to be used to authenticate external users, LDAP is convenient for private sites to authenticate corporate users. Like OpenID, LDAP is a standard that describes how to authenticate against a special LDAP directory server, and is widely used by many applications such as MediaWiki, Apache, JIRA, Samba, SugarCRM, and so on. Also, as LDAP is an open protocol, it is supported by some other directory servers, such as Microsoft Active Directory and Apple Open Directory. For this reason, it is often used by companies as a centralized users' directory and an authentication server.

To allow users to authenticate against an LDAP server, you should add it to the list of supported authentication modes on the **LDAP authentication** page, which is available in the **Administration** menu. To add a mode, click on the **New authentication mode** link. This will open the form:

Authentication modes » New authentication mode (LDAP)

Name *	Packt Publishing LDAP
Host *	ldap.packtpub.com
Port *	636 ☑ LDAPS
Account	cn=ldapadmin,dc=ldap,dc=
Password	••••••••
Base DN *	ou=users,dc=ldap,dc=packtpub,dc=com
LDAP filter	
Timeout (in seconds)	
On-the-fly user creation	☑

Attributes

Login attribute *	uid
Firstname attribute	givenName
Lastname attribute	sN
Email attribute	mail

Create

If the **On-the-fly user creation** option is checked, user accounts will be created automatically when users log in to the system for the first time. If this option is not checked, users will have to be added manually beforehand. Also, if you check this option, you need to specify all the attributes in the **Attributes** box, as they are going to be used to import user details from the LDAP server.

 Check with your LDAP server administrator to find out what values should be used in this form.

In Redmine, LDAP authentication can be performed against many LDAP servers. Every such server is represented as an authentication source in the authentication mode list, which has just been mentioned. The corresponding source can also be seen in the user's profile and can even be changed to the internal Redmine authentication if needed.

Email integration

Redmine email integration can be considered to consist of two components: email delivery (notifications) and email retrieval.

Email delivery

Most likely, if you open the **Email notifications** tab on a recently installed Redmine, you will get the following message:

This message clearly states that you can't fix this issue through the web interface. First, we need to modify the mentioned configuration file and then we can get back here. So, it's time to open the console.

The configuration.yml file

In the `config` subdirectory of the Redmine root directory, you will find the `configuration.yml.example` file. Copy (or just rename) it to `configuration.yml`:

```
$ cp configuration.yml.example configuration.yml
```

Now, open this file in your favorite console editor.

As you can see, it is divided into three blocks: `default`, `production`, and `development`. The `production` and `development` blocks are for environment-specific configuration and the `default` block combines the configuration options of all environments. As we are not going to have any specific configurations for the environments, we will use the `default` block.

The email configuration section starts under the `email_delivery` keyword. In this section you will find commented sample configurations, one of which you can use for your Redmine installation. The only option that is used in all the samples is `delivery_method`, which determines the type of delivery.

The `delivery_method` option accepts the following values: `:sendmail`, `:smtp`, `:async_sendmail`, and `:async_smtp`. The `:async_sendmail` and `:async_smtp` methods deliver emails in separate threads, thus not making users wait for the delivery to complete. Hence, asynchronous methods should be used on installations that involve the delivery of a large number of emails, when a mail (SMTP) server is slow or hardly accessible, or if you are experiencing slow loading of pages that send emails (for example, when you update an issue , when you create a wiki page, and so on).

From the aforementioned delivery methods, I personally recommend the use of `:sendmail` or `:async_sendmail`, as these methods will use the sendmail system tool. This tool is a standard part of **Mail Transfer Agent (MTA)** (software that performs mail delivery); that is, it ships with MTA and uses MTA to send emails. In other words, with the `sendmail` tool, you use the default delivery configuration of the operating system. So, if a system administrator modifies the email delivery configuration of the system, Redmine will automatically use it without any changes on its side. Additionally, such a configuration is easier to maintain as you don't have to care about separate email settings in Redmine:

```
default:
  email_delivery:
    delivery_method: :sendmail
```

You can also use a local or remote SMTP server by choosing the `:smtp` or `:async_smtp` delivery method. In this case, you will additionally need to specify `smtp_settings` to let Redmine know how to connect to the server.

> Avoid using external SMTP servers as in the event of an Internet connection loss, email messages won't be sent at all. Additionally, this will slow down the performance of your Redmine.

So, let's review the options that can be specified inside the `smtp_settings` block:

- The `address` option should contain the IP or hostname of the SMTP server. If you are going to put `localhost` here, consider using `:sendmail` instead.

- The `port` option should contain the TCP port number of the SMTP server. Normally, it is 25 or 587 if the TLS secure protocol is used (for example, TLS is used by Gmail).

- The value of the `domain` option is used for the `HELO SMTP` command. Normally, it's the domain part of the sender's email address. For Gmail (but not Google Apps), you should specify `smtp.gmail.com` here.

- The `authentication` option accepts the `:plain`, `:login` or `:cram_md5` values. You should ask which value to choose to the system administrator of the SMTP server that you are going to send emails through. For Gmail, this should be `:login`.

- Values of the `user_name` and `password` options are going to be used to authenticate the Redmine mailer on the SMTP server.

- Finally, the `enable_starttls_auto` option should be set to `true` if the SMTP server requires TLS (normally, this should be enabled if the port number is 587). Set it to `true` for Gmail.

Avoid using a personal account in `smtp_settings`. Some SMTP servers (for example, Gmail) may override the `from` address of the email message with the address of the authenticated account. Therefore, all Redmine notifications may appear to be coming from your personal email address. Consider creating a special account for this purpose instead.

When you finish editing the `configuration.yml` file, don't forget to save it and restart Redmine.

The Email notifications tab

Let's check out the **Email notifications** tab again. Now it should look as shown in the following screenshot:

These settings are very important as email notifications can annoy users and multiple emails from a single source can be treated as spam. So, let's review them in detail.

The value of the **Emission email address** setting is going to be used as the sender address in email messages, which will be sent from your Redmine. So, its default value, which you can see in the preceding screenshot, should definitely be changed! Normally, people set it to something like no-reply@yourdomain.com, but I would recommend using a real email address here, for example, the email address of your support staff.

If the **Blind carbon copy recipients (bcc)** setting is disabled, notification recipients will be able to see who else has been sent a copy of this notification (what could be treated as a disclosure). So, it's normally a good idea to leave this setting enabled.

The **Plain text mail (no HTML)** setting can be used to make Redmine send all email notifications in the plain text format, that is, without rich text formatting, links, and so on.

However, the most important setting is perhaps the **Default notification** option. It determines which notification mode will be set for new users. As practice shows, users rarely change this setting in their profiles, so the option you choose here is most likely going to be used for most of your users. Let's review the supported modes in detail (also see *Chapter 9, Personalization*):

- **For any event on all my projects**: This option should never be selected by anyone except the users themselves, as in this mode, they are going to receive notifications about all events in all projects that they are members of. From my experience, I can tell you that users (especially if they are not familiar with Redmine) will most likely configure their email clients to move such notifications to a separate folder, and will never read them rather than fix the appropriate notification setting in their profiles. That's why I believe that only the users themselves should select this option. However, if you still want this mode to be the default, be sure to check as few notification actions in the **Select actions for which email notifications should be sent** block as possible.

- **Only for things I watch or I'm involved in**: This option is selected by default. In this mode, users will receive notifications about events in objects that they own (that is, of which they are the authors) or are/were assigned to (if the object is an issue).

- **Only for things I am assigned to**: In this mode, users will be notified about events in issues that they are or were assigned to (this is the same as the previous one, except that authors are not notified).

- **Only for things I am the owner of**: In this mode, users will be notified only about the events in objects that they are authors of.

- **No events**: This mode disables email notifications for the user.

All modes, except **No events**, will still send notifications to users if they are explicitly watching the object that generates these notifications (for example, an issue).

The **Select actions for which email notifications should be sent** block contains the list of events about which Redmine will notify users. Only administrators (and only on this tab) can determine which actions will generate notifications. In other words, if you leave, for example, the **News added** event disabled here, users will never receive emails with any news about any projects (they will need to check it out using the project page or news feeds)! Therefore, I personally recommend that you enable all the available actions here. Otherwise, people may subscribe to some objects assuming that they will get emails on particular events and then get frustrated with the absence of such emails. So, let it be the users who control which notifications they can get.

The next two blocks are self-explanatory. They contain text that will be inserted into the email before and after the notification message. Be sure to change `http://hostname/my/account` to the actual URL here.

Once you have finished configuring the email notifications, you can click on the **Send a test email** link to check whether the email delivery works, and how it works. This link will send a test message to the email address that you have specified in your Redmine account.

Reminder emails

Redmine issues have an optional **Due date** attribute. So what about being notified of the issue due date in advance? Let's do it?

Redmine ships with so-called rake tasks — small Ruby tools intended for different specific tasks that can or should be performed from the console. It also comes with a rake task that can be used to generate notifications about upcoming issue due dates. The name of this task is `redmine:send_reminders`, and it accepts the following options:

- `days`: The number of days before the due date. The value defaults to 7.
- `tracker`: The numerical (internal) tracker ID. If the value is not specified all issue trackers will be checked.
- `project`: The identifier (which is used in the URL) of the project. The task will check all projects if no identifier is specified.
- `users`: The numerical IDs of users and/or groups separated by commas. If the value is omitted all users will be notified.
- `version`: The project version in which the issues are to be resolved. All versions will be checked if the value is not specified.

The syntax of the command that runs the `redmine:send_reminders` task is as follows:

```
$ rake redmine:send_reminders days=7 tracker=1 project=book users=1,5
versions=1.0.0 RAILS_ENV=production
```

Now, let's configure our Redmine to remind all users about the issue due dates a day before they are due, but not on weekends. So, open `crontab` (the file that specifies commands that should be run periodically) using the following command:

```
$ crontab -e
```

> You may need to specify a different user with the `-u` option, for example:
>
> ```
> $ sudo crontab -u www-data -e
> ```
>
> If you are not sure whether the current account can be used, just try running the rake task manually first.

The preceding command will open an editor. Add the following two lines there:

```
0 10 * * 1-4 /usr/local/bin/rake -f /usr/share/redmine/Rakefile
redmine:send_reminders days=1 RAILS_ENV=production
0 10 * * 5 /usr/local/bin/rake -f /usr/share/redmine/Rakefile
redmine:send_reminders days=3 RAILS_ENV=production
```

Run `which rake` to determine the path to the `rake` tool on your server. Be sure to also replace `/usr/share/redmine/` with the correct path to Redmine if you are not using the Redmine package. When you're done, save the changes and exit the editor.

So what do these lines mean? The first line will be executed at 10:00 a.m. on Mondays, Tuesdays, Wednesdays, and Thursdays, and the second line will be executed at 10:00 a.m. on Fridays.

Also note that this rake task will generate reminder emails for issues, the due dates of which are within the specified number of days. So, if you choose 7 days, users will get notifications about issues that are due in 6 days and in 1 day. Running such a task (with `days=7`) every day can really annoy your users. That's why we chose one day in the preceding example. In other words, you should execute this task once in the specified number of days; that is, if you use `days=7`, execute it only, for example, on Mondays.

Email retrieval

While the invention of email predates the invention of the World Wide Web, email is still one of the primary electronic ways to communicate. Thus, while I have a public issue tracker for my projects, I still keep getting emails regarding issues from users. Perhaps that's why email integration is one of the essential features of modern issue trackers, and Redmine does have it.

If you have taken a look at the Redmine directory structure, you might have noticed the `extra` directory, the subdirectories of which contain some scripts and a sample plugin. We are going to review all of these tools in this chapter (except the plugin). Soon, we'll start with `rdm-mailhandler.rb`. As you might have guessed from its name, this script can help Redmine handle incoming email messages.

In addition to `rdm-mailhandler.rb`, Redmine comes with two rake tasks that can be used to retrieve emails, namely `redmine:email:receive_imap` and `redmine:email:receive_pop3`.

The difference between the script and the two rake tasks is in the method in which they are invoked. Thus, `rdm-mailhandler.rb` was designed to be run on the mail server by the **Mail Transfer Agent** (**MTA**), while rake tasks are to be used to fetch emails **from** a remote mail server. Certainly, the script that gets executed by the mail server when an email arrives is better for several reasons: firstly, it runs only when there is a job to do and secondly, Redmine retrieves the email right after it comes to the mail server (that is, the delay is minimal). However, the tool that fetches emails from a remote mail server can be useful as well, especially if the remote mail server is, for example, Gmail (so there is no way to install the `rdm-mailhandler.rb` tool on it).

For the aforementioned reasons, we are going to review both these solutions. But let's start with discussing what exactly Redmine can do with incoming emails.

Handling incoming emails

In incoming emails Redmine expects to see mainly new issues. In addition to issues, Redmine can import issue comments and forum board messages from emails. So, when you receive a notification about a new issue, you can just reply to it and the message that you'll send will be added as a note to this issue. In the same way, you can answer someone's note or other changes in an issue, or someone's message in forums.

> If you want Redmine to receive replies from users via email, you should change the **Emission email address** setting to the address at which you plan to handle such emails. Thereby, this email address will be used automatically by users' email clients when they click on the **Reply** button.

To create a new issue, Redmine needs to know values of several required attributes, that is, the tracker, status, and priority. Luckily, the default values for these attributes can be specified in the tools that are going to be used to process incoming emails. But what if your Redmine also requires some custom fields? Besides, will it not be too limiting to have hardcoded values of such attributes for all issues created via email?

To mitigate the issues that were just mentioned, Redmine can recognize attributes in the message body and supports many more attributes than just the required ones. Check out the sample email body:

```
Hi!

I have an issue...

These are attributes:
Assigned to: Andriy Lesyuk
Tracker: Support
Status: New
Priority: Urgent
Category: Email queries
Target version: 1.0.0
Start: 2016-01-01
Due date: 2016-01-18
Estimated time: 20
Done ratio: 50
Custom field: Value
```

Additionally, values for the issue attributes can be specified in the replies to existing issues. Certainly, whether changes will be applied to the issue, as well as whether a new issue with the specified attribute values will be created, depends on the permissions of the user who authors the email (the user is identified by the `from` email address). Also, to allow changes to the project, tracker, status, priority, and issue category in the email body, you need to list all of these attributes in the `allow_override` or `--allow-override` argument for the appropriate tool (see *Forwarding emails from mail server* and *Fetching emails from IMAP/POP3* subsections).

To prevent attributes and their values from appearing in issue descriptions, issue notes, and forum messages, Redmine allows you to configure which lines the message text should be truncated after. The corresponding lines should be specified under the *Incoming emails* tab of the **Settings** page, that is shown in the following screenshot:

Thus, for our preceding example, we could specify `These are attributes:` here to remove attributes from the issue description or issue note. Of course, such delimiters are to be negotiated with users.

 I believe that it's essential to have the double hyphen line (--) here, as it is often used to separate the message body from the signature.

Also, if the incoming email includes **To** and/or **CC** addresses that are registered in Redmine (that is, there exist user accounts with such emails), the corresponding users will automatically be added to the watchers list of the issue. However, this does not happen for replies.

Finally, if the email includes attachments, they will be attached to the corresponding issue or forum message. Of course, the attachment size limit that is specified on the **General** tab of the **Settings** page is applied to such attachments as well. Additionally, on the **Incoming emails** tab, which was discussed earlier, you can specify the list of wildcarded filenames to skip while importing attachments from emails.

Forwarding emails from mail server

The majority of popular **Mail Transfer Agents** (**MTAs**) can forward incoming email to a third-party script as soon as it arrives in the inbox. And the `rdm-mailhandler.rb` tool, which I have mentioned before, is a script that should be used in this way. When the MTA forwards the email to this tool, `rdm-mailhandler.rb` builds a special HTTP request containing the email message and transmits it to a special **web service** (**WS**) of Redmine. Then, this web service processes the message and performs the appropriate action (for example, creates an issue).

So first, we need to enable the mentioned web service in Redmine. This can be done on the **Incoming emails** tab of the **Settings** page, that is shown in the preceding screenshot. There, you should check the **Enable WS for incoming emails** checkbox and then click on the **Generate a key** link. This will make Redmine generate a special key that will be needed to access the web service.

When ready, copy the `rdm-mailhandler.rb` tool to your mail server and put it into `/usr/local/sbin`. If it's a different server (that is, not the one that Redmine runs on), make sure that you have everything needed to run a Ruby script. If not, install whatever is missing.

But before we proceed, we will check out what arguments are supported by this tool. Let's start with the mandatory ones:

- The `--url` argument should be set to the base Redmine URL, for example, `http://mastering-redmine.com`
- The `--key` argument should be set to the key that we have generated
- Instead of the `--key` argument, you can use `--key-file`, which should be set to the path of the file where the key is stored

Now, let's see what optional arguments are available:

- The `--unknown-user` option accepts values such as `ignore` (the default), `accept`, or `create`. If the default `ignore` value is used, all email messages that come from an unknown email address (that is, an email address that is not associated with any user account in Redmine) will be ignored. If the `accept` value is set, issues created with such email messages will be authored by the special `Anonymous` user. And finally, if the `create` value is specified, new user accounts will be created.

- There are also a couple of other arguments that can be used to control the process of user creation. Certainly, they work only when the --unknown-user argument is set to create. Thus, --default-group can be used to add the newly created users to some special group. The --no-account-notice argument instructs Redmine not to send the account information to the new user. The --no-notification arguments disables email notifications for such users (that is, it enables the **No events** option).

- The --project argument can be set to the identifier of the project in which issues are to be created. If this argument is omitted, the project identifier should be explicitly specified in the body of each email message.

- The --project-from-subaddress argument can be used to tell Redmine which email address can contain the project identifier as a subaddress part of the address (for example, in issues+book@mastering-redmine.com the book is a subaddress and a project identifier). In this way, users will be able to select the project right in the email address. Also note that Redmine will look for such addresses in to, cc, and bcc email headers.

- The --fixed-version argument can be used to set a target version for new issues.

- The --tracker argument can be set to the name of the tracker that will be used for newly created issues.

- The --status argument can be specified to set a different initial status for issues that are created from incoming emails (the default issue status is configured per tracker what will be reviewed in the next chapter).

- The --category argument can be used to set a special category for issues that are created from emails.

- The --priority argument can be used to set a different priority for issues that are created from incoming emails.

- If the --private argument is used, all created issues will be made private.

- The --allow-override argument can be used to restrict the issue attributes, which can be specified in the message body of the incoming email. The issue attributes that are supported by this argument are the six aforementioned ones: project, tracker, status, category, priority, and private (multiple attributes should be separated by commas).

- If the --no-permission-check argument is used, new issues, comments and forum messages will be created, even if the author of the email does not have appropriate permissions.

- Finally, two special arguments, --no-check-certificate and --certificate-bundle, can be used to bypass SSL certificate errors.

The `rdm-mailhandler.rb` script is intended to be executed in the shell, that is, it's just a console script. So here is a sample of the command:

```
/usr/local/sbin/rdm-mailhandler.rb --unknown-user create --project book
--url http://mastering-redmine.com --key mvF868NBavZZVWinIejC
```

The rest of configuration depends on which mail transfer agent are you using. As we can't review all the available MTAs here, let's assume that you are using Postfix, which is configured to use a plain-text file for aliases, such as `/etc/aliases`.

So, open the `/etc/aliases` file and add the following line:

```
issues: "|/usr/local/sbin/rdm-mailhandler.rb --unknown-user create
--allow-override=project,tracker,status,category,priority --project book
--url http://mastering-redmine.com --key mvF868NBavZZVWinIejC"
```

Here, `issues` is the username part of the email address (the full address can look like `issues@mastering-redmine.com`). The string that starts with the pipe (|) instructs Postfix to forward messages that come to this email address to the standard input of the `rdm-mailhandler.rb` tool.

After this, your Redmine should be able to receive issues, notes, and forum messages via email.

Fetching emails from IMAP/POP3

Nowadays, many companies host their email on external mail servers that they do not own (for example, on Google). So, it's impossible for them to integrate the `rdm-mailhandler.rb` tool with the server's MTA. Especially for such cases, Redmine provides two additional rake tasks that can fetch emails from remote IMAP and POP3 servers. As the IMAP protocol is more advanced, the IMAP rake task has more features than the POP3 one, but which one to use depends on what protocol is supported by your mail server. Many servers (including Gmail) support both.

So let's see what the command for fetching emails from IMAP looks like:

```
$ rake redmine:email:receive_imap host=imap.gmail.com port=993
ssl=1 username=issues@mastering-redmine.com password=LIIWLmedev6M9yAJ
RAILS_ENV=production
```

Now, let's review the options that are available for the IMAP and POP3 rake tasks. Here they are:

- The `unknown_user` option, like the `--unknown-user` argument of `rdm-mailhandler.rb`, supports values such as `ignore`, `accept`, and `create`. The meanings of these values are the same as that ones for `rdm-mailhandler.rb`.

- Like `rdm-mailhandler.rb`, the rake tasks support special options: `default_group` and `no_account_notice`. These options can be used to control the process of user creation (to add the user to a group and to disable the account information notification correspondingly).

- The `project`, `status`, `tracker`, `category`, `priority`, `fixed_version`, `private`, and `allow_override` options also accept the same values and have the same meanings as the corresponding arguments of `rdm-mailhandler.rb`.

- The `no_permission_check` option can be used to allow creating issues, comments, and forum messages by users who do not have the appropriate permissions in Redmine.

- The `host` option should be set to the IP or hostname of the mail server. Its default value is `localhost`.

- The `port` option should contain the port number of the mail server. For IMAP the default value is `143`, and for POP3 it is `110`.

- The `ssl` option should be set to `1` if the mail server supports SSL.

- The `starttls` option is available only for IMAP. It should be set to `1` if the IMAP server supports this protocol extension.

- The `username` and `password` options specify the credentials that should be used to connect to the IMAP or POP3 server.

- The `folder` option, which is supported only for IMAP, specifies the name of the mail folder on the server to process. The default folder is `INBOX`.

- The `apop` option can be used to select the APOP authentication for the POP3 server.

- By default, the POP3 rake task keeps email messages that it failed to process on the mail server (because, for example, they can be intended for a human). So the special `delete_unprocessed` option can be used to instruct the task to remove such emails.

The IMAP protocol allows moving email messages between server folders. To use this feature, the IMAP rake task supports the following additional options:

- The `move_on_success` option specifies the name of the folder to which the successfully processed emails should be moved.

- The `move_on_failure` option specifies the name of the folder to which the ignored email messages should be moved.

Now that we know what options we can use, let's make the rake task check the IMAP server for new emails once in an hour. To do this we'll add it into `cron` using the command:

```
$ crontab -e
```

This command will open the editor. Add there a line that looks like this:

```
45 * * * * /usr/local/bin/rake -f /opt/redmine/redmine-3.2.0/Rakefile
--silent redmine:email:receive_imap host=imap.gmail.com port=993 ssl=1
username=issues@mastering-redmine.com password=LIIWLmedev6M9yAJ
unknown_user=create allow_override=project,tracker,status,category,
priority RAILS_ENV=production
```

This line tells `cron` to run the `redmine:email:receive_imap` rake task on the 45th minute of every hour. Here, `/usr/local/bin/rake` is the full path to the `rake` tool, which can be obtained using the `which rake` command, and `/opt/redmine/redmine-3.2.0` is the root directory of the Redmine installation. Also, make sure you replace the credentials with your own ones.

The `redmine:email:receive_pop3` rake task can be run in a very similar way.

Repository integration

Repository integration is an awesome feature of Redmine. I just can't imagine this application without it! So, I believe that you will like Redmine for having it. But as soon as you get to know how deep this integration can be, I'm sure you will love Redmine even more!

We will start by configuring repositories and ensuring that the basic integration works. Then we will discuss how to turn Redmine into a repository manager.

The Repositories tab

So, here we come to the last tab on the **Settings** page — the **Repositories** tab:

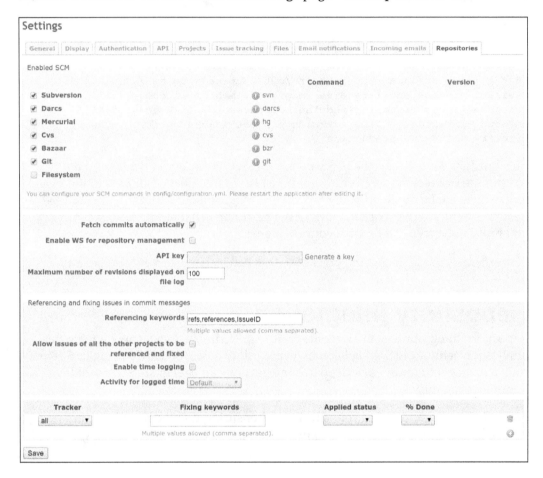

The exclamation mark near the name of an **Source Control Management (SCM)** command indicates that there is some issue with this SCM. The small text below the checklist in the **Enabled SCM** block advises that you may need to specify proper paths to the commands in config/configuration.yml. But you should do this in rare cases, for example, if you have installed SCMs from sources. And in most other cases, the exclamation mark just means that the SCM is not installed (as in this case).

So, let's shortly review how to install these SCMs on Ubuntu/Debian. Of course, you are not likely to need all of them (you should have decided which SCM to use after having read *Chapter 1, Getting Familiar with Redmine*).

SCM	Installation command
Subversion	`$ sudo apt-get install subversion`
Darcs	`$ sudo apt-get install darcs`
Mercurial	`$ sudo apt-get install mercurial`
CVS	`$ sudo apt-get install cvs`
Bazaar	`$ sudo apt-get install bzr`
Git	`$ sudo apt-get install git`

If you have installed any of these SCMs, do not forget to restart Redmine to make it pick them up. Afterwards, if you go to the **Repositories** tab, you should see check marks instead of exclamation marks near the commands and SCM version numbers in the **Version** column:

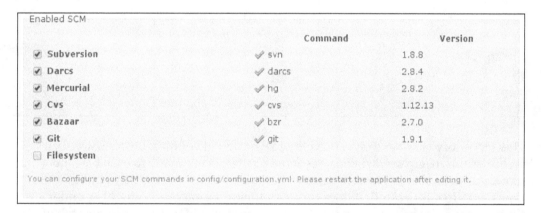

If any of the listed SCMs are not installed (or exclamation marks are still shown for them for some other reasons), you should disable them here by unchecking the corresponding checkboxes.

Before enabling the **Filesystem** SCM, you should set the `scm_filesystem_path_regexp` option in `config/configuration.yml` to a regular expression that will ensure that a proper path is used! Otherwise, users who have the **Manage repository** permission can get the ability to read the filesystem of the server that runs Redmine.

Other blocks of the **Repositories** tab are reviewed in the following subsections.

Fetching commits

The main feature of Redmine SCM integration is the repository browser, which is available under the **Repository** tab of a project. Here is the screenshot that shows how it looks on Redmine.org:

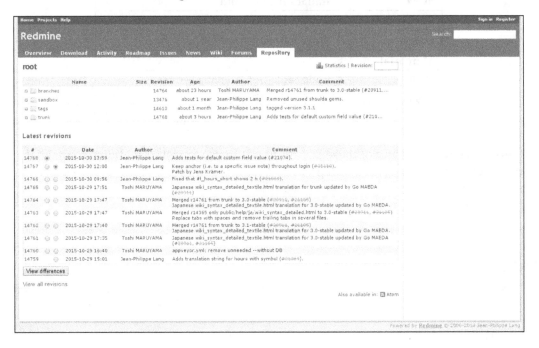

This repository browser can be used to view or download files, browse directories and revisions, compare revisions, see what changes were made to each file, and more. But to be able to see new changes, Redmine needs to fetch them from the repository first. By default, it does this each time a user accesses anything under the `projects/<project>/repository` URL (that is, under the **Repository** tab of the project).

In other words, Redmine fetches new commits from the repository when you click on the **Repository** tab, on the `trunk` directory of the repository, on a file of such a directory, and so on! If Redmine does not have to serve many users at the same time and the repository is local, this should not be a big problem. But what if the Redmine installation is heavily loaded and uses remote repositories?

This default behavior is enabled by the **Fetch commits automatically** setting, which can be found on the **Repositories** tab of the **Settings** page. So, to make Redmine stop updating commits on each user visit, you just need to disable it. But how will Redmine fetch new data in this case? Without such updates, the **Repository** view of the project is going to become outdated sooner or later.

Luckily, Redmine offers several other solutions for fetching new commits from repositories. Which one to use depends on whether the repository is local or remote and from where the update can be initiated. Generally, there are two places where you can initiate this process—from cron or from an SCM hook.

Using cron

Cron can be used to trigger an update of repositories within Redmine. However, this can be done only on the same server where Redmine is running. Still, it's better than the default update-on-request option, as you can control how many times the update is executed.

To trigger the update, you need to use the following command:

```
$ rails runner "Repository.fetch_changesets" -e production
```

So, this command should be put into `crontab` as follows:

```
*/30 * * * cd /opt/redmine/redmine-3.2.0 && /usr/local/bin/rails runner
"Repository.fetch_changesets" -e production
```

Don't forget to replace `/opt/redmine/redmine-3.2.0` with the actual path to your Redmine installation.

This line will trigger the fetching of commits for *all* projects every 30 minutes.

> This command can also be used to make Redmine load data from a huge repository that was just added to a project. Doing this from the browser (using the **Fetch commits automatically** mode) can be troublesome.

The second option is more advanced and flexible, and it is to be used on the server where the SCM is running.

Using an SCM hook

All SCMs—at least the ones that I used to work with—support **hooks**. Hooks are scripts that are located in a special directory or are listed in a configuration file of the repository. Thus, for Subversion this directory is `hooks`. For Mercurial hooks are to be specified under the [hooks] section in `.hg/hgrc`. For CVS, they can be specified in the `commitinfo` file. For Bazaar, they can be either put into the `.bzr/hooks` directory or listed in the `bazaar.conf` file. For Git, they should be put into the `.git/hooks` directory. These scripts are triggered when an event occurs, for example, when a user makes a commit to the repository. And this is exactly where we should initiate fetching the commits for Redmine!

To do this, we need to use another special **web service (WS)** that is provided by Redmine and that can be accessed using the following URI: sys/fetch_changesets. But first, we need to enable it on the **Repositories** tab of the **Settings** page:

Fetch commits automatically	☐
Enable WS for repository management	☑
API key	oVVm1CmvXJnpRVmTZ5ii Generate a key
Maximum number of revisions displayed on file log	100

Check the **Enable WS for repository management** checkbox here and click on the **Generate a key** link. Then press **Save**.

Now, you need to create a hook script for your SCM (check out the SCM's documentation for the format, the name of the script, and the location) and put the following command there:

```
curl -o /dev/null "https://mastering-redmine.com/sys/fetch_changesets" -d
key=oVVm1CmvXJnpRVmTZ5ii > /dev/null 2>&1
```

Replace https://mastering-redmine.com with the actual URL of your Redmine installation and oVVm1CmvXJnpRVmTZ5ii with the key that was generated for you.

 Use the HTTPS protocol in the URL (if available) to encrypt the key when it is sent over the Internet.

Different projects usually use different repositories, which can be located on different servers, and even use different SCMs. For such cases, this web service supports an additional parameter: id. This parameter should contain the project identifier, like in the following example:

```
https://mastering-redmine.com/sys/fetch_changesets?key=oVVm1CmvXJnpRVmTZ5
ii&id=book
```

Actually, this is the right approach—each repository should be configured to update only the project to which it belongs. But, this means that each repository is to be configured separately, which can be a headache (especially if your Redmine installation hosts many projects). However, Redmine will otherwise update all repositories in all projects when a commit is made to any of them.

The Git SCM supports only local repositories in Redmine, but it's possible to make a clone from GitHub and then keep the local copy up to date using Jakob Skjerning's GitHub Hook plugin:
`https://github.com/koppen/redmine_github_hook`

Do not forget to disable the **Fetch commits automatically** setting on the **Repositories** tab when you have configured all your repositories to trigger the update of commits through the web service.

Automatic creation of repositories

In the previous subsections of this section, we discussed how to configure Redmine as a repository browser, which is a well-known feature of this application that actually works out of the box (if the SCM is installed). Now let's speak how to turn Redmine into a repository manager.

Redmine comes with a special tool intended for creating repositories for projects that do not have a repository yet. The name of this tool is `reposman.rb`, and it's located in the `extra/svn` directory of Redmine. It is to be executed periodically by cron on the SCM server. When it is run, it connects to Redmine, fetches its projects list, checks whether a repository exists for each of the projects, and creates a repository if the project does not have a repository yet. But note that it expects the project's repository to have exactly the same name as the project itself (it uses the project identifier). Also note that to use it, you'll need access to the server that hosts SCM (or is going to host it).

To proceed, you need to know where the repository files are to be located. If the SCM server has already been configured, figure out what the path for repositories is and which SCM is to be used. If no SCM server exists yet, let's just create a directory for repositories for now; later on, in the next subsection, we'll configure the server.

It is assumed that you are going to use Subversion. To conform to the FHS, let's select `/var/lib/svn` as the directory for the Subversion repositories:

```
$ sudo mkdir /var/lib/svn
```

If you have not enabled the web service for repository management, as described in the *Using an SCM hook* subsection of this chapter, do it now. This web service is going to be used by the `reposman.rb` tool to check the repositories list.

Also, before creating a repository, we need a project that this repository will be added to. This can be either a test project or a real one. A new project can be created using the **New project** link, which becomes available when you click on the **Projects** item in the top-left menu. So please create it, if you don't have a project yet.

When ready, open the console on the SCM server and test the `reposman.rb` tool by running it in the following way:

```
$ sudo /opt/redmine/redmine-3.2.0/extra/svn/reposman.rb --owner=www-
data --svn-dir=/var/lib/svn --url=file:///var/lib/svn --redmine-
host=mastering-redmine.com --key=oVVm1CmvXJnpRVmTZ5ii --verbose -test
```

Change the paths, the hostname, and the API key to the correct ones.

 If the SCM server is located on a different physical server, you'll need to copy `reposman.rb` there and possibly install Ruby.

Let's review the various options that are supported by this tool:

- The `--svn-dir` option should point to the directory under which new repositories are to be created.

- The `--redmine-host` option should hold the IP or hostname that will be used by the `reposman.rb` tool to connect to Redmine.

- The `--key` option specifies the API key of the web service.

- The `--owner` option specifies the name of the system user who will own the repository files on the SCM server.

- The `--group` option can be used to specify the name of the group to which the repository files will belong.

- The `--url` option specifies the URL that can be used to access repositories externally (for example, `http://mastering-redmine.com/svn`).

- The `--scm` option should be specified if any other than the Subversion SCM is to be used (its possible values are `Subversion`, `Darcs`, `Mercurial`, `Bazaar`, `Git`, and `Filesystem`).

- The `--command` option can be used to specify a custom command for repository creation, and it is required for SCMs other than Subversion and Git.

- The `--key-file` option can be used as an alternative to `--key` as it allows you to store the API key in a file.

- The `--test` option can be used to check what the tool is going to do.

- By default, the `reposman.rb` tool creates a repository only if the corresponding project does not have any repository yet. This can be changed by the `--force` option, which instructs the tool to always create the repository with the project's identifier in its name, if such a repository is missing.

- The `--verbose` option can be used to get more information about what the tool is doing.

- The `--quiet` option is to be used if you do not want the tool to give any output to the console.

If the test run worked fine, we can use `cron` to make the tool be run periodically and create repositories, when new projects are registered. To do this, add the following line to `crontab`:

```
15 * * * * /opt/redmine/redmine-3.2.0/extra/svn/reposman.rb --owner=www-
data --svn-dir=/var/lib/svn --url=file:///var/lib/svn --redmine-
host=mastering-redmine.com --key=oVVm1CmvXJnpRVmTZ5ii --quiet
```

This tells `cron` to run `reposman.rb` on the 15th minute of every hour.

From now on, *all* your projects should have repositories created for them automatically.

> **The SCM Creator plugin**
>
> For easy repository creation, you can also use the SCM Creator plugin. This plugin currently supports Subversion, Git, Mercurial, and Bazaar. For all of these SCMs, except Git, it can create only local repositories (located at the same server on which Redmine is running). For Git, it can create local and remote GitHub repositories. You can check it out at:
>
> `http://projects.andriylesyuk.com/project/redmine/scm-creator`

Advanced repository integration

If you check a role's permissions on the **Roles and permissions** page of the **Administration** menu, you will see the **Commit access** permission. This permission has nothing to do with Redmine as a web application, as no commit access is, in fact, possible within Redmine. Actually, it is for what is called advanced repository integration. Thus, this permission is going to be checked by an extra tool called `Redmine.pm`, if it has been properly integrated. And like other similar tools this one can be found in the `extra/svn` directory of Redmine.

Normally, a Subversion server uses the Apache web server with the WebDAV module. The same configuration can be used for a Git and a Mercurial server. And the `Redmine.pm` tool is actually another module for Apache that handles authorization.

So how does it work? When users request access to a repository, Apache asks `Redmine.pm` whether it should authorize or forbid them. To give the answer, `Redmine.pm` reads data from the Redmine's database. Access is granted or denied depending on the user's role and permissions. Thus, if the user's role in the project has the **Commit access** permission, the user is allowed to commit changes to the project's repository.

> If you want to allow read-only access to the repository for anonymous users, make the corresponding project public and grant the **Browse repository** permission to the **Anonymous** role.

Let's now see how to configure advanced integration for Subversion:

1. We'll start with installing and configuring the Subversion server. It is assumed that you are going to use Debian/Ubuntu to run the SCM server and you have already installed Apache. Execute the following command:

    ```
    $ sudo apt-get install libapache2-svn libapache2-mod-perl2
    libapache-dbi-perl
    ```

    This command will install the WebDAV and ModPerl modules for the Apache and the Perl DBI library.

2. Now, copy `Redmine.pm` into the `Authn` subdirectory of the `/usr/lib/perl5/Apache` directory:

    ```
    $ sudo mkdir /usr/lib/perl5/Apache/Authn
    ```

    ```
    $ sudo cp /opt/redmine/redmine-3.2.0/extra/svn/Redmine.pm /usr/
    lib/perl5/Apache/Authn/
    ```

3. Next, we need to know where the repositories are going to be located. If you have chosen the path in the *Automatic creation of repositories* subsection, use that path. Otherwise, let's use `/var/lib/svn`:

    ```
    $ sudo mkdir /var/lib/svn
    ```

    At the moment, we have all that we need to start configuring Subversion with Apache.

    There are two options for adding the Subversion configuration to Apache configuration files: use an existing `<VirtualHost>` directive if you want Subversion to be accessible under a path such as `/svn`, or add a new `<VirtualHost>` directive, if you want to use Subversion under a subdomain, (for example, `svn.mastering-redmine.com`). We will choose the first option (for the second option, you need to create a new virtual host first). Also, we will use the `redmine.conf` file that we created while installing Redmine on Ubuntu using the official tarball (see the *Installing Redmine from sources* section of *Chapter 2, Installing Redmine*).

4. Open the configuration file of the virtual host and add the following lines before the closing `</VirtualHost>` directive:

```
PerlLoadModule Apache::Authn::Redmine
<Location /svn>
        DAV svn
        SVNParentPath /var/lib/svn

        Order deny,allow
        Deny from all
        Satisfy any

        AuthType Basic
        AuthName "Mastering Redmine SVN Server"
        PerlAccessHandler Apache::Authn::Redmine::access_handler
        PerlAuthenHandler Apache::Authn::Redmine::authen_handler

        RedmineDSN "DBI:mysql:dbname=redmine;host=localhost"
        RedmineDbUser redmine
        RedmineDbPass your_password_here

        <Limit GET PROPFIND OPTIONS REPORT>
            Require valid-user
            Satisfy any
        </Limit>
        <LimitExcept GET PROPFIND OPTIONS REPORT>
            Require valid-user
        </LimitExcept>
</Location>
```

Instead of the credentials that are used in this sample configuration (the database name, username, and password), use the real ones. If you are not sure about them, take them from the Redmine's `database.yml` file.

 You will also need to replace `localhost` with the IP or hostname of your Redmine installation if you are using a separate server for Subversion. Additionally, you may need to modify the bind-address option of the MySQL server in this case.

5. When ready, restart Apache:

```
$ sudo service apache2 reload
```

This is it! You are now ready to go with advanced Subversion integration.

Advanced Git integration can be configured in a very similar way (with some Git-specific configuration steps). The same can also be done for Mercurial and Bazaar. However, it would be unfair to only additionally review Git in this section, and it would be too much to review all SCMs here. So for other SCMs, you should check out the official tutorials for advanced integration at `http://www.redmine.org/projects/redmine/wiki/HowTos`. See the **Source Code Management (SCM)** section there.

Troubleshooting

No one is lucky enough to never have an issue with an application. So, it's essential for a user to know where to ask for assistance, how to do it, and what information should be provided to make the issue as clear as possible. That's what we'll discuss now.

Before asking a question, it's always worth ensuring that no one has asked it before and that the answer has not been given yet. Besides Google, you can search for issues similar to the one that you experience on `http://www.redmine.org/`, using the search form `http://www.redmine.org/search`. Check the following screenshot:

In most cases, the answer — if it exists — is found in **Issues** or **Messages**. The answer to a frequently asked question can also be found in **Wiki pages**.

If you can't find the answer using this search form, the first thing to check is whether the issue is really related to Redmine itself. Thus, it can be related to one of the plugins that you are using. The easiest way to check this is to try to disable all plugins (or to disable them one by one to determine which plugin causes the issue). This can be done by simply renaming the plugins' `init.rb` files, using the following command for example:

```
$ mv redmine_scm/init.rb  redmine_scm/init.rb.bck
```

This command should be executed for each subdirectory (`redmine_scm` is such a subdirectory) of Redmine's `plugins` directory (this is where plugins are located). Also, don't forget to restart Redmine after executing this command.

If it appears to be an issue in a third-party plugin, contact its author or the community. To find the home page of the plugin check out the **Plugins** page in the **Administration** menu (but note that not all plugins specify the home page). Alternatively, you can try finding the contact details for the plugin using the already mentioned search form (choose **Redmine plugins**).

Now it's the time to prepare the details. Let's start with getting information about the environment under which we are running Redmine. Execute the following command:

```
$ RAILS_ENV=production ruby bin/about
```

For http://mastering-redmine.com/, this command currently gives the following output:

```
Environment:
  Redmine version                3.1.1.stable
  Ruby version                   1.9.3-p484 (2013-11-22) [x86_64-
linux]
  Rails version                  4.2.4
  Environment                    production
  Database adapter        Mysql2
SCM:
  Subversion                     1.8.8
  Filesystem
Redmine plugins:
  no plugin installed
```

Keep this information, as it should be provided in the issue that you are going to report to developers.

Before asking Redmine developers or the community to help you with your issue, you should also check out the Redmine log files. In many cases, logs can give you a hint about the source of the problem, so you can even understand how to resolve it on your own. Anyway, error messages from your log files, if any, should be always given to the people whom you ask for help.

Usually, Redmine stores its logs under the own log directory. However, if you use the Redmine package from the Debian/Ubuntu repository to install Redmine, the log files will be under the redmine subdirectory of /var/log. The name of the file that contains logs should be production.log (for the production environment).

Normally, a log file consists of blocks like this:

```
Started GET "/admin/plugins" for 23.197.12.199 at 2015-10-30 20:45:06
-0500
Processing by AdminController#plugins as HTML
  Current user: s-andy (id=1)
  Rendered admin/plugins.html.erb within layouts/admin (4.6ms)
  Rendered admin/_menu.html.erb (7.6ms)
  Rendered layouts/base.html.erb (21.0ms)
Completed 200 OK in 49ms (Views: 38.9ms | ActiveRecord: 1.2ms)
```

This is a block without errors.

An erroneous block looks like the following:

```
Started GET "/users/1" for 192.168.0.1 at 2015-10-30 14:13:17 +0000
Processing by UsersController#show as HTML
  Parameters: {"id"=>"1"}
  Current user: s-andy (id=1)
  Rendered users/show.html.erb within layouts/base (4.3ms)
Completed 500 Internal Server Error in 277ms (ActiveRecord: 19.3ms)


ActionView::Template::Error (undefined method `mail' for
#<User:0x00000007a420c0>):
    10:        <li><%=l(:field_login)%>: <%= @user.login %></li>
    11:    <% end %>
    12:    <% unless @user.pref.hide_mail %>
    13:        <li><%=l(:field_mail)%>: <%= mail_to(@user.mail, nil, :encode
=> 'javascript') %></li>
    14:    <% end %>
    15:    <% @user.visible_custom_field_values.each do |custom_value| %>
    16:    <% if !custom_value.value.blank? %>
  app/views/users/show.html.erb:13:in `_app_views_users_show_html_erb___8
01144951909033840_62290640'
  app/controllers/users_controller.rb:77:in `block (2 levels) in show'
  app/controllers/users_controller.rb:73:in `show'
  lib/redmine/sudo_mode.rb:63:in `sudo_mode'
```

If you are getting something like this, then it's definitely an error in the code.

Usually such an error is accompanied by the following message in the browser:

Or it will be something like this if you use Passenger:

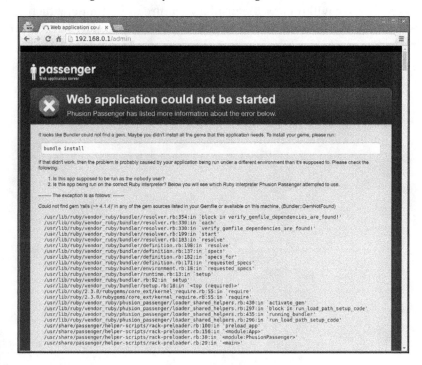

So, if you get such messages, look for errors in your logs!

 If the error message says could not find gem, try running bundle install. If the stack trace contains a plugin's file (a file under the plugins directory), then the error could be caused by this plugin.

If your issue is not yet resolved, go to `http://www.redmine.org/` and create a new issue or post a message on its forums.

But if you find a possible security vulnerability, report it to `security@redmine.org` instead.

Summary

I guess you have become a bit tired with all these general details, installations, configurations, integrations, and so on. We have been walking around Redmine for three chapters, but have not really worked with it (besides the settings, of course). This was the last such chapter. In the upcoming chapters, you will be learning how to use its main features (through the web interface).

In the next chapter we will review the primary feature of Redmine, which is really well implemented and which made Redmine so popular. This feature is **issue tracking**.

4
Issue Tracking

It's difficult to determine whether Redmine is rather a project management tool or an issue tracker. Issue tracking is not possible without a project (while some project management is still possible without issues). Even so, we spend most of our time working with Redmine as an issue tracker. This appears to be a fundamental component of Redmine that nevertheless depends on its other components. So, to use Redmine effectively, you have to learn it. For these reasons, we will start reviewing Redmine's functionality from its issue tracking capabilities.

In other words, the Issue tracking module is too deeply tied to other Redmine modules to be reviewed separately. But the opposite is also true—other modules use issues too extensively to skip issue tracking and start from reviewing other components. So, in this chapter, we will try to concentrate on issue tracking while also mentioning other modules if and where they are applicable. But don't worry if you are not familiar with mentioned modules yet! I will let you know where you'll be able to check them quickly.

In this chapter, we will cover the following topics:

- Creating an issue
- The issue page
- The issue list
- Updating an issue
- Issue reports
- Importing issues
- Keeping track of changes
- Issue-related settings

Creating an issue

In order to be able to create an issue, you need to have a project already. So, create one if you haven't done this yet (use the **New project** link that can be found under the **Projects** menu item). You can also jump to the *Creating a project* section in *Chapter 5, Managing Projects*, where project creation is described, and then come back here.

If you already have a project, or after you have created it, navigate to the **New issue** tab in the **Projects** menu. You will see the following form:

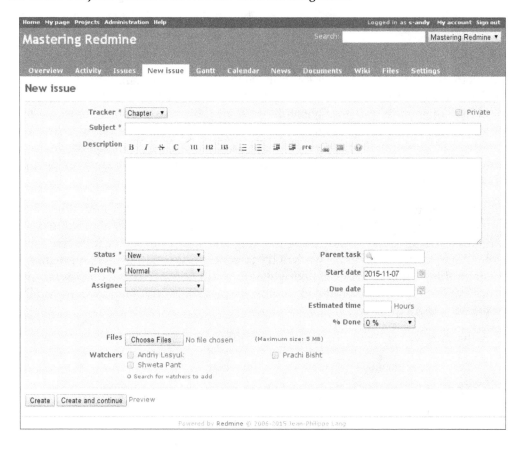

This is the form that Redmine users use to create issues. Fields that are marked with the red asterisk * are mandatory.

> Issues can be also created via email if you have configured the email retrieval (as described in the *Email retrieval* subsection of *Chapter 3, Configuring Redmine*), or through third-party tools if you have enabled the REST API.

Let's discuss each element of this form:

- In Redmine, the **Tracker** name is used to describe the type of the issue. Thus, the appropriate element in JIRA (a popular commercial alternative to Redmine) is named literally **Issue type**. By default, Redmine comes with the following trackers:

    ◦ **Bug**

    ◦ **Feature**

    ◦ **Support**

    You can delete, modify, or add trackers using the **Trackers** page of the **Administration** menu, which will be reviewed in *Chapter 7, Access Control and Workflow*. For my demo project, I have added a new tracker called **Chapter**, which you can see selected in the previous screenshot.

- The **Private** checkbox can be used to make the issue visible only to you and other members of groups that you are a member of. If the project is private as well, such users are also required to be members of the project.

- The **Subject** field should briefly describe the issue (like, for example, an email subject describes the message). In most cases, the tracker and the subject of the issue (in addition to the unique numerical identifier) are the only fields that users see on other Redmine pages that mention the issue. For this reason, the content of this field should be chosen with care.

> The subject should give the basic idea about the issue and should not be ambiguous or too long.

- I believe that the **Description** field does not need an explanation. But it's worth mentioning that for this field you can use rich text formatting. To get an idea about its capabilities, you can click on the last button ⚙ of the upper toolbar. We will review the appropriate Wiki syntax in *Chapter 6, Text Formatting*.

> Remember that rich formatting can help you draw the eye to the key messages and highlight specific data, such as code blocks, in the issue description. This in turn can improve the overall perception of the issue.

- The **Status** field indicates the status of the issue, such as whether it is active, whether anyone is working on it, whether it is already resolved, and so on. In the previous screenshot, the status was set to **New** as that was a new issue, and this status was selected by default (I just did not change it). The available issue statuses, their order and the default status can be configured on the **Issue statuses** and **Trackers** pages of the **Administration** menu.

- The **Priority** field reflects how urgent or critical the issue is. The values for this field and their order can be managed on the **Enumeration** page of the **Administration** menu. There, you can also select the default value (which is **Normal** by default).

- The **Assignee** field holds the name of the user who will be responsible for handling the issue. Only members of the project or the original issue author can be selected here. That is, if you want to assign an issue to someone, you must first ensure that that person is a member of the project (new members can be added under the **Members** tab of the project's **Settings** page).

- The **Parent** task field can hold the numerical identifier of another issue to which the new issue will be added as a subtask. To help you identify the right issue, when you type a value Redmine shows the autocomplete box with a list of matching issues and their subjects.

- The **Start date** and **Due date** fields can be used to set the period during which the issue has to be resolved. Nonetheless, they don't have to be specified together. These attributes, if both are set, are used to display the issue on the project's Gantt chart. Also, each of these attributes is used to display the issue on the calendar. By default Redmine sets the **Start date** field to the current date, what can be disabled under the **Issue tracking** tab of the **Settings** page in the **Administration** menu.

- The **Estimated time** field can be used to specify how many hours it should take to resolve the issue. This attribute can be especially useful if you are using the, Time tracking project module (which is described in *Chapter 8, Time Tracking*), as it allows you to control the time spent on the issue.

> Normally, you should not set the estimated time for an issue, unless it is assigned to you or you are a manager for the person to whom the issue is assigned.

- The **% Done** field, also known as the done ratio, indicates how much percentage of the issue has been resolved. Thus, it should ideally be 0% by the start date, and by the due date, it should be 100%. The value specified here is shown on the Gantt chart and is used for the project roadmap to show the overall progress for the corresponding version.

- Redmine allows you to add any number of attachments to an issue. Each attachment can have a description (the special textbox for the description appears as soon as you upload a file to the issue form). The size of each file is limited by the **Maximum attachment size** setting, which can be found under the **General** tab of the **Settings** page in the **Administration** menu.

> It's a good idea to describe the file that you attach to the issue, using this special textbox. You should do this, even if it's the only attachment in the issue, as other users can add more files later (for example, with the same name).

- Each issue can be watched. By watching the issue, you will:
  - Be able to see a list of issues that you watch on **My page** (if you have enabled the **Watched issues** block there; this page is going to be reviewed in *Chapter 9, Personalization*). In this way, you can have a kind of a list of *favorite* issues.
  - Be notified via email about any changes made to the issue (if email notifications have been enabled and properly configured; refer to *Chapter 3, Configuring Redmine*, to learn how to do this).

- The new issue form, which you can see in the previous screenshot, includes checkboxes only for members of the project. To add non-members to the **Watchers** list, you need to click on the **Search for watchers to add** link.

- When you have finished editing the issue, you can click on the **Create** button to submit it and open its page. Alternatively, if you need to add another issue, you can click on the **Create and continue** button to save the current issue and get the new issue form again.

- The **Preview** link can be used to preview the issue description, in particular to check how the Wiki markup will be rendered.

Some of the discussed form elements, which are also known as standard fields, can be disabled for particular trackers on the **Trackers** page of the **Administration** menu. Most of them can also be made required or read-only per issue status, member role, and tracker on the **Workflow** page of the same menu. Both of these pages will be reviewed in *Chapter 7, Access Control and Workflow*.

Additionally, Redmine supports custom fields for issues, which can add their own elements to the issue form as well. Custom fields are going to be reviewed in *Chapter 11, Customizing Redmine*.

Even so, these are not all the elements that this form can include. There can be more elements added when you configure the project. The project configuration is discussed in detail in the very next chapter. Now let's talk about only those things that add new elements to the new issue form.

Issue categories

In many cases, having just the tracker (the issue type) is not enough to describe an issue. To see what I mean, let's take the **Feature** tracker. Is an issue of this tracker for a UI feature? Is it for a new functionality of the project? Is it, maybe, for an API feature? As you can see, for some complex projects, you may need an additional attribute to make the issue more concrete. And Redmine does provide such an issue attribute. But why did not we see it? Because we need to add at least one value for this field to make it appear on the issue form.

Such values can be added in the **Issue categories** tab, which can be found in the project's settings (the **Settings** tab of the project menu). Here is what this tab looks like:

As you can see, there are no issue categories here for now. To add an issue category, you need to click on the **New category** link. Then you'll see the following form:

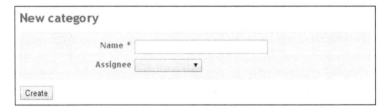

The **Assignee** field of this form can be set to a user to whom issues of this category should be automatically assigned (unless of course the assignee was specified explicitly). Thus, if you have different employees responsible for different parts of the project, you can create categories named after those parts and specify the corresponding employees here as assignees for those categories. In this way, a reporter will only need to select a part of the project and the issue will automatically get assigned to the corresponding employee.

But wait! How will reporters select the issue category? If you check out the new issue form after you have added an issue category, you will see an additional field there, as shown in this screenshot:

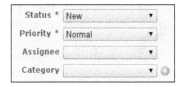

The ⊚ icon at the right-hand side of the field appears only for users who have the **Manage issue categories** permission. Such users may add issue categories right from the issue form.

 Some examples of good issue categories are **API**, **Reporting**, **Front-end**, **Back-end**, and **UI**.

Issues and project versions

Normally, a project has multiple planned versions. If so, in which of them is a particular issue planned to be resolved? This question draws attention to the need to be able to assign an issue to a project version. However, the issue form that was shown earlier did not include any field for this. Well, the project that I used did not have any version either.

As soon as you add a version to the project using the **Versions** tab, which can be found on the project's **Settings** page, the new field appears on the form, as shown in the following screenshot:

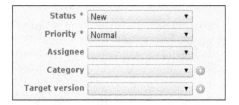

The new **Target version** field should be set to the name of the version in which the issue should be resolved. If it's set, the issue will also be listed on the project roadmap and in the version's change log (both will be reviewed in *Chapter 5, Managing Projects*).

Similar to the one near the **Category** field, the ⊕ icon allows you to add a version directly from the issue form. Of course, to be able to do this, you must have the **Manage versions** permission. You will learn more details about version management in the next chapter.

The issue page

When you finish creating an issue by clicking on the **Create** button, you get redirected to the issue page, which looks like this:

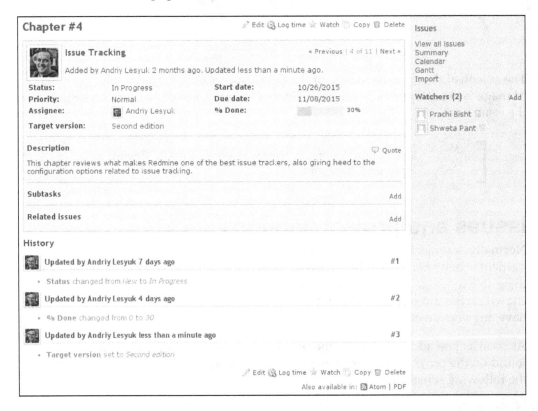

This page not only shows information about the issue but also gives you all the instruments that you need to work with it.

The content of the issue, including its attributes, is located inside the big yellow block. In the top-right corner of this block, you can see the **Previous** and **Next** links. These links can be used to navigate through the issue list (for example, issue search results).

Below the yellow block, you can see the **History** section. It lists changes that were made to the issue and includes information on what exactly was changed, when it was changed, and by whom.

The sidebar of this page contains the contextual links (most of which will be reviewed in *Chapter 5, Managing Projects*) and the **Watchers** section, which can be used to manage the watchers of the issue.

Subtasks

In the previous screenshot, at the bottom of the yellow box, you can see two empty sections. The first of them is **Subtasks**. If you click on the **Add** link to the right of its label, you will be redirected to the new issue form, with the **Parent task** field pre-filled with the current issue number. In this way, you can create subtasks.

But, what are subtasks? Let's check out the following screenshot:

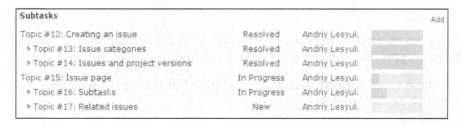

These are the subtasks that I added to my demo project. Besides being shown in the hierarchical structure, subtasks (usually) also define the priority (the highest priority of all subtasks is used), the start date (the earliest date is used), the due date (the latest date is used), the done ratio (calculated), and the estimated time (the sum is used) for the parent task. Certainly, Redmine does not allow you to specify values for these attributes of the parent task explicitly in such cases. However, this behavior can be changed from the **Issue tracking** tab of the global **Settings** page (we will review this tab later in this chapter).

The Smart Issues Sort plugin

Redmine has an issue with displaying the hierarchical tree of tasks, as it strictly keeps the sort order. In the previous screenshot, the hierarchy is preserved because issues are sorted by numbers and they are sequential. So, to have the hierarchical tree of issues, you need either to keep their numbers sequential by creating them in the appropriate order, or to use the Smart Issues Sort plugin by Vitaly Klimov, which resolves this issue:

```
http://www.redmine.org/plugins/redmine_smart_
issues_sort.
```

Related issues

Another empty section at the bottom of the yellow box on the issue page is **Related issues**. If you click on the **Add** link of this section, the following form will appear inside it:

This form can be used to associate other issues with the current one. For each such related issue, you should specify the type of relation.

Some of these types not only describe the relation but also provide implicit functionality. So, let's review each of them:

- **Related to**: This is one of the relation types that does not do anything. You can use it just to mark that the issues are somehow related. Also, this type is selected by default, as it can be seen in the previous screenshot.

- **Duplicates**: This type tells Redmine that the current issue should be closed when the related one is closed.

- **Duplicated by**: This type is the inverse of **Duplicates**. It forces the related issue to be closed when the current one is closed.

- **Blocks**: This type does not allow the related issue to be closed until the current one is open.

- **Blocked by**: This type is the inverse of **Blocks**. It tells Redmine to prevent the closure of the current issue until the related one is open.

- **Precedes**: This type forces the start date of the related issue to follow the due date (plus an optional delay in days) of the current one.

- **Follows**: This type is the inverse of **Precedes**. It forces the start date of the current issue to follow the due date (plus an optional delay in days) of the related one.

- **Copied to**: This type marks the related issue as a copy of the current one and is automatically set by Redmine when an issue is copied. This relation type should not be set manually.

- **Copied from**: This type marks the current issue as a copy of the related one and is automatically set by Redmine when an issue is copied. This relation type should not be set manually either.

As the **Precedes** and **Follows** relation types support an additional delay, the relation form includes the special **Delay** field for these two types, as shown in the following screenshot:

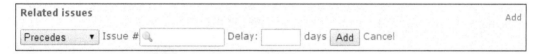

In this field, you can specify the number of days that should pass between the due date of the preceding issue and the start date of the following issue.

 The described implicit functionality can become a source of confusion. Thus, if two duplicate issues are assigned to different employees, closing one of them will lead to closure of another one, and this can come as a surprise to the assignee of the latter. Also, adding a preceding issue with empty start and due dates can lead to clearing the dates of the following issue. For these reasons, you should be careful while managing issue relations.

When added, related issues are shown in the **Related issues** section, as you can see in this screenshot:

Related issues				Add
Follows Chapter #3: Configuring Redmine	Resolved	10/12/2015	10/25/2015	
Precedes Chapter #5: Managing Projects	New	11/09/2015	11/22/2015	

The issue list

Now that you have learned how to create issues and check their details, let's move on to the **Issues** tab of the **Projects** menu, where they are listed:

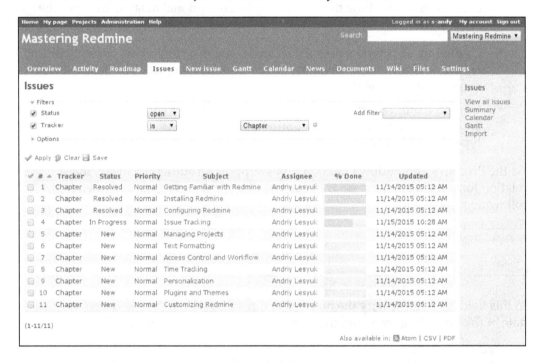

On the sidebar of this page, you can see the same **Issues** section that you could see on the single issue page. The **View all issues** link of this section can be used to open the issue list with all view parameters reset to their default values. The form under the **Issues** title in the main content area and above the list is actually the one that you can use to modify the parameters of the list. Let's discuss this form in detail.

By default, issues are filtered by their status, so only open issues are listed. But you can add more filters using this form. Thus, you can also filter issues by **Tracker**, **Priority**, **Author**, **Assignee**, **Category**, **Target version**, **Subject**, **Start date**, **Due date**, the done ratio, the issue relation, and much more. The following screenshot shows some of the filters that are available:

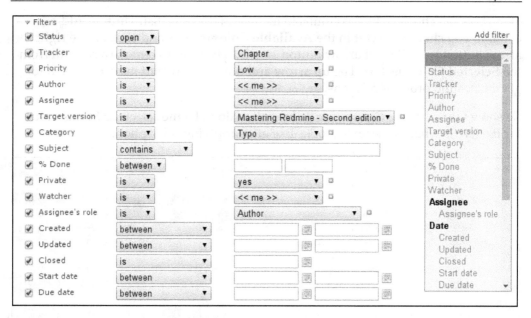

Each of these filters has a set of its own conditions. For example, the **Subject** filter can check a part of the subject, the **Tracker** filter can look for several trackers (the little plus icon ⊡ enables the multi-select mode), and date filters support relative conditions (such as, for examples, **less than days ago**, **this week**, **in more than (days)**, and so on). The best way to learn these filters is perhaps by playing with them—if you don't have enough issues on your Redmine installation, you can do this at http://www.redmine.org/.

Below **Filters**, you can see the **Options** label. If you click on it, the following form elements will be shown:

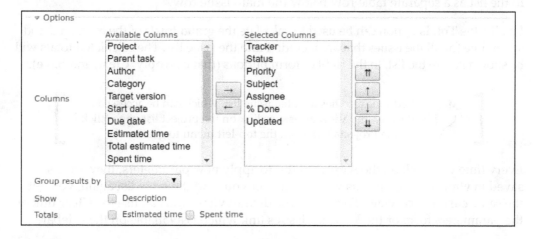

Here, you can choose which columns to include in the issue list. Thus, to add a column, you should select it in the **Available Columns** box and click on the right arrow button →. The left arrow button ← is to be used to remove a column from the **Selected Columns** box. The up arrow and down arrow buttons can be used to get the desired order of columns.

To show you what the **Group results by** option does, let me select the **Status** value for it. Here is what the issue list looks like after applying this option:

✓	# ▲	Tracker	Status	Priority	Subject	Assignee	% Done	Updated
⊟ New								
☐	5	Chapter	New	Normal	Managing Projects	Andriy Lesyuk		11/14/2015 05:12 AM
☐	6	Chapter	New	Normal	Text Formatting	Andriy Lesyuk		11/14/2015 05:12 AM
☐	7	Chapter	New	Normal	Access Control and Workflow	Andriy Lesyuk		11/14/2015 05:12 AM
☐	8	Chapter	New	Normal	Time Tracking	Andriy Lesyuk		11/14/2015 05:12 AM
☐	9	Chapter	New	Normal	Personalization	Andriy Lesyuk		11/14/2015 05:12 AM
☐	10	Chapter	New	Normal	Plugins and Themes	Andriy Lesyuk		11/14/2015 05:12 AM
☐	11	Chapter	New	Normal	Customizing Redmine	Andriy Lesyuk		11/14/2015 05:12 AM
⊟ In Progress								
☐	4	Chapter	In Progress	Normal	Issue Tracking	Andriy Lesyuk		11/15/2015 10:28 AM
⊟ Resolved								
☐	1	Chapter	Resolved	Normal	Getting Familiar with Redmine	Andriy Lesyuk		11/14/2015 05:12 AM
☐	2	Chapter	Resolved	Normal	Installing Redmine	Andriy Lesyuk		11/14/2015 05:12 AM
☐	3	Chapter	Resolved	Normal	Configuring Redmine	Andriy Lesyuk		11/14/2015 05:12 AM

As you can see, the list gets divided into groups. Each group has a label with the number of issues in it. Also, these groups can be collapsed or expanded (using the gray plus ⊞ or minus ⊟ icon correspondingly).

The **Show** option, if the **Description** checkbox is checked, adds the issue description to the list as a separate table row below the main issue row.

Finally, the **Totals** option can be used to calculate the grand totals of the estimated and spent time for all the issues that are included into the issue list. The calculated totals will be shown before the list, to the right of form buttons (that is, **Apply**, **Clear**, and **Save**).

 Redmine also has a global issue list, which can be accessed through the **View all issues** link on the project list page (click on the **Projects** link from the top-left menu to get there).

Every time you click on the **Apply** button to apply new parameters, they are also saved in your browser. In this way, whenever you load the issue list again, you get the same customized view. To reset to the default view, you can use the **Clear** link of the parameters form or the **View all issues** link which is available on the sidebar.

Custom queries

All new users, when they come to your Redmine website—despite their roles—will see the same issue list with the same columns, the same filters applied to the list, and so on. Actually, this is fine, unless you want them to be able to get the list of issues that they are interested in with just one click (and without the need to customize the view). So, how can you do this?

By customizing the issue list you can show: issues that are to be tested to your testers, features in future versions to public users, feature requests to your developers, and so on. All you need to do is to share such a customized view with the appropriate users. You can do this by clicking on the **Save** link of the parameters form, which was discussed previously. This will open the query form, which is shown in the following screenshot:

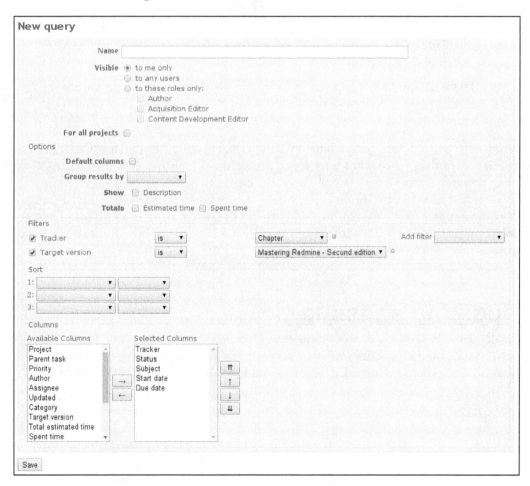

Most elements of this form are already known to you, so let's discuss only those that may need an additional explanation:

- As you can see, such custom queries can be private (**to me only**), public (**to any users**), or visible only to selected user roles (**to these roles only**).

- By default, a custom query is created for the current project only. So in order to make it available for all projects, you need to check the **For all projects** checkbox.

 When you create a public custom query, be sure that it won't appear to be unsolicited for most of your users (especially if you are creating such query for all projects).

- If using the **Columns** element of the **Options** block you have selected columns which fit your needs but are not likely to be useful for others, you can enable the **Default columns** option to use the default columns in the saved custom query.

- The **Sort** option can be used to select the default sorting mode for the saved query. This can always be changed by just clicking on a heading of the issue list.

When you save a newly created custom query, it gets added to the new **Custom queries** section on the sidebar where you can access it anytime. If you are currently using a saved custom query (by the way, the currently used query is saved in the browser just like the current view parameters), it is highlighted on the sidebar and its name appears as the title of the page instead of **Issues**. Also, the **Edit** and **Delete** links appear in the top-right corner of the main content area. These links can be used to modify or delete the saved query.

Updating an issue

Finally, let's check out how to update issues. To open the issue update form, you need to click on the **Edit** link, which is located in the top-right corner of the issue page (in the contextual menu). This will open the following form below the last history entry:

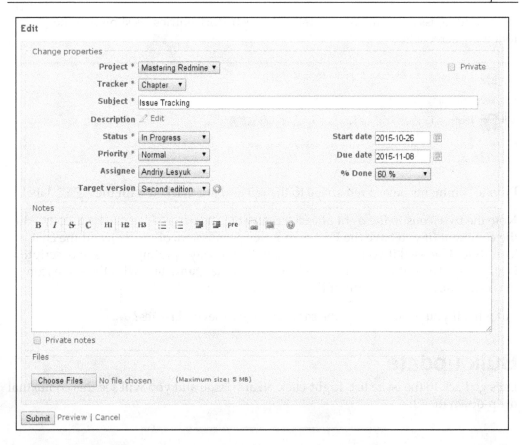

Most of the fields of this form should already be known to you. The missing text area for the **Description** field is hidden to save space and can be revealed by clicking on the **Edit** link (with the pen icon).

A new element in this form is the **Notes** box. As you can see, the text area inside this box supports Wiki formatting (like the one for the **Description** field). This is the text area where you can enter your comments on the issue. If the **Private notes** checkbox is checked, such comments will be visible only to those project members who have the **View private notes** permission.

When added, issue comments are rendered as history entries, as shown in the following screenshot:

Private comments have a red stripe to the left and are marked with the PRIVATE label.

Note the two icons to the right of each comment. The pen ✏ icon can be used to edit the comment (if you have the **Edit own notes** permission, of course), and the chat 💬 icon should be used if you want to quote it. By the way, quoting the issue description is also easy. To do this, you just need to click on the **Quote** link with the same icon that can be found to the right of the issue description.

But what if you need to make the same change to several issues?

Bulk update

Let's go back to the issue list. Right-click on any issue and you will see this contextual drop-down menu:

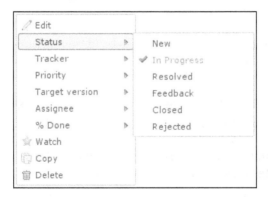

This menu provides you with a quick way of setting one value at a time for the **Status, Tracker, Priority, Target version, Assignee,** or **% Done** fields of several issues (you can select multiple issues in the list and then right-click on one of them).

 However, it's not, recommended to make one change at a time, unless it's really going to be the only one. If you make multiple single changes separately, all of them will be represented as separate issue history entries and notifications about them will be sent in separate emails.

If you need to change several fields of multiple issues at a time, you should use the **Edit** item of this contextual menu. This item activates the following bulk edit form:

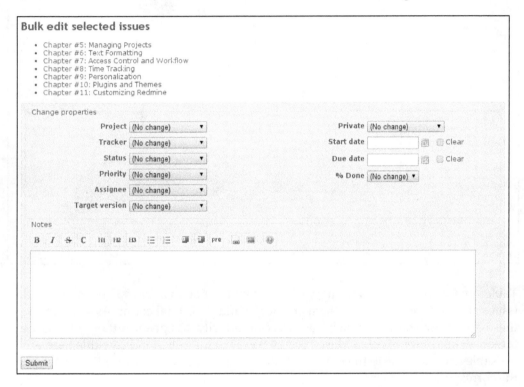

Issue reports

If you click on the **Summary** link, that can be found in the **Issues** section on the sidebar of the aforementioned issue pages, you will be redirected to the issue reports index, which is shown in the following screenshot:

Tables on this page show summary of issues by their status, that is, how many of the issues are open, how many of them are closed and their total count. As you can see, these counts are shown for each tracker, issue priority, assignee, author of the issue, target version, subproject, and issue category. Every number and row title here is clickable and redirects to the issue list with the appropriate filters applied to show the corresponding issues.

If you click on the 🔍 icon near a table caption, you will be redirected to the detailed report for the corresponding issue property. Thus, clicking on this icon near the **Tracker** caption will open the report, which is shown in the following screenshot:

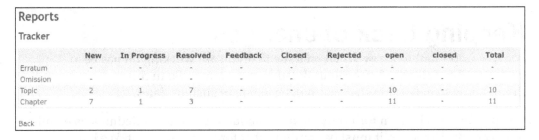

As you can see, the detailed report shows counts for each issue status and not just for open and closed issues.

Importing issues

You have probably noticed that it's possible to export an issue list to a CSV file using the corresponding link in the **Also available in:** block, which can be found below each issue list. The opposite—to import issues from a CSV file—is also possible.

The **Issues** section on the sidebar, which we discussed in the previous section, also contains links such as **Calendar**, **Gantt** (about which we'll speak in the next chapter), and **Import**. The latter one can be used to import new issues from a CSV file. When you click on this link, a wizard-style dialog will be opened and you'll be asked to upload a file. After you do this, the following form—a part of the wizard—will be shown:

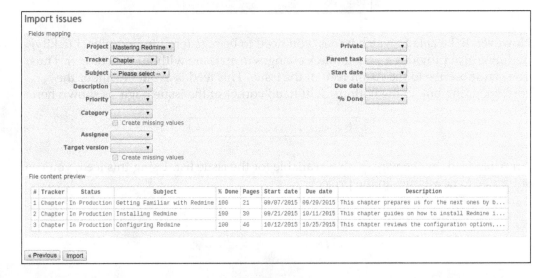

Using this form, you should select which columns of the CSV file correspond to which issue properties. Additionally, you can specify an explicit value for some of them and even chose to import new values for others.

Keeping track of changes

It's very important to know when an issue that you are working on has been updated, especially if it has been updated by a customer. So in this section, we will discuss how to make sure that you will be aware of such updates.

The primary mechanism for notifying users about any events in Redmine is email notifications. However, it must be configured before you can use it. We have discussed how to do this in *Chapter 3, Configuring Redmine*. Also, for notifications to work for changes in issues, email notifications must be enabled for issue updates, what can be done under the **Email notifications** tab of the **Settings** page in the **Administration** menu (using the **Issue updated** checkbox). Finally, for a user to be able to receive email notifications, any notification type except **No events** should be selected in his/her profile, as this type, in fact, disables email notifications for this particular user (we'll discuss this in detail in *Chapter 9, Personalization*).

If it was you who created the issue, or if this issue is or was previously assigned to you, you should already be receiving email notifications about changes in it. If it's not so, you need to subscribe to changes in a particular issue using the watching mechanism. To do this, you just need to open the page of the issue and click on the **Watch** link in its contextual menu. This menu is located in the top- and bottom-right corners of the issue page and looks as follows:

However, to be able to watch issues, you need to be registered in Redmine. Luckily, Redmine also provides a way to track changes in an issue without watching it. Thus, you can subscribe to the **Atom** feed of the issue. This feed is available under the corresponding link in the bottom-right hand corner of the issue page, as shown here:

An **Atom** feed, by the way, is also available for the issue list. Using this feed, you can subscribe to new issues in the project.

You can also configure email notifications to be sent when a new issue is added to the project. To do this, go to your profile (using, for example, the **My account** link in the top-right menu), select the **For any event on the selected projects only** option under **Email notifications**, and choose the projects for which you want to get such notifications. But note that in this case, you'll be notified about all events on the selected projects.

Configuring issue tracking

Let's now see what configuration options are available in Redmine for issue tracking.

The Issue tracking module

Everything you have read in this chapter so far can actually be disabled for a project with just one click. However, I'm not sure who might need to do this and why... Anyway, just in case you got Redmine with issue tracking disabled by someone else or whatever, let's discuss how Issue tracking can be enabled (or disabled) for a project.

Open the project settings by selecting the **Settings** tab in the **Projects** menu. Then select the **Modules** tab of the **Settings** page. Make sure that the **Issue tracking** module is checked, as shown in this screenshot:

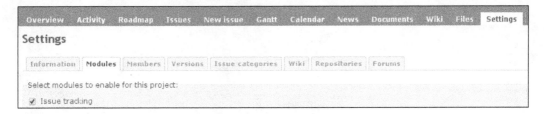

If this checkbox is unchecked, issue tracking won't be available for the project.

The Issue tracking module can also be enabled for all projects by default. This can be done under the **Projects** tab of the **Settings** page of the **Administration** menu.

The Issue tracking tab

Remember that we skipped several tabs of the **Settings** page in the **Administration** menu in the previous chapter? It's now time to discuss one of them—**Issue tracking**:

So let's go through the available settings:

- By default, you can mark an issue as related to another one only if both are in the same project. But if projects hosted on Redmine are somehow related, it can be useful to link issues from different projects. So, to make this possible, you need to enable the **Allow cross-project issue relations** setting.

- If the **Link issues on copy** setting is set to **Yes**, the copied issue will be added to the original one as related using the **Copied to** relation type, and the original issue will be added as a **Copied from** issue to the copy. If this setting is set to **Ask** (which is the default), Redmine will ask you what to do each time you copy an issue.

- By default, subtasks are required to be from any subproject of the topmost project at any level. This is controlled by the **Allow cross-project subtasks** setting, which is set to **With project tree** by default. To allow subtasks from any projects, you need to use **With all projects** for this setting. To allow subtasks from any subproject or any parent project (but not their other subprojects), use **With project hierarchy**. Finally, to allow subtasks only from subprojects, use **With subprojects**.

- By default, you can't assign an issue to more than one user. However, by enabling the **Allow issue assignment to groups** setting, you can make it possible to assign an issue to a group. Groups can be created and edited on the **Groups** page of the **Administration** menu.

> Note that assigning an issue to a group may end up with nobody taking responsibility for the issue, especially if the issue is boring.

- There were times when the first thing I did after creating a new issue was removing the current date from its **Start date** field. So, I was quite happy to see that the **Use current date as start date for new issues** setting was added to Redmine. Disable this setting unless you are sure that all your users will create issues on the day on which these issues should start, or unless you just need any value in this field for some reason.

- The **Display subprojects issues on main projects by default** setting is an option that can lead to confusion. If your subprojects are highly related to their parent projects, you may want to enable this setting to have issues of subprojects included in issue lists of their parent projects. But remember that having forgotten about this feature or not having noticed it, users may eventually navigate to a subproject and then wonder where the other issues have disappeared. Also, some users may wonder why certain settings (such as issue categories and custom fields) that are configured for the parent project do not work for some issues.

- Despite what it may sound like, the **Calculate the issue done ratio with** setting is actually about choosing between the manual and automatic done ratios.

If this option is set to **Use the issue status**, the % **Done** issue field disappears from the issue edit form, so there will be no way to set the done ratio explicitly. Also, for the automatic done ratio to work, you must configure the done ratios for your issue statuses on the **Issue statuses** page of the **Administration** menu, as shown in this screenshot (otherwise, the done ratio will always be empty):

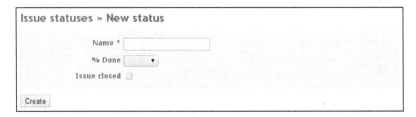

 The % **Done** field for issue statuses is available only when the **Calculate the issue done ratio with** setting is set to **Use the issue status**.

After switching to the automatic done ratio (or updating the done ratios of the issue statuses), you should click on the **Update issue done ratios** link in the top-right corner of the **Issue statuses** page to recalculate all done ratios for all issues.

 The **Update issue done ratios** link is not available if **Calculate the issue done ratio with** is set to a value other than **Use the issue status**.

Finally, if the **Calculate the issue done ratio with** setting is set to **Use the issue field** (the default value), users will need to specify the done ratio on their own.

 Unfortunately, in practice they often don't specify the done ration on their own. I guess this is the reason support for the **Use the issue status** option was added. So, you should consider using this option, if the done ratio is important to you.

- Using the **Non-working days** setting you can select which week days should not be considered to be working. This setting affects the Gantt chart and calculation of issue date properties.

- Two other settings in the main block, which are **Issues export limit** and **Maximum number of items displayed on the gantt chart**, can be used to limit the number of issues that can be exported to a CSV file and included into a Gantt chart correspondingly.

- The **Parent tasks attributes** block contains settings that allow you to control how the **Start date**, **Due date**, **Priority**, and **% Done** fields are determined for parent tasks (that is, issues that have subtasks). If these settings are set to **Calculated from subtasks**, the values of the corresponding fields of parent tasks are calculated as described in the *Subtasks* subsection of **The issue page** section of this chapter. If the **Independent of subtask** value is selected, these fields are to be set manually.

- The last block, which is **Default columns displayed on the issue list**, can be used to select different default columns for issue lists on your Redmine installation. Thus, instead of making each user select the columns that he/she wants to see in the issue list, you should determine (in a way that is out of scope here) which columns are most commonly needed by your users and select them on this page.

- In the last block, using the **Totals** setting you can also choose to show grand total counts of the estimated and/or spent time of the included issues in the issue list by default.

Issues and repository integration

To check other settings that are related to issues, we need to go to the **Repositories** tab of the **Settings** page in the **Administration** menu. We will speak about the part of this page which is shown in the following screenshot:

The **Referencing keywords** setting holds the words that, if found in commit messages before an issue number (# plus a number), generate a *reference* for the appropriate issue. In practice, however, you most likely will want to specify an asterisk (*) here, which means that no special word is required for a reference to be created (only the issue ID is enough). Also, such a reference can be created for several issues at a time. To do this, you need to list these issues in the commit message separated by commas, spaces, or ampersands (&).

But, what is a reference? Let's check out the issue shown in the following screenshot:

The gray block that you can see under the **Associated revisions** title contains an issue reference. It was created by an SVN commit command like this (the **Fixing keywords** field was set to *, that is, an asterisk):

```
$ svn commit -m "Fixed that wiki start page can't be changed (#11085)."
```

An issue can have any number of such references.

Special issue references can also be used to modify the status and/or the done ratio of the issue. As it can be complicated to find suitable universal words for all available trackers, Redmine allows you to specify different **Fixing keywords** for different trackers for such references. As you might have guessed, this can be done in the table at the bottom of the settings page.

Let's review a sample: say, if **Applied status** was set to **Closed**, % **Done** was set to **100%**, and **Fixing keywords** included `closes`, the following SVN command would close the issue and set its done ratio to **100%**:

```
$ svn commit -m "Fixed that wiki start page can't be changed (closes
#11085)."
```

Finally, the **Allow issues of all the other projects to be referenced and fixed** setting decides whether users will be able to reference and fix issues of projects to which the repository does not belong. This is unlikely to be needed, unless all your projects are highly related.

Summary

Having learned the Issue tracking module, you may consider that you have actually learned Redmine, as issue tracking is its main feature that most people work with. Other modules are, in fact, not as critical to know for a usual user, and, as it has been mentioned, the entire Redmine interface is quite easy to understand. However, as this book is not named *Redmine: The very basics*, I assume that you want to learn more to be able to not only use Redmine but also master it.

The next chapter is intended mostly for project managers and site owners, as it describes the capabilities of Redmine as a project management and a project hosting tool. But it should also be interesting for usual users as it teaches how to navigate through the project and how to find information. Additionally, it shares some best practices.

5
Managing Projects

Unfortunately, or fortunately, this chapter is not about the project management bit which is part of software engineering, but about managing projects in Redmine. Despite this, it is actually targeted at project managers (as well as project owners and the like). Thus, it describes what tools are available for projects and how they can be used. Even so, this chapter should not be ignored by regular users as it teaches them how to find the needed information, where to put requests, how to keep a track of changes in a project, and much more.

If the previous chapter described Redmine as an issue tracker, this one reviews it as a project management and project hosting solution. This is a kind of secondary role served by Redmine.

In this chapter, we will cover the following topics:

- Modules
- The global configuration
- Creating a project
- The project pages
- The project configuration
- Closing a project
- The project list
- Project maintenance best practices
- Administering projects

Modules

I have already mentioned modules several times, for example, the Issue tracking module that we discussed in the previous chapter. Thence, you have probably concluded that a module is a part of a functionality, and that's correct. But to be more precise, this is a part of the functionality that is used for projects. This is why Redmine modules are also often called **project modules**.

Actually, modules are like bricks, with which you can build a website for your project. On the other hand, they can also be used to disable functionality that is not needed. But generally, modules are nothing more than virtual units, as they are not plugins, their files are not stored separately from the core, and so on.

Certainly modules can also be provided by plugins, but we are going to discuss only core project modules here. Even so, not all of them will be reviewed in this chapter. Thus, as we have discussed the Issue tracking module in the previous chapter, we will skip it here. However, we will review the **Roadmap** tab of the project menu that is provided by the Issue tracking module because it has not been reviewed yet. Also, we will skip the Time tracking module, as it will be reviewed in *Chapter 8, Time Tracking*.

We start this chapter with reviewing modules because later you will have to choose which modules to enable for your projects. And how can you do this without understanding what is provided by those modules?

The Issue tracking module

As I have already mentioned, the whole of the previous chapter was about what this project module does. However, the Issue tracking module also provides the **Roadmap** page, which we have not reviewed yet. So, let's do that now.

The Roadmap page

When enabled, in addition to the **Issues** and **New issue** tabs (which have been already discussed), the Issue tracking module adds the **Roadmap** tab. This is what it looks like:

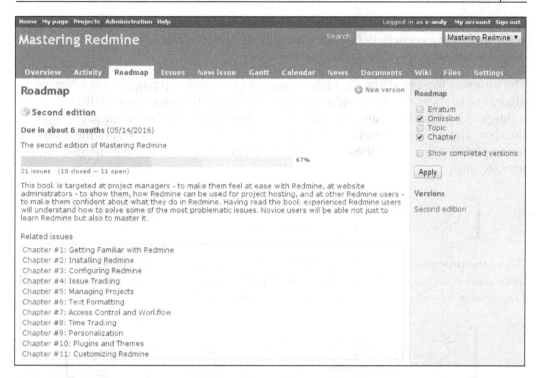

This page shows the overall progress for versions of the project and lists the closed and open issues for some trackers, thus producing feature lists for the versions.

On the sidebar, under the **Roadmap** label, you can select trackers that should be listed on this page. By default, only those trackers for which the **Issues displayed in roadmap** option is enabled (on the **Trackers** page of the **Administration** menu) are selected and listed here.

Also by default, the roadmap shows only open versions. But you can change this by enabling the **Show completed versions** option (and clicking on the **Apply** button).

If the project has subprojects, there will also be the **Subprojects** option. This option can be used to make the roadmap include versions and issues of subprojects.

Under the **Versions** label, you can see a list of available versions (my project has only one version, which is **Second edition**). Completed versions, if they exist in the project, will be available under the toggle box with the title **Completed versions**.

The **New version** link that you see in the top-right corner of the content area is a shortcut for adding a new version (we will review this in *The Version tab* subsection of *The project configuration* section of this chapter).

As you might have guessed, the **Second edition** label near the yellow box icon () is the title of the version. Below the title, you see the effective date, which is shown only if it has been specified for the version.

The progress bar — perhaps the main element of the roadmap page — uses a simple algorithm to show the done and completeness ratios (the latter has a slightly lighter color). The done ratio indicates how many issues are closed out of the total number. The completeness ratio indicates what percentage of the rest of the issues is completed. For both of these ratios, Redmine attempts to take the estimated hours into account.

> You can click on the issue counts below the progress bar to see the list of referenced issues.

Below the progress bar and above the issue list, Redmine shows the content of the associated Wiki page. We will review later what this page is and how can it be specified (*The Version tab* subsection of *The project configuration* section).

> You can also right-click on an issue in the issue list to get the contextual pop-up menu. This menu can be used to manipulate the issue.

The Version page

If you click on a version title on the roadmap page, you will be redirected to the version page, which looks like this:

As you can see, the version page contains generally the same information as the roadmap, but it's about a single version. Also, unlike the roadmap, the version page lists all issues of the version in the **Related issues** block.

Additionally, this page contains a contextual menu that can be used to modify the version (the **Edit** link), edit the associated Wiki page, or delete the version.

Also, it has the special **Issues by** block that allows you to check completeness ratios per different values of an issue attribute. Thus, it's possible to see completeness progress bars for different categories, trackers, statuses, priorities, authors, and assignees of issues of the version. To change the mode of this block, just select a different issue attribute in the drop-down list.

If you have enabled the Time tracking module, this page will also show the total estimated time and the total spent time for issues of the version in another separate block.

The News module

It's essential that all major changes made to a project are accompanied by official news from the owners of the project. Therefore, Redmine would not be a good project hosting solution without the News module.

When enabled, the News module adds the **News** tab to the project menu, as shown in this screenshot:

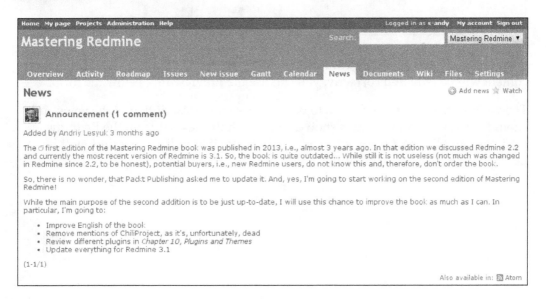

Under this tab, you can see the list of all news about the project. To subscribe to these news feeds, you can click on the **Watch** link in the top-right corner.

 You can also subscribe to project news using the **Atom** link and your favorite feed reader.

If you have the **Manage news** permission, you will also see the **Add news** link in the contextual menu. Clicking on this link shows the following form above the news list:

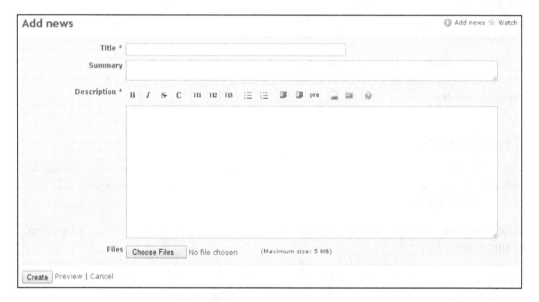

As you can see, the news description supports Wiki formatting. To ensure that the content will be rendered correctly, you can use the **Preview** link below the form.

The value of the **Summary** field is to be used as a short description of the news and should always be specified. It is shown along with the news title on the Redmine start page and the start page of the project, but note that unlike **Description**, this field does not support Wiki formatting.

If you click on the news title, you'll be redirected to the news page, which is shown in this screenshot:

If you have the **Comment news** permission, you will see the **Add a comment** link on this page. Clicking on this link opens the form containing only one text area, which also supports Wiki formatting. Using the trash 🗑 icon to the right of the comment, users with appropriate permission can remove the comment.

If you are interested in getting notifications about new comments in the news, you can click on the **Watch** link in the contextual menu of the news page (after this, the link will change to the **Unwatch** link). If you have authored the news, watching will be enabled for you automatically. Other links in this menu can be used to edit and delete news.

The Documents module

The Documents module can be useful if the project has a lot of documentation. Let's see what this module can do for you.

When enabled, this module adds the **Documents** tab to the project menu, which is visible only if the user has the **View documents** permission. This tab is shown in the following screenshot:

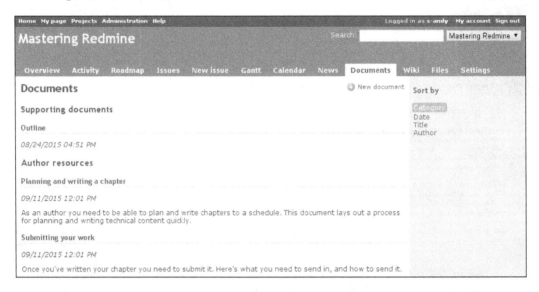

Here, the **Outline**, **Planning and writing a chapter**, and **Submitting your work** links are document titles. Below each title, you can see the date when the document was added and an optional short description.

In the previous screenshot, the documents are listed by categories. Thus, **Supporting documents** and **Author resources** are their names. Document categories are global (that is, for all projects) and can be managed from the **Enumerations** page of the **Administration** menu, as shown here:

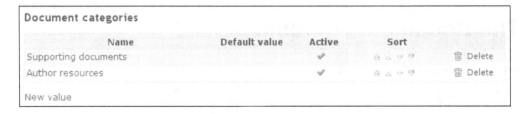

Additionally, it's possible to list documents by date, title, and author. To change the display mode, you just need to click on the corresponding link on the sidebar.

Thus, when documents are listed by titles, only the first letter of the document title is used for groups, as follows:

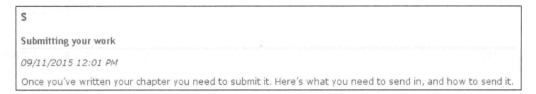

Now let's see how to add a document. To do this, you need to click on the **New document** link. It will open the following form:

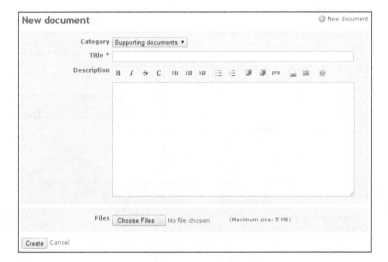

In Redmine, a document is a documentation object that can include, for example, images, chapters, and so on as separate files. For this reason, the document form can be used to upload multiple files one by one—when you choose a file, it gets uploaded and the **Choose Files** button becomes available again.

To edit a document, click on its title to be redirected to the document page and then click on the **Edit** link there. In the same way, you can use the **Delete** link to remove a document.

> **The Document Management System Features plugin**
>
> A more featureful document management solution is provided by the DMSF plugin, which was originally written by Vít Jonáš (it is now maintained by Daniel Munn). You can get this plugin at:
>
> https://github.com/danmunn/redmine_dmsf

The Files module

You will need the Files module if you want users of your project to be able to download project files (for example, releases). When enabled, this module adds the **Files** tab to the project menu, which looks like this:

Project files can optionally be associated with a particular version. Thus, in the preceding screenshot, all the files belong to **Second edition**. The file list can be sorted by filename, date, size, and download count (that is, **D/L**).

If you click on the **New file** link, you'll get this form:

As you can see, with this simple form, you can upload multiple files at once.

What is the difference between files and documents?

Unlike documents, files can be added to a particular project version. Only for files Redmine provides MD5 hashes and saves the download count. Files are available right under the **Files** tab, whereas to download documents, you need to locate and open the documentation object first.

The Wiki module

Under this subsection, we will review what is provided by the Wiki module. The Wiki syntax will be reviewed in the next chapter.

> Don't confuse Wiki formatting with the Wiki module.
> The former is a feature of Redmine that is widely used
> by its components, and the latter is a virtual module that
> implements the **Wiki** tab of the project. Thus, Wiki formatting
> still remains available for issues, project, and document
> descriptions, and so on if the Wiki module is disabled.

The Wiki tab plays the role of the entry point to the project's Wiki system. However, by default, there are no Wiki pages in the project, that is, the landing page for the Wiki system does not exist either. Therefore, when you click on the **Wiki** tab, you get the Wiki page edit form (or an error if you don't have permission to edit the Wiki page). This form looks as follows:

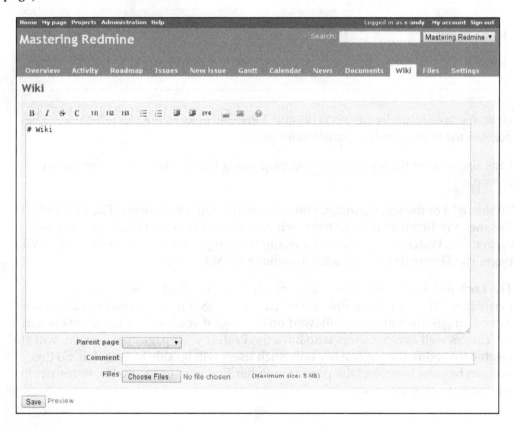

Certainly, the content field of this form supports Wiki syntax. A short description of this syntax becomes available when you click on the last button 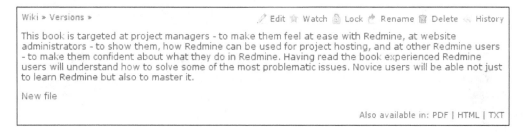 of the toolbar. When the page content is ready, you can click on the **Preview** link to check how it is going to be rendered. The preview of the page will be shown below the form.

This form also has the special **Comment** field. This field should be used to specify what changes were made to the Wiki page. For new pages, I usually write *Created* here. A little later, I will show you what these comments are used for.

Using the file upload element of this form, you can add any number of files to the Wiki page. Usually, these will be images that will be shown on the page.

The **Parent page** field can be used to make the page a child of another page. This will affect the index of the Wiki pages (which we'll discuss later in this subsection). Additionally, child pages will get breadcrumbs:

> Wiki » Versions »   ✏ Edit ☆ Watch 🔒 Lock ↪ Rename 🗑 Delete ↺ History
>
> This book is targeted at project managers - to make them feel at ease with Redmine, at website administrators - to show them, how Redmine can be used for project hosting, and at other Redmine users - to make them confident about what they do in Redmine. Having read the book experienced Redmine users will understand how to solve some of the most problematic issues. Novice users will be able not just to learn Redmine but also to master it.
>
> New file
>
> Also available in: PDF | HTML | TXT

Here, the breadcrumbs are the **Wiki** and **Versions** links in the top-left corner. They point to the corresponding parent Wiki pages.

Let's also discuss the layout of a Wiki page using the previous screenshot as an example.

To the right of the breadcrumbs, you can see the contextual menu. The **Edit** link in this menu redirects to the edit form, which is similar to the one that we discussed earlier. The **Watch** link allows subscribing to changes that will be made to this Wiki page. The **Delete** link can be used to remove the Wiki page.

The **Lock** link is only available for users who have the **Protect wiki pages** permission. The title of this link is a bit confusing, as it may be considered that no more changes are going to be allowed on the page if you click on it, but this is not so. You, as well as other users who have the **Protect wiki pages** permission, will still be able to modify the page. Also, only such users will be able to unlock it. So this link can be used to protect the page from other Redmine users, that is, to restrict its editing to trusted users only.

Before we discuss the **Rename** link, let's figure out how to create a Wiki page. Similar to many other Wiki systems, a Wiki page in Redmine can be created in the following two ways:

- **By adding the page name to the URL**: For example, if the URL for the project is `http://mastering-redmine.com/projects/book`, you can create a page with the name `Test-page` by adding this name to the URL as follows: `http://mastering-redmine.com/projects/book/wiki/Test-page` (note the additional `/wiki/` path). Going to this URL will invoke the previously discussed edit form, where you will be able to specify the content for the page (if you have permission to do this, of course).

- **By adding a link pointing to the new page on any existing page**: The new Wiki page that you are going to create should be referenced from somewhere. So, just add a link to this not-yet-existing page there. The syntax for adding a link to a page is as follows:

  `[[Test-page|Any display text]]`

  This link will be rendered in red, which means that the referenced page does not exist.

  Any display text

  If you click on this link, you will be redirected to the edit form just as with the previous method (in fact, it's the same as going to the URL of a new page).

 The latter method is easier and should be preferred, as it also sets the page that contains the link as the parent page automatically. So, don't forget to clear the value of **Parent page** if this is not what you want.

But what if you've made a mistake in the page name? This is what the **Rename** link is available for in the contextual menu. Clicking on this link redirects to the form shown here:

Title here is actually the name of the Wiki page, as it can be seen in the URL. This name is also used when you reference the page on other Wiki pages. Therefore, the **Redirect existing links** option has been checked. If this option is checked, the renamed page will still be accessible by the old name (and URL). Additionally, this form allows you to change the parent page and even the project of the page (that is, it allows you to move the page to another project).

> Always enable the **Redirect existing links** option if the page has been available under the old name for some time. This is recommended not only because users could have referenced it on other pages or have saved the old URL in their favorites, but also because search engines could have already indexed it.

The last link from the contextual menu of the Wiki page that is to be reviewed is **History**. When you click on it, you will see something like the following:

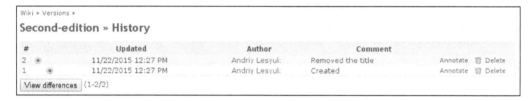

This is where comments discussed earlier are shown. By choosing the versions (for example, **1** and **2**) and clicking on the **View difference** button, you can see what changes were made between them:

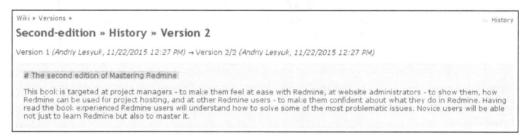

The **Annotate** link, which is located to the right of the version on the **History** page, can be used to check who authored which line of the Wiki page. And the **Delete** link near it can be used to clear the history from redundant entries, if you have the **Delete wiki pages** permission. This, however, won't remove the changes themselves, unless you delete the latest version of the page.

On each Wiki page, below the content you can also see the **Also available in:** block of links. Using these links you can export the page content in **PDF**, **HTML**, and **TXT** formats.

On the sidebar of each Wiki page, you will see the navigation menu, which looks like this:

Navigation in a Wiki system is usually implemented using the Wiki syntax (that is, through links). But if the authors of Wiki pages have failed to maintain the navigation, you can always use this navigation menu to find the page you need.

Custom content on the sidebar under the Wiki tab

Redmine allows you to add custom Wiki content to the sidebar of the Wiki module. To use this feature, you need to create a Wiki page named Sidebar. Its content will be automatically shown on each Wiki page above the navigation menu. However, note that the sidebar content should start with a ### (h3.) title to look similar to other titles on the sidebar.

The index of Wiki pages mentioned earlier is available under two links—**Index by title** and **Index by date**. The index that can be accessed by the former link also displays the structure of the Wiki pages, like this:

As you might have noticed, this index can be watched. And if you watch it, you will be notified about every new Wiki page that gets added to the project. In addition to watching, you can subscribe to this list using the **Atom** link.

The Redmine Wiki Extensions plugin

You might want to install the Wiki Extensions plugin by r-labs. It allows you to add tags and comments to Wiki pages, use Wiki pages as tabs in the project menu, and much more. Check it out at http://www.r-labs.org/projects/r-labs/wiki/ Wiki_Extensions_en.

The Repository module

Redmine was designed mainly for software projects. Each software project has source code, so it's essential for Redmine to have a source code browser. Nowadays, software projects use revision control systems for collaboration. Therefore, Redmine needs to support such systems as well. In Redmine, all such functionality is provided by the Repository module, which adds the **Repository** tab to the project menu and the **Repositories** tab to the project's **Settings** page.

So, let's review the latter first. Go to the **Settings** tab of the project menu and select the **Repositories** tab. You should see something like the following:

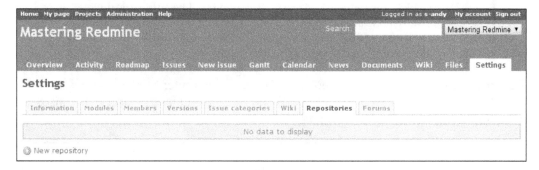

By default, there is no repository in the project. To add one, you need to click on the **New repository** link. This is what you will see next:

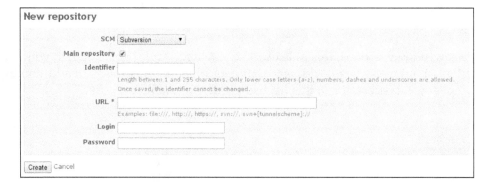

The **SCM** field of this form contains only those SCMs that have been permitted by an administrator on the **Repositories** tab of the **Settings** page in the **Administration** menu. That page and tab were discussed in *Chapter 3, Configuring Redmine*.

The **Main repository** checkbox must be checked for one of the repositories of the project (it can be any). If you are adding the first repository for the project, the **Main repository** option will be enabled anyway, even if you disable it in the form. Then, if you enable it for any next repository of the project, this option will be automatically disabled for the previous main repository. In this way, Redmine ensures that there is only one main repository in the project.

The **Identifier** field is required if you have or are going to have many repositories in the project, as it is used to distinguish them.

What other fields are available in this form depends on the type of SCM (for example, **Subversion**). To determine the correct values for those fields, you need to contact the administrator of your repository.

The Git repository is slow?

If you have commits with a huge amount of modified files and directories, loading the Git repository can become slow. To resolve this issue, try disabling the **Report last commit for files and directories** option.

Redmine expects all the repositories that you add using this form to be already available. In other words, this form just registers them in Redmine. However, you can configure the automatic creation of repositories using the `reposman.rb` tool, which was described in *Chapter 3, Configuring Redmine*.

The SCM Creator plugin

You can also use the SCM Creator plugin for Redmine. It allows you to create repositories directly from the discussed form. Check it out at `http://projects.andriylesyuk.com/projects/scm-creator`.

After you have registered a repository, it gets added to the repository list of the project, as shown in the following screenshot:

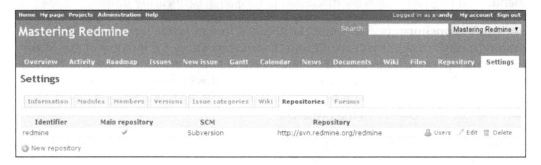

Every commit in revision control systems is associated with a username. This username, however, can differ from the one in Redmine. In such cases, Redmine won't be able to detect the correct users for commits. That's what the **Users** link is for. When you click on this link, Redmine opens a form that can be used to associate repository usernames with Redmine users. By default, Redmine assumes that the same username means the same user. And, if Redmine fails to find an appropriate user, it will just show the repository username as it is (without the link to a Redmine user).

I am not sure whether you have noticed, but in addition to the repository that appeared in the repository list, the project now has a new **Repository** tab (just before **Settings**). This tab is also provided by the Repository module, but it appears only when at least one repository is available in the project.

So, let's check out what's under this new tab:

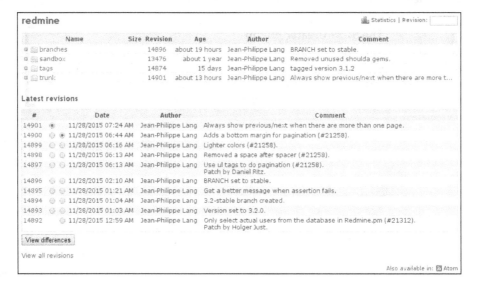

The upper part of the screen can be used to browse the source code. You can either click on the directory names to go to a separate page with their content, or use the plus icon ( ) to show the content in place. The lower part displays the information about the last 10 commits that were made to the repository. To view all the commits, you can click on the **View all revisions** link. Finally, to view some basic statistics about when commits were made and who committed the changes, use the **Statistics** link in the top-right corner.

 You can also subscribe to commits using the **Atom** link.

If you click on a revision number, you will see a brief summary of the changes that were made in this revision. Here is a sample:

So, to see what exactly was changed, you can do any of these actions:

- Click on the **View differences** link on this page (for the entire commit)
- Click on the **diff** link near the filename on this page (for this particular file)
- Select the revisions and click on the **View differences** button on the main (previous) screen (for differences between revisions, which can include several commits)

You will get something like this:

```
Revision 14899

View differences:  ◉ inline  ○ side by side

trunk/public/stylesheets/application.css
494 494
495 495 input#content_comments {width: 99%}
496 496
497     span.pagination {margin-left:3px}
    497 span.pagination {margin-left:3px; color:#888;}
498 498 .pagination ul.pages {
499 499   margin: 0 5px 0 0;
500 500   padding: 0;

503 503 .pagination ul.pages li {
504 504   display: inline-block;
505 505   padding: 0;
508     border: 1px solid #888;
    506 border: 1px solid #ccc;
507 507   margin-left: -1px;
508 508   line-height: 2em;
509 509 }
510 510 .pagination ul.pages li a,
511 511 .pagination ul.pages li span {
512     padding: 4px 10px;
    512 padding: 3px 8px;
513 513 }
514 514 .pagination ul.pages li:first-child {
515 515   border-top-left-radius: 4px;

                                    Also available in: Unified diff
```

If you click on a filename in the main screen of the repository browser, you will be redirected to a page about that file. It will contain the following four links in its upper part:

```
History | View | Annotate | Download (875 Bytes)
```

All of these links, except **Download**, open a separate page:

- **History**: This page lists only those revisions that have affected this file. On this page, you will also be able to select two revisions and click on the **View differences** button to see what changes were made to the file between them.

- **View**: This page just shows the content of the file with highlighted syntax.

- **Annotate**: This page shows the content of the file too, but additionally, it includes information about who authored each line of the file and in which revision, like this:

```
redmine / trunk / lib / redmine / version.rb @ 14899          Statistics | Revision: 14899

History | View | Annotate | Download (875 Bytes)

 1    824    jplang    require 'rexml/document'
 2
 3    453    jplang    module Redmine
 4                        module VERSION #:nodoc:
 5  14027    jplang        MAJOR = 3
 6  14893    jplang        MINOR = 2
 7                         TINY  = 0
 8   5549   tmaruyama
 9   2036    jplang        # Branch values:
10                         # * official release: nil
11                         # * stable branch:       stable
12                         # * trunk:               devel
13                         BRANCH = 'devel'
14    453    jplang
15  10616    jplang        # Retrieves the revision from the working copy
16    824    jplang        def self.revision
17  10616    jplang          if File.directory?(File.join(Rails.root, '.svn'))
18    824    jplang            begin
19  10616    jplang              path = Redmine::Scm::Adapters::AbstractAdapter.shell_quote(Rails.root.to_s)
20                               if `svn info --xml #{path}` =~ /revision="(\d+)"/
21                                 return $1.to_i
22   5549   tmaruyama            end
23                             rescue
24                               # Could not find the current revision
25                             end
26                           end
27  10616    jplang          nil
28    824    jplang        end
29
30                         REVISION = self.revision
31   5549   tmaruyama      ARRAY    = [MAJOR, MINOR, TINY, BRANCH, REVISION].compact
32                         STRING   = ARRAY.join('.')
33   6521   tmaruyama
34   5549   tmaruyama      def self.to_a; ARRAY  end
35   6521   tmaruyama      def self.to_s; STRING end
36    453    jplang      end
37                      end
```

- **Download**: This link just triggers the file download.

Also, you're probably wondering how the **Repository** tab looks if more than one repository is used in the project. It looks the same. In the case of many repositories, the sidebar just contains links that allow quick switching between the repositories, as shown in the following screenshot:

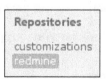

Now, you can play with the repository browser more on your own to see all its pages and features. In my opinion, the Repository module is the most visually beautiful core module of Redmine, so it's really worth playing with. (If you don't have a repository to play with, you can check out http://www.redmine.org or http://mastering-redmine.com.)

The Forums module

The Forums module is often undeservedly ignored by Redmine users. Therefore, in practice it is underused. So what is the use of this module?

A project needs to provide some means to support its users, answer their questions, and so on. The Forums module adds discussion boards that make this possible. A board can have an unlimited number of threads, called **topics**. Each topic can have any number of posts, which are called **messages**.

However, in practice, users rarely use forums to ask for support. Most likely, they will use issues for this, especially if Redmine comes (and it does by default) with the **Support** tracker that is intended for such use. So, why not? Why should you use forums instead?

Let me explain:

- Firstly, support issues will get mixed in with others (bugs, features, and so on). This will make the issue list harder to read and will require users to configure filters.

- Secondly, when you resolve an issue, you should close it! And closed issues are going to be hidden, while forum threads remain open and visible even after they have been resolved. In this way, with forums, you will build a troubleshooting database, while with issues, you are going to get duplicates.

- Thirdly, topics can be categorized using boards. While issues also support categories, users can't subscribe to them. And they can subscribe to boards and topics. The possibility of subscribing will also let volunteers help you support your customers.

- Fourthly, forums and issues use different permission sets. This means that you can have a special role for community supporters and you won't need to take them into account when granting permissions for issues.

As you can see, forums are better for customer support to some extent.

 If you have decided to go with forums, consider removing the **Support** tracker to avoid confusion.

Before we proceed with checking out the capabilities of this module, we need to configure it. Its configuration can be done on the project's **Settings** page under the **Forums** tab, which is shown here:

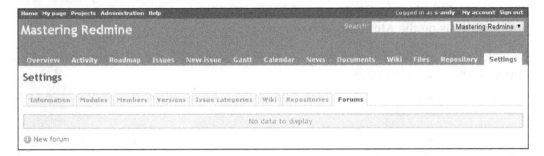

Click on the **New forum** link to add a new discussion board. This will open the form:

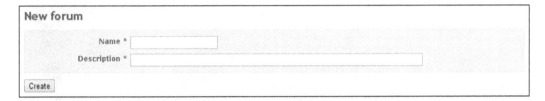

The value of the **Name** field should briefly describe the topic of the forum. The **Description** field should contain a longer description. Thus, good examples of the values are the following:

Name	Description
General discussions	If no other forum fits, write here
Help	If things do not work, ask here
Development	Anything about development should be written here

As soon as you create the first forum in the project, the **Forums** tab will be added to the project menu:

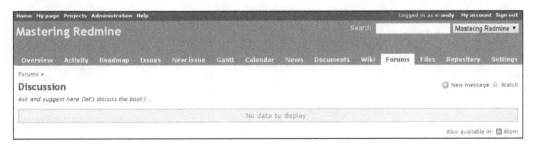

If you have only one forum, you will see its topic list under the **Forums** tab. But if you have more forums, then under the **Forum** tab, you will see the list of forums first.

You can watch the forum by clicking on the **Watch** link or by subscribing to the **Atom** feed. If you have more than one forum, you will also be able to subscribe to new forums using the **Atom** link on their index page.

Now, let's add a topic. If you click on the **New message** link, the following form will appear above the topic list:

Certainly, forum messages also support Wiki formatting.

If the **Sticky** option is enabled, the topic will always appear at the top of the message list. If the **Locked** option is enabled, no more replies will be allowed for that particular topic (consider it like closing the discussion).

When the message is saved, you are redirected to the page of the newly created topic, which looks as follows:

The first message in a forum creates a new topic. The user who creates a topic is automatically added to its watcher list (that's why we have the **Unwatch** link in the preceding screenshot).

To reply to a message, you can use either the **Quote** link, which will insert the quoted content of the original message into your reply, or the **Reply** link. In both cases, an additional form that contains just a text area is shown under the **Reply** link. Replies are added to the existing topic as messages.

Now let's check out the forum page again (I have added several other topics):

Here, you can see how sticky and locked topics are shown. The **RE: A demo topic for the book** link is a quick shortcut to the last message in the topic. The message list can be sorted by the **Created**, **Replies**, and **Last message** columns.

The Calendar module

The Calendar module adds a tab with the same name to the project menu. It looks like this:

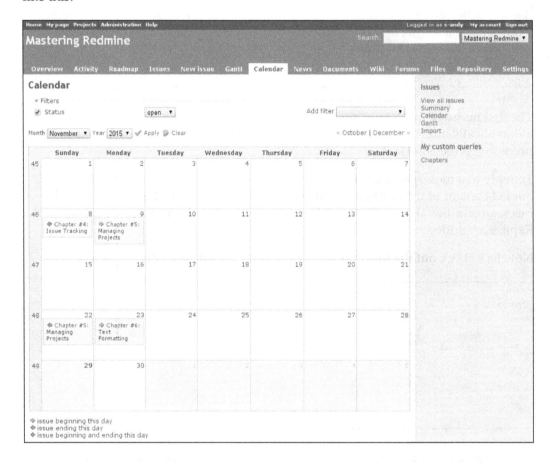

As you can see, the calendar shows the start and due dates of issues, if they are specified. Thus, the start date is shown with a green arrow pointing forward ⇨, and the due date with the red arrow pointing backward ⇦. If the start and due dates are the same, a red rhombus (◆) is shown.

Hovering the mouse cursor over an issue opens a box with its details. These details include the assignee name, priority, status, and so on:

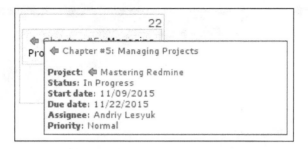

If a version has the due date, it will also be shown on the calendar, as follows:

Here, **Second edition** is the name of the project version.

Also, you might have noticed that the calendar page contains a filter similar to the one we saw on the issue list. In fact, this can be considered to be the same filter, as its configuration is retained when you move between the **Issues**, **Calendar**, and **Gantt** tabs.

The Calendar module is really useful if issue reporters and/or assignees always specify the start and due dates. But if an issue has neither, it won't be displayed on the calendar at all.

The Redmine ICS Export plugin

This plugin allows you to export issues and versions into ICS format, which is compatible with most major pieces of calendar software. Refer to `https://github.com/buschmais/redmics`.

The Gantt module

It seems that no project management software is complete without the Gantt chart, as this type of bar chart is perfect for representing the flow of work in a project in terms of time and resource availability.

In Redmine, such a chart is available under the **Gantt** tab of the project menu, but only if the Gantt module is enabled, of course.

It's good that I worked on the book with quite a big delay (not so good, but…) as you can see how delays are displayed on the Gantt chart. The delay is marked in red on the graph. Also, issues that should have been closed according to their due date have red titles here (this time it's fine, as the chapters are going to be closed during the rewrite phase of the book). Finally, the issue that is in progress has an orange title.

The blue arrows on the Gantt chart indicate issue relations (next chapters follow previous ones).

Like the calendar, the Gantt module uses the same issue filter that is used by the issue list, what means that you can configure what to show on the Gantt chart using the **Issues** tab. The **Zoom in** and **Zoom out** links allow zooming of the chart down to weeks or days or up to months, respectively.

The **Previous** and **Next** links under the chart allow movement between periods. For example, if the chart shows *January – June 2015*, the **Previous** link will move to *July – December 2014* and the **Next** link will move to *July – December 2015*.

Additionally, a Gantt chart can be exported as a PDF document or a PNG image.

Also, as with the calendar, when you hover your mouse cursor over a bar, a box with detailed information about the issue is shown.

 To be able to export a Gantt chart in PNG, you need to have RMagick installed.

The global configuration

There is still one tab on the **Settings** page of the **Administration** menu that we have not discussed yet. It's the **Projects** tab. So let's check it out now:

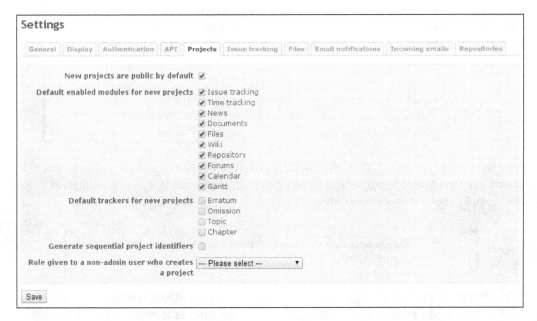

A project in Redmine can be either public or private. A public project is visible to everyone, even to unregistered users (unless you have restricted access to the whole of Redmine by enabling the **Authorization required** option under the **Authentication** tab). Of course, access to some pages of the project can still be restricted, but even if every page is restricted, the public project will still be visible! It will just appear to be empty. A private project is the opposite—it cannot be seen by non-members, whatever you do! Thus, you can let unregistered users and non-members see everything, but still such projects won't be visible to them.

So, the **New projects are public by default** setting should be enabled only if all of your projects are to be public. Otherwise, it is possible that a project that was meant to be private is accidentally left public. However, even if you want all of your projects to be public, you may still want to disable this setting to avoid the appearance of empty projects in the project list, as users may need some time to put data into them (later, when their projects are ready, they can change this). You should consider this especially if you are positioning your Redmine installation as a list of active and up-to-date applications so that your users won't get frustrated when they see no data in a project.

The next setting is the reason we started this chapter with a review of project modules. Now, I believe that you can easily determine which modules you need. Remember, however, that on this page you select modules that are going to be enabled by default for all new projects. Also note that users will still be able to enable modules that are not selected here and disable the ones that you selected.

> Perhaps, it's a good idea to uncheck all modules here, except **Issue tracking**. In practice, users often skip configuration of modules when they create a project and leave it as it is. This results in empty and unused news, documents, files, Wiki, and so on.

Like the previous setting, **Default trackers for new projects** can be used to select which trackers should be enabled for new projects by default. Here, you should enable only those trackers that are going to be common for all your projects.

> Please note that if you select no trackers here, Redmine will assume that all trackers are to be enabled by default.

Each project in Redmine has a unique identifier—a short string with letters, digits, dashes, and underscores. The main goal of this identifier is to replace the numerical project ID, which is used internally, by something more readable and memorizable.

For this reason, I'm not sure why one may need to enable the next setting. Perhaps, it was added for cases when users do not care about the readability of project identifiers. In other words, if you just don't want users to think up project identifiers and do not care about their ease of remembrance, you can enable the **Generate sequential project identifiers** setting. When it's enabled, Redmine generates sequential identifiers for new projects. Thus, if the identifier of the previous project was `redmine`, the next suggested identifier will be `redminf` (not very smart, is it?), and if the previous identifier was `chapter-1`, the next one will be `chapter-2`.

For the **Role given to a non-admin user who creates a project** setting, you should select a role that will be assigned automatically to the user who creates the project. Certainly, this should be a role with project management permissions. If you don't do this, such users will get the first role from the role list (which can be checked in **Roles and permissions** under **Administration**). So, using this setting you can avoid confusion when users discover that some things are not available for them in their just-created projects (because their automatically assigned role does not have the appropriate permission).

Creating a project

Now that we have chosen the default values for some project fields, let's create a project. This can be done in two ways: using the **New project** link on the project list (click on the **Projects** top menu item to get there), or using the link with the same name on the **Projects** page of the **Administration** menu. The latter is available only for administrators, however. In both cases, you will get the following form:

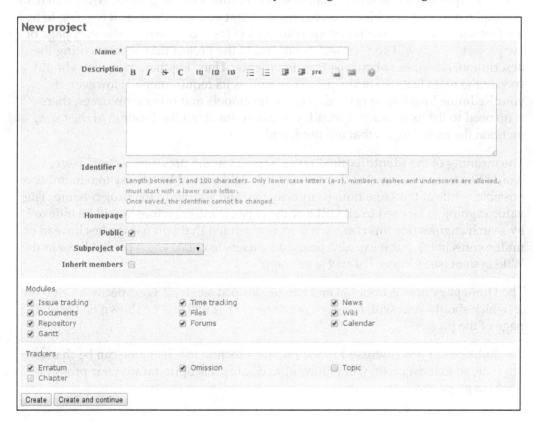

Not much to explain here, right? But let's speak about the best practices for filling this form. It's perhaps the most important form in Redmine because it is where you actually create the face of your project.

 To be able to create projects, a user must have the **Create project** permission. If you want to allow any registered user to create projects, you need to grant this permission to the **Non member** built-in role.

The value of the **Name** field, which is required, should be as short as possible but still descriptive. Usually, you will want it to be identical to the project name. However, if your project is a part of another system, you may also want to prefix it with the name of that system, for example, `Redmine SCM Creator`, where `SCM Creator` is the project name and `Redmine` is the name of the system the project was created for.

The **Description** field should contain a short summary of the project. While this field is actually optional, it is highly recommended that you specify it, as it is going to be the first source of information about your project (as it is shown on the start page of the project, which will be reviewed soon, and in the project list). While writing the description, remember about the target audience. Thus, for customers, you should specify the main features of the project as well as its requirements. However, if your Redmine installation is used only by developers and other employees, there is no need to list its features. Instead, you can write about the location of the team, mention the technologies that are used, and so on.

The meaning of the **Identifier** field was discussed in the previous section. Here, I would like to emphasize that the value of this field should be as easy to remember as possible, while at the same time be informative and similar to the project name. This value is going to be used in all URLs of the project, and therefore, it will be indexed by search engines (for this reason, it is recommended that you use dashes instead of underscores here). But it can also be used by users to create cross-project links in the Wiki system (see *Chapter 7, Text Formatting*).

The **Homepage** field is optional and can be skipped safely. If you specify a value for it (which should start with `http://` or `https://`), it will just be shown on the start page of the project.

The **Public** field was discussed in the previous section too. Its value can be changed anytime, so in most cases, you will want to disable this option until your project is ready to go public.

Each project in Redmine can have any number of subprojects, each subproject can have any number of its own subprojects, and so on down to any nesting level. But in what cases should subprojects be used?

Taking into account their implementation, I come to the conclusion that subprojects should be projects that are closely related to the main project but still independent. They should not be like repository branches, as branches share source code and subprojects don't. They should not be like project modules either (like Forums for Redmine), as the latter can't be used or distributed separately. (Subprojects can have their own files under the **Files** tab, so plugins for Redmine fit better than modules here.) They can be related to versions of the parent project (as Redmine can share versions with subprojects). They can share the workflow with the parent project (and the roadmap of the parent project can include issues and versions of subprojects). Issues in subprojects can be related to issues in the parent project (and the issue list of the parent project can include issues from subprojects). Different people can work on the parent project and on its subprojects (but members can be "inherited" — see the next option of this form). And so on.

These are not rules or official recommendations (and I'm not aware of any official recommendations, by the way). These are implementation limitations and features that you should consider while using subprojects. I just wanted to give you a general idea of what can be put into subprojects.

Redmine users often use this feature to implement project categories, which are unfortunately missing in Redmine. While this works, I would recommend that you avoid doing this. The side effect of such "categories" are empty projects with empty tabs, with a huge grand total time (it's about time tracking) that was spent on all subprojects, with activity lists (which include activities on subprojects), with issues of all subprojects, with some weird members (for example, users who have **Create subprojects** permission and were added especially for the purpose of creating subprojects), and so on.

Generally, the subprojects feature seems to be incomplete, as users often face different limitations, even when they use it in the right way (for example, issue categories are not shared). So, the decision to create a project as a subproject should be based on the available features and not the visual representation (which is the main reason behind using parent projects as categories).

> **The Project Sections plugin**
>
> An implementation of project categories is provided by the Project Sections plugin, which can be found at `http://projects.andriylesyuk.com/project/redmine/project-sections`.

But why did I write all this? All this is about the **Subproject of** option, which can be used to make the project a subproject of another one.

 You can also add subprojects using the **New subproject** link on the overview page of the parent project (which we will soon discuss). Clicking on this link opens the same new project form, but with a pre-filled value for the **Subproject of** field.

Subprojects can't share members of the parent project, but they can "inherit" them. That's what the **Inherit members** option was added for. When you enable it for a new project, all members of the parent project (if any) are copied to the new project. When you disable it for an existing project, all "inherited" members will be removed from the project.

Now, we come to the modules again. Luckily, we already know what each module does, so it should be easy to choose which modules to enabled for the project. The only thing that you should take into account while doing this is that you should not enable them unless you are going to use them right away. It is better to enable a project module later—right before using it. Thus, if you have enabled **Wiki**, be sure to add a Wiki page; if you've enabled **News**, be sure to write news (for example, about creating the project); and so on. Avoid users' disappointment when they reach an empty page of an unused module.

In the new project form, you should also choose trackers for your project. Here, you can see just their names, but the associated workflows are what you actually need to consider. However, it's a bit too early to discuss these things, as they are going to be reviewed later in this book (in *Chapter 7, Access Control and Workflow*). Also, which trackers you need depends on the project (for example, I doubt that you will need the **Chapter** tracker for your projects). So, the only thing that I can recommend right now is enabling as few trackers as possible, because a large number of trackers may confuse your users.

The project pages

Certainly, not all tabs in the project menu are provided by modules. Thus, even if all project modules are disabled for the project, it will still have the three core tabs—**Overview**, **Activity**, and **Settings**.

The **Overview** and **Activity** tabs are public and the **Settings** tab is visible only to project managers. We will talk about the **Settings** tab in *The project configuration* section. Right now, let's speak about the first two tabs.

The Overview tab

The overview page is the landing page for the project. That's why it combines all of the information that can be of interest to users. However, it needs to be stated that users who use Redmine intensively rarely come to this page, as they know where they can find the information they need. On the other hand, new users of the project, especially first-time users, come to this page more often. So, it can be concluded that the overview page is intended mostly for new users. Still, this page contains some information that you won't find elsewhere.

So, let's check out the **Overview** tab:

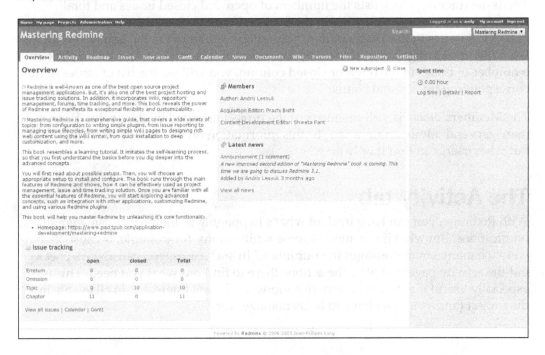

The description of the project that you can see under the **Overview** label is what you specify in the **Description** field of the project form. Below the description, you can see the value of the **Homepage** field of the same form. Towards the right from the **Overview** label is the **New subproject** link. This link opens the new project form with the **Subproject of** field set to the current project. All of these elements are already known to you.

Near the **New subproject** link, you can see the **Close** link. This link will be discussed later in this chapter. On the sidebar, you can see the grand total of the time spent on this project and the related links. The whole **Spent time** block is provided by the Time tracking module, which we'll discuss in *Chapter 8, Time Tracking*.

The content of the **Latest news** block should already look familiar to you, as it contains the latest news provided by the News module, which was discussed earlier. This block also contains the **View all news** link, which redirects to the **News** tab.

The next two blocks are available only on this page.

The **Issue tracking** block lists the numbers of open and closed issues and total number of issues for each tracker in the project. If you click on the tracker name or a number of issues in the **Total** column, you will be redirected to the issue list with the issue filter preconfigured to show only the issues of this tracker. And if you click on a number of issues in the **open** or **closed** column, you will get the list of issues of the corresponding tracker and status.

The **Members** block lists all members of the project grouped by their roles. Project managers and administrators can see this information on the project's **Settings** page, but other users can find it only here.

The Activity tab

With Redmine, you can keep track of what's happening in the project using email notifications. But what if you missed some notifications, for example, because there were too many email messages in your inbox? In such cases, you can always check out the activity page and filter the actions there to find out what you need. This is especially useful if you don't use notifications or you are interested in all events in the project (and you don't have to be its manager for this).

The activity page that I'm referencing is available under the **Activity** tab, which is shown in the following screenshot:

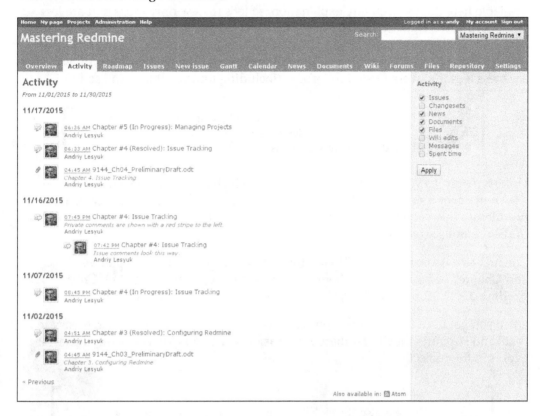

By default, the activity page shows a summary of events in the project for the last 30 days. This period can be configured using the **Days displayed on project activity** setting, which can be found under the **General** tab of the **Settings** page in the **Administration** menu. The dates for which the activities are shown can be seen under the **Activity** label. At the bottom of the activity list, you can see the **Previous** link. This link allows you to move to the previous 30 days (that is, before **11/01/2015**). If you go there, to the right from the **Previous** link, you will see the **Next** link. This link can be used to move back to the current period. So, using these links, you can navigate the history of project events.

Additionally, you can subscribe to the activity feed using the **Atom** link which you can see below the list.

The sidebar of the activity page contains the already mentioned filter that allows you to select what kinds of events you want to see. Most of the event types that are available here do not need any explanation, so let's review only those that are less obvious. Thus, if the **Issues** checkbox is checked, the activity list will include changes of the issue status and notes. If the **Changesets** action is enabled, the list will also include repository commits. And, if the **Messages** checkbox is checked, you will also see messages that were posted to forums (including topics, replies, and so on).

> Note that the issue events shown here are not the same as the issue history entries shown on the issue page. The latter include many more details.

Unfortunately, as you can see, it's not obvious which item is for which event type. Different event types have different icons, but to learn which one is for which, you need to use this page for some time. Anyway, let me tell you what events you can see in the previous screenshot.

The first two items for **11/17/2015** are the status changes for the **Chapter #4** and **Chapter #5** issues. Below them, you can see the upload of the **9144_Ch04_PreliminaryDraft.odt** file. For **11/16/2015**, you see notes for the **Chapter #4** issue.

Once you get used to this page, you will love the listing, as it is compact, is easy to read, and supports the filter—there is no easier way to quickly check out the latest events in the project.

> **Global activities**
>
> There is also the global activity page that shows events on all projects (to which a user has access, of course). This page can be useful for employees who work on different projects, for example, company directors who want to know what's happening on all projects. To get there, click on the **Projects** item of the top menu and then click on the **Overall activity** link.

The project configuration

In this section, we are going to discuss topics intended solely for Redmine project managers, that is, users who have permissions that allow them to edit some project attributes (or other attributes that are somehow related to projects). It's easy to check whether you are among of them—if you see the **Settings** tab in the project menu, it means you can manage this project (or at least some of its attributes).

So, let's move on to this tab:

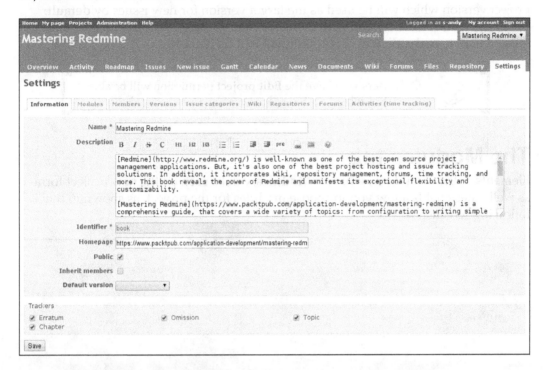

Here, you see the settings of the project. As you can see, these settings also use tabs. Let's discuss them.

In this section, we will skip the **Issue category** tab, as it has been discussed in the previous chapter. We will also skip the **Repositories** and **Forums** tabs as they have been reviewed along with the appropriate modules. Also, we won't review the **Activities** (**time tracking**) tab because it's going to be reviewed in *Chapter 8, Time Tracking*.

The Information tab

The first tab of the settings menu that gets opened by default and which you can see in the previous screenshot is the **Information** tab. Generally, it contains the same fields that can be found in the new project form.

The only new field in this form is **Default version**. Using this field you can select a project version which will be used as the target version for new issues by default. Thus, you can create a version with the name, for example, *Next major release* and select it here to make all new issues assigned to it by default.

 Only users who have the **Edit project** permission will be able to see this tab.

The Modules tab

Elements of the second tab, which is **Modules**, can be seen on the new project form as well. These fields allow you to choose modules for the project, as shown in the following screenshot:

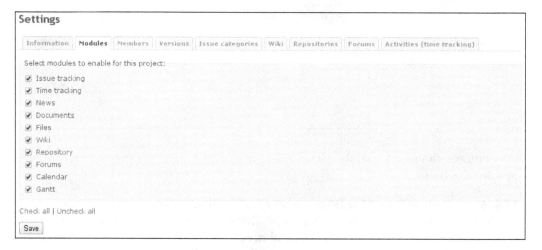

On this tab, you can enable (or disable) modules anytime—for example, when you are ready to fill out their pages.

 Only users who have the **Select project modules** permission will be able to see the **Modules** tab.

The Members tab

The next tab is **Members**. Check it out in this screenshot:

This is the page where you can manage the members of the project.

 To get access to this tab, the user must have the **Manage members** permission.

If you click on the **New member** link, it will open the following dialog:

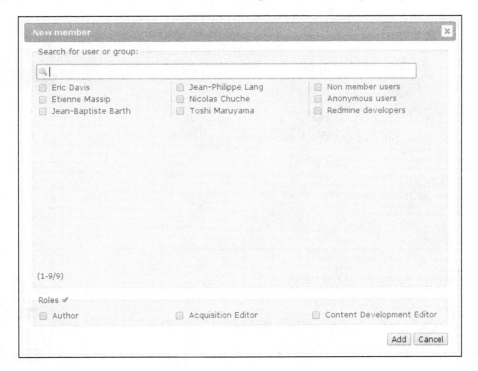

As you can see, in this dialog, you can choose several users and several roles at the same time (a user can have multiple roles in a project). Notice that the user list also contains groups, for example, **Redmine developers**. In this way, you can add all members of a group as members of the project.

The search field can be used to filter users and groups by parts of their names. Thus, if I type `Jean` in this field, the list will contain only **Jean-Philippe Lang** and **Jean-Baptiste Barth**. The green check mark (✅) near the **Roles** label can be used to quickly select or unselect all listed roles.

Maybe you have noticed that the user/group list contains only those users who are not members of the project yet. To assign a different role to an existing member of the project, you need to use the **Edit** link in the member list. When you do this, the following form is revealed in the member's row:

After you have saved the changes or clicked on the **Cancel** link, this form disappears and the member's row gets updated accordingly.

The Versions tab

Now, let's see what's under the **Versions** tab:

This is where we manage the versions of the project.

 If you don't have the **Manage versions** permission, you won't see this tab.

Project versioning is extremely important for software projects. Thus in Redmine, project versions can be referenced by issues (and you can specify in which version the issue is going to be resolved), project files can be uploaded for a specific version, versions are shown on the roadmap, the calendar can show version dates, the Wiki syntax supports links to versions (we will speak about this later), custom fields support the **Version** type, and so on. In other words, by ignoring versions, you literally limit the functionality that is available for your project in Redmine.

However, it's also important to manage versions correctly. Let's check out the new version form that becomes available when you click on the **New version** link. This form is shown in the following screenshot:

New version

Name *	
Description	
Status	open ▼
Wiki page	
Date	📅
Sharing	Not shared ▼

Create

Here, **Name** is usually a version number but also can be just a string (such as *Second edition* in my case). However, it's not recommended to use strings for this field, as you can end up with a broken order of versions (which can be corrected by using the **Date** field though, which we'll discuss soon). This is also the only required field.

The **Description** field is optional and should contain a very short description of what is special about this version, for example, *Maintenance release*. This description is going to be shown on the roadmap and the version page.

The value of the **Status** field can be **open, locked,** or **closed**. Here, "locked" means that the version is in a *frozen* state and all associated issues have been fixed but not yet tested. Also, you can't change the **Target version** of an issue to a locked or closed version.

The **Wiki page** field contains the name of the Wiki page that describes changes that were made in this version. The content of this page will be embedded in the version's section on the roadmap and the version page. Such a Wiki page can contain, for example, the changelog for the version.

Remember about **SEO** while choosing the a name for the associated Wiki page. Thus, you can use the word `Changelog` plus the version name, for example, `Changelog-1-0-2`.

When you save the version, the value of the **Wiki page** field turns into the link that points to the associated Wiki page (see the **Second-edition** link in the first screenshot of this subsection). The same Wiki page is also going to be referenced by the **Edit associated Wiki page:** link on the version page.

The **Date** field is not just for showing the due date of the release. Thus, the value of this field affects the order of versions, as shown in the following screenshot:

Version	Date	Description	Status	Sharing	Wiki page		
2.5.0	03/02/2015		open	Not shared		Edit	Delete
3.2.x	12/06/2015		open	Not shared		Edit	Delete
2.6.x			closed	Not shared		Edit	Delete
3.0.x			closed	Not shared		Edit	Delete
3.1.x			closed	Not shared		Edit	Delete
4.0.x			open	Not shared		Edit	Delete

Usually, more recent versions are shown at the bottom of the list, but if a version has **Date**, it gets moved to the top. So, other versions appear as newer. In other words, an empty **Date** field is treated as distant time in the future.

 Actually, you should not mix versions with dates and versions without dates, as your version list may become disordered. Nevertheless, you can still use dates for old and current versions and leave them empty for future versions.

Additionally, the value of the **Date** field is used to determine whether the version is completed, but we will get back to this a little later in this subsection.

The last field of this form — the **Sharing** field — accepts the following values:

- **Not shared**: This version won't be shared. This means that it will be available only for this project. This is the default value.

- **With subprojects**: This version will be available for all subprojects of this project down to any nesting level.

- **With project hierarchy**: This version will be available for all subprojects as well as all parent projects of the current one, but not for other subprojects of parent projects. To be able to choose this option, the user must have the **Manage versions** permission for the parent project as well.

- **With project tree**: This version will be available for all subprojects of the current project as well as all subprojects of all parent projects of the current one. Moreover, it will be available for all parent projects of the current project. As with the previous option, to be able to select this option, the user must have the **Manage versions** permission for the parent project.

- **With all projects**: This version will be shared among all projects that are available on this Redmine installation! As this is a very wide sharing method, this option is available only for administrators. Certainly, you have to be extremely careful when choosing this option.

Any of these fields can be modified later by clicking on the **Edit** link next to the version in the version list. This link opens the same form that we have just reviewed. Additionally, you can remove the version by clicking on the **Delete** link.

There is, however, one more thing related to versions that we have not discussed yet. It's the **Close completed versions** link, which can be seen on the right-hand side under the version list (see the first screenshot in this subsection).

A completed version can be considered to be a not-yet-closed version that nonetheless meets all the conditions to be closed. Remember that when we were reviewing the **Date** field, I promised to get back to it? That's here! If the value of the **Date** field is in the past and there are no more open issues for the version, such a version is considered to have been completed. So, using the **Close completed versions** link, you can close all such versions with just one click.

The Wiki tab

The last tab of the project's **Settings** page that we will review in this section is **Wiki**, which is shown here:

In this tab, you can specify the landing page for the project's Wiki, which is *Wiki* by default. In other words, using this form, you can change the Wiki page that is opened when you click on the **Wiki** tab of the project menu. Thus, you may need to do this if you have prepared a special page for the next release of your project.

The **Delete** link in the bottom-right corner can be used to delete the start page. However, it not only deletes the Wiki page itself but also removes the name of the landing page in the form! So after this, the **Wiki** tab of the project menu (not of the project's **Settings** page) disappears, as the start page no longer exists. Actually, I believe that a more gracious way to do the same is to just disable the Wiki module.

Closing a project

Some companies may work on many small projects. In several years, such companies end up with a huge list of projects, the majority of which are not used anymore (that is, there are no new issues, files, Wiki pages, updates on forums, and so on). However, removing such projects can be unacceptable as some of them can potentially be renewed in future, others can be forked and some data of the original project can still be needed for a fork, the data of others can be needed for reference, and so on. At the same time, leaving such projects in the list can also be problematic, as in that case, the project list can become unusable. This is when the **Close** link on the project's **Overview** page comes in handy.

When clicked on, and after a confirmation, this link puts the projects into a read-only state. In this state, all project information remains available and all read permissions are preserved, but nothing can be changed or added. Also, the **Overview** page of the project gets this warning:

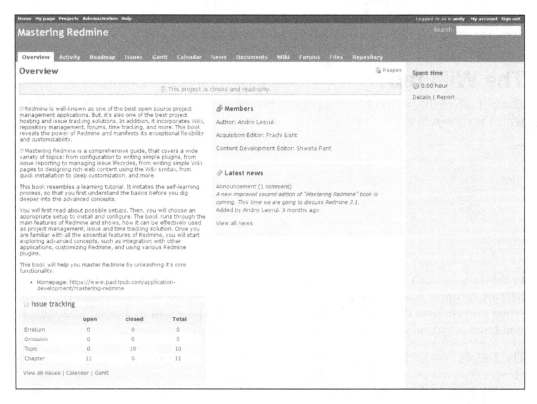

As you can see, the **Close** link has changed to **Reopen**, which can be used to open the project again. Also notice that the project does not have the **New issue** and **Settings** tabs anymore (as these tabs are to be used to modify the project).

[Only project members who have the **Close / reopen the project** permission can use this feature.]

By the way, the project list does not include closed projects by default.

The project list

Let me say a few words about the page where projects are listed. You have probably seen this page, as it's where we can find the **New project** link as well as the **View all issues** and **Overall activity** links, which have been mentioned in this and the previous chapters. So, you can now see them here:

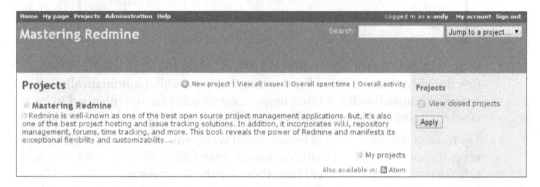

This page lists projects that are accessible to the user. The list includes a shortened description of each project. If a project has a yellow star ☆ near the name, it means that you are a member of that project. If a project is a subproject, it will be shown with an additional margin to the left.

As mentioned in the previous section, the project list does not include closed projects by default. Therefore, on the sidebar of this page, you can see a form with the **View closed projects** option that allows you to change this.

Also, it's possible to subscribe to the list of projects and be notified about new projects when they are added. To do this, just copy the **Atom** link and paste it in your favorite feed aggregator.

Project maintenance best practices

As of now, we have reviewed the functionality that is available for projects in Redmine. However, in my opinion, it's not enough to learn what functionality is available. It's much more important to learn how to use it properly. So now, I would like to share some of my experience of what should be done and what should be avoided. In other words, in this section, I would like to list some best practices for better project maintenance. So let's go:

- Always specify the target version when you close an issue, as it is used for the roadmap.

- Have a future version added to the version list. If you are unsure what version name or number this will be then name it, for example, *Next version*. You can always change the name later. If no future version is available, a developer won't be able to select a value for the **Target version** field.

> Redmine developers use the following version names for future versions: *Candidate for next major release* and *Candidate for next minor release*.

- Write a changelog for each released version, using the associated Wiki page functionality. Just the list of fixed issues that is provided automatically is not enough because this list is often huge, issue subjects are not intended to be clear enough for a changelog, and so on.

- Try to keep the done ratio of issues actual while you work on it. There are several reasons for this. Firstly, customers may follow the issue and its done ratio in particular, so this will help them see the progress (while 0% can be frustrating). Secondly, the grand total of the done ratios is used to show the overall progress of the project version.

- Write news every time you make a release. Customers who are waiting for a new release of your project may subscribe to the news of your project and expect to get news about the new release.

Custom queries

You should not expect your users to learn how the issue filter works and configure it to their needs on their own. Wherever possible, you should ensure that they feel comfortable while browsing your issue lists. And this is not only about your customers but also—and even especially—about your project members.

Check out the following examples of custom queries. Some of them will possibly be useful for you. The others, I hope, will give you an idea about custom queries that you may need:

Name	Filters	
	Field/Option	Condition/Value
My open issues	Status	open
	Assigned to	"<<me>>"
My open issues in the next version	Status	open
	Assigned to	"<<me>>"
	Target version	"Next version"
Issues watched by me	Status	open
	Watcher	"<<me>>"
Unassigned issues	Status	open
	Assignee	none
New features in the next version	Tracker	Feature
	Target version	"Next version"
Changelog for current stable version	Target version	"Stable"
	Sort	Tracker
Roadmap	Status	open
	Group results by	Target version
Issues grouped by assignees and sorted by priority	Status	open
	Group results by	Assignee
	Sort	Priority
Issues by trackers sorted by status	Group results by	Tracker
	Sort	Status

The issue filter and custom queries were described in detail in the previous chapter.

Administering projects

Redmine also has another list of projects. This list, however, is available only for administrators. You can check it out on the **Projects** page of the **Administration** menu. It looks as shown in this screenshot:

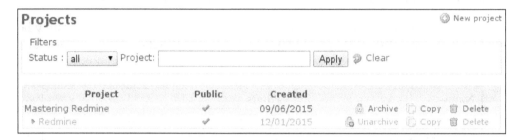

Here, you can see all the projects that I have on my demo Redmine installation. This page has a very simple form that allows you to filter projects by their statuses and by a part of the name. The **Clear** link can be used to reset values of this form.

Available statuses are: **all**, **active**, **closed**, and **archived**. If the status filter is set to **active** (which is the default), the list won't include closed and archived projects. You already know what a closed project is. You will read about archived projects in the *Archiving projects* subsection. Also note how the subproject, that is, **Redmine**, is shown.

Additionally, on this page, you can see another **New project** link, which was mentioned earlier in this chapter. This link opens the new project form that we have discussed as well.

New things on this page are the **Archive** (and **Unarchive**) and **Copy** links. Regarding the **Delete** link, I guess there is no need to explain what it does (note that it does this asking for a confirmation). So now, let's talk about other links.

Copying projects

Let's see what happens when we click on the **Copy** link:

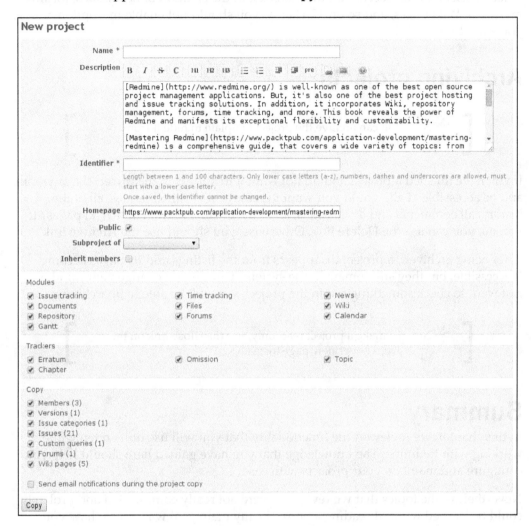

This form is very much the same as the new project form, except that it uses some values and states of the original project and has the additional **Copy** block.

In some circumstances, projects hosted in Redmine can be very similar. For such cases, with this **Copy** link, Redmine provides a way to create a project template and then copy it into new projects.

The **Copy** block allows you to choose what types of objects should be copied to a new project. The **Send email notifications during the project copy** option controls whether users should receive notifications about the creation of new issues, forums, messages, Wiki pages, and so on. Certainly, you should not enable this option, unless you want to "spam" them.

Archiving projects

 You can archive the project template to hide it from users.

If you have finished a project and do not want it to appear in the project list anymore and be accessible at all, would you want to remove it? With all issues, all of the history, all comments and discussions, all of the documentation and Wiki pages? If you do, you can use the **Delete** link. Otherwise, you should use the **Archive** link.

After being archived, a project disappears from the listings and its pages become inaccessible, but they still remain in the system. Thus, if you change your mind or just want to check something out in the project, you will be able to unarchive it.

 To make a project read-only, use the **Close** link on the project overview page instead.

Summary

In this chapter, we reviewed the functionality that you will use quite often while working with Redmine. The knowledge that you have gained here should help you configure and maintain your projects with ease.

Nevertheless, the topics that we reviewed were not really complicated and probably could be learned without reading a book. So, my main goal was not to show you the basics of managing projects in Redmine, but to show things that you should consider while doing this. I also tried to share my experience about best practices for configuring and maintaining Redmine projects. I hope I have succeeded in this.

With each chapter, we learn more and more and you probably wonder, "What else can be in the next chapters?" But do we know enough? For example, we know that we can use the Wiki syntax almost everywhere in Redmine, but have we discussed this syntax? That's what we are going to do in the next chapter.

6
Text Formatting

As a developer, I can assure you of the importance of rich text formatting in user requests—especially in issue descriptions—for good text comprehension. It is especially important if the one who is going to comprehend an issue (for example) is constantly dealing with a lot of such issues. In practice, users unfortunately neglect rich formatting often, what results in bad readability and sometimes distorted message layouts (when some characters are treated as formatting markers). Therefore, I believe that familiarity with Redmine text formatting is essential for using this application. Luckily, the syntax of the formatting language is not too complicated, as it's based on a plain-text markup language.

Redmine currently comes with native support for two markup languages—Textile and Markdown. However, we will focus mainly on the former (while mentioning the latter whenever possible). There are two reasons for this. Firstly, most Redmine installations (still) use Textile, as it was supported by Redmine long before Markdown was added. Secondly, Textile is less used in other applications, so you most likely won't be able to learn it elsewhere.

The Textile markup language attempts to add rich formatting to plain text while not breaking its readability. Thus, list items begin with * or #, italic text is enclosed in _ (underline), and so on. This way, if someone writes text not using any formatting markers, such text will be rendered just fine (in most cases). Moreover, Textile is able to add rich formatting to plain text that does not include any special Textile rules. For example:

- Pieces of text that are separated by empty lines are rendered as paragraphs
- Paragraphs that start with > are rendered as quotes
- Strings that start with, say, `http://`, are rendered as links

In other words, Textile is very simple and easy to learn. At least, most of its syntax is. However, this book is not aimed at simple things that you can learn on your own, so in this chapter you will also find some complicated advanced topics.

We will cover the following topics in this chapter:

- Formatting text in Redmine
- The Wiki syntax

Formatting text in Redmine

Initially in Redmine, rich text formatting was implemented mainly for the integrated Wiki system that is provided by the Wiki module, which was described in the previous chapter. That's why it is still often called Wiki formatting (and that's the name I will use to refer to it from now on). Right now, however, the Wiki syntax is used not only for the Wiki pages but also for issue descriptions, comments, news, project descriptions, and so on.

The underlying markup language used for Wiki formatting can be selected on the **General** tab of the **Settings** page, which can be found in the **Administration** menu. Check out the following screenshot:

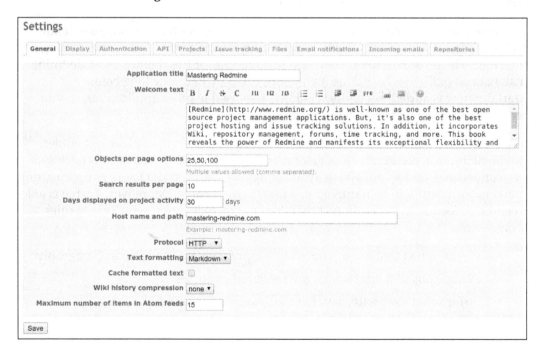

Thus, if the **Text formatting** setting is set to **none**, the content that you put into a Wiki-syntax-enabled text area will be shown as is, that is, any formatting will be ignored. This will also apply to the Wiki system, what means that Wiki pages will lose their formatting. However, the Wiki syntax for Redmine's internal linking (such as links to issues and Wiki pages), which will be covered further, will still be functioning! Otherwise, the Wiki system would become completely useless, particularly without support for cross-page links.

As before, for fresh Redmine installations with a fresh audience, I would recommend that you choose **Markdown** for the **Text formatting** option (see *Chapter 2, Installing Redmine*). Certainly, this chapter would become less useful for you in that case. Less useful but not totally useless, as the Wiki syntax has a part that is common to both Textile and Markdown.

The Wiki toolbar

Almost every text area for a field that supports Wiki formatting comes with the Wiki toolbar:

This toolbar does not convert the text area into a **What You See Is What You Get (WYSIWYG)** editor, however. It just provides an easy way to paste the most commonly used formatting markers. Unfortunately, a well-working WYSIWYG solution for Redmine currently does not exist as far as I know.

 For Markdown, this toolbar does not include the underline button, ᵤ , as this markup language does not support this style.

The last button in the toolbar, ◉ , opens a quick reference for the Wiki syntax. The page that gets opened also includes a link to more detailed documentation.

None of the buttons in the toolbar open a dialog. All of them just paste the syntax markers at the current position in the text area. Also, if the user selects part of the text in the text area, clicking on these buttons formats the selected text accordingly. Thus, if the user clicks on the ʙ button, the selected text will be enclosed in * (the bold marker). If the user selects several lines of the text and clicks on the ≔ or ≣ button, * or # (list markers) will be prepended at the beginning of each selected line accordingly.

The Wiki toolbar is really helpful when you have just started using Redmine and therefore do not remember all the markers. After you become a more experienced user, I believe you will prefer to type them directly in the text area (at least I do). Also, the Wiki toolbar does not cover all the available markers, so you won't be able to completely avoid typing them anyway. For this reason and because we have not covered the available syntax yet, we won't review these buttons here. However, you may play with them on your own.

To get a hint of what a button does, hover the mouse cursor over it.

Preview

In most cases, forms with Wiki-syntax-enabled text areas include the **Preview** link, an example of which is shown here:

This link can, and should, be used before submitting the content to Redmine to check whether it's going to be formatted correctly. When you click on this link, the preview of the content of a Wiki syntax-enabled text area will be rendered beneath the form.

Always use the **Preview** link, if available, before submitting content to the server. Do this even if you are sure that the markup is correct and even if you did not use any markers at all, as the content can still include some special characters or sequences of characters that may be treated as formatting markers by the core Redmine formatter or third-party extensions.

Of course, in most cases, you will be able to fix the content later after submitting it. However, if users are subscribed to the content, they will most likely get the initial version and not the fixed one. Also, further changes are sometimes logged in the change history of the resource (for example, the issue history), thus clogging it.

Where to store linked images?

Wiki content can use linked images. Here, the word linked means it's hosted on the same Redmine installation, and possibly stored in the same resource (for example, an issue) and embedded in the Wiki content of the resource using the Wiki syntax. While the Wiki syntax allows the linking of images that are hosted on external websites, this can be inadmissible in many cases, for example, for security reasons or due to the load speed. So, let's discuss where you can store your linked images.

If the resource (such as an issue or a Wiki page) for which you are writing the content lets you attach files, attach your images to it. Thus, for issue notes, attach images to the issue.

However, not all resources can have attachments (that's why I have written this subsection, actually). For such resources, some users store linked images under the **Files** tab of the project menu, but I don't recommend doing this. Under the **Files** tab, your users expect to see files for downloading, for example, installation packages, documentation, samples, and so on. So, they may conclude that these images are somehow related to the project (for example, they may think of them as diagrams) and should be downloaded as well.

Therefore, I believe that in such cases the best option is to attach linked images to a specially created and dedicated Wiki page, for example, *Linked-images*. There, you will also be able to describe the purpose of the page and annotate images that are attached — if you want, of course. Also note that if this page won't be referenced from any other Wiki page, it will be seen only on Wiki index pages, such as **Index by title** and **Index by date**, which is perhaps good.

 If you have disabled the Wiki module, you can use a special closed issue instead.

But what URL should you use if you store the image in a separate resource? For the same resource, it's easy (use just the filename; see the *Images* subsection of *The Wiki syntax* section), but what about a separate resource? Not so easy, but not too difficult either. To get the URL, right-click on the name of the attached file and copy the link address, as follows:

You should get a URL that ends with /attachments/<id>/<filename>. This is the URL you should use when embedding the image in a Wiki content! Also, always use the relative URL. I mean the one that starts with /, for example, /attachments/<id> or /redmine/attachments/<id> (this depends on whether your Redmine uses a subdomain — redmine is the subdomain here). And yes, <filename> is actually optional, so it can be omitted.

The Wiki syntax

So far, we have discussed the way in which text formatting is integrated into Redmine. Now we'll focus exclusively on the syntax rules.

The basics

The supported syntax rules can be divided into special rules (for example, lists and tables) and the rest. So, the rest actually includes not only the basics but also rules that are very simple and therefore do not need a separate subsection. Moreover, these are the rules that you are going to learn right now. But let's start with the basic principles.

A Textile or Markdown document is a plain-text document. The new line character in such a document is treated as a <br /> tag in HTML; that is, the rest of the text after the new line character in the current paragraph is moved to a new line.

A paragraph is separated from the previous and next paragraphs by an empty line, that is, two new line characters. Thus, the following text will be formatted as a single paragraph:

```
Redmine is a flexible project management web application.
Written using the Ruby on Rails framework,
it is cross-platform and cross-database.
```

Alternatively, you can start each paragraph with p. (there should be a space after the dot):

```
p. Redmine is a flexible project management web application.

p. Written using the Ruby on Rails framework,
it is cross-platform and cross-database.
```

But again, paragraphs must be separated by an empty line. Otherwise, the p. in the third line will just be ignored and shown as is inside the paragraph.

 The p. marker works only with Textile.

The p. marker stands for *paragraph* and is converted into the HTML <p> tag. But in fact, the effect of using p. is usually the same as not using it, because Textile uses the HTML <p> tag for every paragraph that does not have any marker at the beginning of the line anyway.

 The p. marker can be used to keep the indentation consistent for all paragraphs in a document. Thus, you can write a code paragraph as follows:

```
p. <code>...</code>
```

Similar to p., the h1., h2., h3., h4., h5., and h6. markers are converted into HTML's <h1>, <h2>, <h3>, <h4>, <h5>, and <h6> tags accordingly. These markers can be used to add headings to a Wiki content. To see how all the heading levels are formatted, let's use the following code:

```
h1. First heading

h2. Second heading

h3. Third heading
```

```
h4. Fourth heading

h5. Fifth heading

h6. Sixth heading
```

This code is rendered as shown in the following screenshot:

First heading

Second heading

Third heading

Fourth heading

Fifth heading

Sixth heading

As you can see, these headings define sections of the Wiki document, each of which can be edited independently using the pen icon ✎ on the right. Headings down to the fourth level will also be shown in the table of contents (I will explain how to enable it later in this chapter).

 In Markdown, headings can be specified using the # marker. The level of heading is specified by the number of hashes. Thus, to add an <h6> heading to Wiki content, place six hashes at the beginning of the line, as follows:

```
###### Sixth heading
```

These are the basic blocks that define styles for paragraphs. Now it's time for basic inline styles.

Let's start with checking how the following text will be formatted:

```
This is the difference between *strong* and **bold**.
Inline cite looks ??this way??.
Inline text can be +inserted+ or -deleted-.
This is the difference between _emphasize_ and __italics__.
Also Redmine supports ^superscript^ and ~subscript~.
```

Here is the corresponding screenshot:

This is the difference between **strong** and **bold**.
Inline cite looks *this way*.
Inline text can be <u>inserted</u> or ~~deleted~~.
This is the difference between *emphasize* and *italics*.
Also Redmine supports ^superscript^ and ~subscript~.

 The superscript and subscript markers should be separated from other words by spaces. Thus, the supports^superscript^ code won't work, as there is no space between supports and ^. However, this does not apply to Markdown.

You should have noticed an odd thing about strong and bold, as well as emphasized and italic styles. In most cases, * and **, as well as _ and _ _, are the same (and look the same), except that they are converted to different HTML tags. Here is the full list of HTML analogs of these Textile markers (and their Markdown analogs):

Textile	HTML	Markdown
...	`<strong>...</strong>`	**...**
...	`<b>...</b>`	
??...??	`<cite>...</cite>`	
+...+	`<ins>...</ins>`	
-...-	`<del>...</del>`	~~...~~
_..._	`<em>...</em>`	*...*
_ _..._ _	`<i>...</i>`	
^...^	`<sup>...</sup>`	^...
~...~	`<sub>...</sub>`	

 Explaining the difference between the `<strong>` and `<b>` tags is beyond the scope of this book and is related to HTML. Basically, `<b>` and `<i>` are just styles, while `<strong>` and `<em>` are intended to emphasize the content.

Sometimes, you may want to use short names or phrases for something that can need a more detailed explanation. In such cases, you can use footnotes and acronyms to let readers quickly check out the details.

A **footnote** consists of two parts. The first part is a number, which should be specified inline using square brackets, for example, Some text[1] (there should be no space between the text and the marker). The second part should be specified separately — preferably at the bottom of the document — using fnX., where X is the footnote number. Like p. and hX., this marker should be at the start of the line. Also, as this is a so-called block marker, each footnote should be separated from other lines by empty lines.

> In Markdown, footnotes can be specified using this syntax: [^X] (inline) and [^X] : Note (at the bottom of the document).

Acronyms are specified inline using parentheses. Their syntax is ABC(Text), where ABC is an all-caps word that is going to be shown on the page, and Text is the description that will be shown when the user hovers the mouse arrow over the visible part. Also, as with footnotes, there should be no space between the acronym and its description.

So now, let's check out how the following Textile code will be formatted:

```
In Redmine[1] Wiki pages can be exported to PDF(Portable Document
Format), HTML(HyperText Markup Language) and TXT(Plain text).

fn1. Flexible project management web application written using Ruby on
Rails.
```

This is what we get:

> In Redmine[1] Wiki pages can be exported to PDF, HTML and TXT.
>
> [1] Flexible project management web application written usin HyperText Markup Language

To visually separate parts of the text, you can use - - - (dashes), ***, or _ _ _ (underscores) between paragraphs (separated from the paragraphs by empty lines). These markers will produce a horizontal line (made with the HTML <hr> tag). All of these markers work in Markdown as well.

Sometimes, the formatting needs to be disabled. If this is the case, to disable the processing of some part of the text by Textile, use the special <notextile> tag. Here is an example:

```
<notextile>This text will be shown *as is*.</notextile>
```

But note that this won't disable link generation—it will turn off only the formatting. New line characters and empty lines won't be processed either, so the no-textile (the text inside `<notextile>`) text will always be shown in a single paragraph.

Quotes

For applications such as Redmine, it's important to be able to embed quotes, especially in issue comments and forum messages. Luckily, the Redmine Wiki formatting implementation allows us to do this. Moreover, the appropriate forms usually provide UI elements for quoting original messages.

In Redmine, quotes can be embedded in two ways:

- By default, to format a text as a quote, Redmine uses the > marker at the beginning of the line (yes, it's another block marker). As this marker supports nesting, you can use it as follows:

  ```
  >> Initial message
  > Reply to initial message
  ```

  Here is a screenshot that shows how this text will be rendered:

  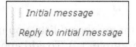

  Initial message

  Reply to initial message

  This syntax works for both Textile and Markdown, but in Textile, the > marker does not have to be separated by an empty line from the previous paragraph. Moreover, the empty line will break the left gray line, which indicates that the paragraph is a quote. On the contrary, in Markdown, the empty line is required.

- Textile supports one more way of specifying quotes—with the `bq.` marker. Generally, both ways produce visually identical results (because both rely on the HTML `<blockquote>` tag), but `bq.` does not support nesting. However, the `bq.` marker, like the `<blockquote>` tag, supports the `cite` parameter:

  ```
  bq.:http://www.redmine.org Redmine is a flexible project
  management web application. Written using the Ruby on Rails
  framework, it is cross-platform and cross-database.
  ```

  Here, the syntax is as follows:

  ```
  bq.:cite Text
  ```

  Note that `cite` can be an absolute or relative URL or a named anchor (that starts with #). This parameter is not displayed or used by browsers, but it can be used by search engines to locate the original message.

Lists

Redmine Wiki formatting supports bulleted and numbered lists. Bullet list items can be created with the * marker, and numbered list items can be created with the # marker. Both should be placed at the start of the line and followed by a space (unlike the strong * marker, which should be followed by a word).

Bulleted and numbered lists can be nested. To add a nesting level, just add another marker at the beginning. Let's see how the following example will be rendered using Textile:

```
# The first item
## Nested item
### Next nesting level
# The second item
```

The following screenshot shows the result:

```
1. The first item
       1. Nested item
              1. Next nesting level
2. The second item
```

In Markdown, for numbered lists, you need to use a number and a dot (for example, 1.). To add another nesting level, you need to prepend spaces before the marker.

You can also mix types of nested lists. For example, check out the following code:

```
# The first item
#* Nested item
#** Next nesting level
# The second item
```

Images

Images can be embedded in Wiki content using the ! rule, the syntax of which is as follows:

```
!Options.ImageURL(Title)!:HREF
```

Here, `Options.` (with the dot), `(Title)`, and `:HREF` are optional.

 For Markdown, the syntax is `![Title](ImageURL)`. But note that you should always specify `Title`, even if it is empty, that is, `[]`.

The image URL can be absolute or relative. Thus, to embed an image that was attached to a different resource (described in the *Where to store linked images?* subsection of the *Formatting text in Redmine* section), you need to use the relative URL:

```
!/attachments/110!
```

Of course, in this case, users who have access to the current Wiki content will also be required to have access to the resource to which the image is attached.

Images that are attached to the current resource can be embedded just by using their file names, like in this example:

```
!9144_06_15.png!
```

The optional `HREF` parameter can be used to turn the image into a clickable link that points to a URL:

```
!redmine-logo.png!:http://www.redmine.org
```

The optional `Options` parameter can be used to align the image relative to the text. Supported alignment options are `<`, `=`, and `>`. These options align the image to the left, center, and right correspondingly. For example, let's check out how the following markup is rendered:

```
!<.redmine-logo.png!

Redmine is a flexible project management web application.
Written using the Ruby on Rails framework, it is
cross-platform and cross-database.
```

This is what we get:

 Redmine is a flexible project management web application. Written using the Ruby on Rails framework, it is cross-platform and cross-database.

Resizing images

You can resize the image in the browser using CSS width and height properties, as follows:

```
!{width:64px;height:64px;}.<ImageURL>!
```

Finally, the `Title` parameter can be used to specify the alternative text for the image. This text is going to be displayed when the browser fails to load it (it's an analog of the `alt` attribute of the HTML `<img>` tag).

The alternative text may also be shown by email clients when the Wiki content is sent in email notifications (thus, many clients do not show Internet resources by default). So, it's a good idea to always specify the title.

Links

Redmine's Wiki formatting supports two types of links: normal and internal.

Normal links

If the text contains strings that start with `http://`, `https://`, `ftp://`, `ftps://`, `sftp://`, or `www.`, they will be rendered as links automatically. The same will be done with email addresses—they will be converted into `mailto:` links.

Also, normal links can be created using the following syntax:

```
"Anchor(Text)":Link
```

Here, `Anchor` is the text that is going to become clickable, `Text` is the optional link title that will be displayed when the user hovers the mouse arrow over `Anchor`, and `Link` is the URL that the link will point to.

For Markdown, the syntax is `[Anchor](Link "Title")`.

Internal links

Redmine Wiki formatting would be incomplete without support for internal links. In particular, its Wiki system would be useless without cross-page links.

The syntax for internal links was developed especially for Redmine, so it's common to both formatters: Textile and Markdown.

Wiki links

It's essential for any Wiki system to support cross-page links, as such links are the only way to navigate the Wiki (other than the awkward Wiki index).

In Redmine's Wiki, cross-page links can be created using this syntax:

```
[[Project:Page#NamedAnchor|Title]]
```

Everything except `Page` is optional here. `Page` is the name of the Wiki page, that is, the last component of the page URL. For example, in the URL `http://www.redmine.org/projects/redmine/wiki/RedmineWikis`, the page name is `RedmineWikis`.

 A free-form page name will also be converted to a proper URL path. Thus, `[[Free form page name]]` will link to the page with the name `Free_form_page_name`.

Sometimes, you may need to create a link to a section of a Wiki page. Sections that are created using the `h1.` to `h4.` markers always include **named anchors**, which can be referenced in links. Moreover, the named anchor is always automatically generated from the title of the heading. Therefore, we can use just the heading title as `NamedAnchor`. Here is an example:

```
[[Wiki#First heading]]
```

 In the URL, `NamedAnchor` is used as a component that is also known as the fragment identifier. As not all characters are URL-safe, Redmine sanitizes heading titles and values that you specify in Wiki links. However, if in some cases you need to specify the already sanitized named anchor, you can determine it by hovering your mouse arrow over the heading and then over the **pilcrow** (¶) that will appear to the right of the heading . The sanitized value will be seen in the URL, that should be shown on the status bar, after the # sign (that is, as the URL fragment).

In practice, you will rarely want to use the page name as the title of the link (which is also known as the anchor). And, to use a different piece of text, you should put it into the Wiki link as `Title` (after the | sign). Here is an example:

```
See [[Another-Wiki-page-name|this page]] for details.
```

Finally, if the page that you are about to link to belongs to a different project, you should prefix its name in the Wiki link with the project name or identifier, as follows:

```
[[Mastering Redmine:Wiki-page-name]]
```

Don't hesitate to put cross-page links in places where you think they will be suitable. Remember that, with the `Title` parameter, you can turn a part of the text into a cross-page link. A sufficient number of such links will only improve your Wiki's structure.

Project links

If the projects that you host on your Redmine installation are somehow related, you may want to create links from some projects to others. For such cases, Redmine supports project links that have this syntax:

```
project:Name
```

Here, `project` is the keyword that indicates the project link, and `Name` is the project name or identifier. If the project name contains special characters, for example, spaces, it should be put in double quotes.

Project links point to the overview page of the project and always use the project name as the anchor (that is, visible text).

Version links

Linking to a version is a very useful feature, and I personally use it quite often. Thus, it can be used in news, when you describe the new features of a version; in issues, if you want to specify which version is affected; and so on. Version links point to the version page and always use the version name as the anchor. The syntax is like this:

```
version#ID
version:Name
```

Here, `version` is the keyword that indicates that this is a version link, `Name` is the version name (which can be enclosed in quotes), and `ID` is the numeric ID, which can be seen in the URL of the version page (the last component).

To link to a version in a different project, prefix it with the project identifier, like in this example:

```
redmine:version:3.1.0
```

Issue links

Most likely, you will use issue links even if you don't plan to. That's because their syntax is very natural and obvious. It's just #X, where X is the issue number.

If the issue is closed, its anchor, that is, the issue number, will be formatted as strikethrough. If the user hovers the mouse arrow over the issue link, the hint box will show the subject and status of the issue.

Resolving an issue is a process that often engages not only the assignee, but also users, customers, QA engineers, and more. In such cases, it is very useful to be able to reference a particular note (history entry) of the issue, especially if that note explains some details. To create a link to an issue note, use this syntax:

```
#X-Y
#X#note-Y
```

Here, Y is the number of the history entry, which can be seen on the issue page.

Attachment links

While the ability to attach files to a resource can be used to store images that will be embedded in Wiki content of that resource, the main goal of attachments is actually different. Thus, we usually store files in a Wiki page, an issue, a forum topic, or any other resource just to let users download them. In such cases, we need to reference the attached files somewhere in the Wiki content. To do this, instead of using text such as "check the file attached to this page" we can use the following syntax:

```
attachment:filename.ext
```

This will produce the link to the attached file, which will trigger its download when users click on it. Instead of `filename.ext`, use the actual filename of the attachment. Enclose the filename in quotes if it contains spaces or other special characters.

However, note that the file that you link to in Wiki content must be attached to the resource that this Wiki content is part of. This means that you can't create links to project files (the ones that are under the **Files** tab).

News links

Sometimes, you may want to mention news about the project in your Wiki content. In such cases, you can use the `news` syntax rule, as follows:

```
news#ID
news:Title
```

Here, ID is the numeric ID of the news. This ID can be seen in the URL of the news page (the last component). Title is the title of the news (which can be enclosed in quotes). When rendered, news links always use the title as the anchor.

If the news that you are about to link to is in a different project, you should prepend the syntax rule with the project identifier, like this:

```
project-identifier:news#ID
project-identifier:news:Title
```

Document links

The very same rule is available for documents:

```
document#ID
document:Title
```

Here, ID is the numeric ID of the document, which can be seen in the URL of the document page, and Title is the document title (which can be put in quotes).

To create a link to a document in a different project, use the project identifier at the beginning, as follows:

```
project-identifier:document#id
project-identifier:document:Title
```

Forum links

Linking to forums is very much the same:

```
forum#ID
forum:Name
```

Again, ID is the numeric ID of the forum (you know how to find it) and Name is the name (title) of the forum.

 If you have only one forum, it's not so easy to determine its ID. In this case, look for it in other URLs of this forum (for example, you can use the new message URL). Such URLs should contain boards/ID/, where ID is what you are looking for.

Forum links can be used, for example, to advise users on where they can discuss their questions. However, in practice, you will most likely want to link to a specific topic of the forum or even to a specific message in a topic (for example, because it contains details about the issue).

From a technical point of view, a reply in a topic is the same object as the topic itself (a topic is just the first message in a thread). So, to link to both of them, you need to use message links. The syntax for such links is as follows:

```
message#ID
```

Here, `ID` is the unique numeric ID of the message.

Unfortunately, the message ID which is to be used in such links is not shown in the list of topic messages, and individual replies do not have URLs to take it from. This means that it should be determined in a special way. Check out this screenshot:

As you can see in the previous screenshot, when you hover your mouse arrow over the message subject, on the status bar of the browser, you should see the reply URL. In this particular case, it is the following:

```
http://mastering-redmine.com/boards/1/topics/2?r=4#message-4
```

Let's discuss what this URL tells us. The message ID of the reply is **4** (`#message-4`). The first message of the topic has ID **2** (`topics/2`) and is actually the topic. Also, the numeric ID of the forum is **1** (`boards/1`).

As in the case of other links, to make a reference to a forum or message in another project, just prepend the project identifier with a colon (`:`) at the end.

Repository links

Repository support is one of the most powerful features of Redmine, so it is not surprising that the Wiki syntax comes with support for many repository-related links.

As you might know, SCM systems are intended for managing and tracking revisions. Each revision that is created by a commit contains changes that were made to files. So, links to revisions may be needed to let users know when, by whom, and how files were changed. However, the way to create such links depends on the type of revision ID, which in turn depends on the type of SCM.

Some SCMs, such as Subversion, use numeric IDs for commits. To link to revisions in such SCMs, you should use this syntax:

```
Repository|rX
```

Here, X is the revision number and `Repository` is the repository identifier, which should be specified if you have more than one repository in the project. Also, the `Repository|` part is optional. Here are some examples:

```
r128
Core|r9868
```

Other SCMs, such as Git, use string IDs for revisions (for example, special hashes). For them, you should use the following syntax:

```
commit:Repository|ID
```

Here, ID is the revision ID, `commit` is the keyword, and `Repository` is the optional repository identifier. Let's see some examples:

```
commit:0e1a622a
commit:Core|9fde11f9
```

 I would recommend that you always use the repository identifier in your repository links. Otherwise, if you add another repository to your project or change the main one, old links will become broken (as they will point to a wrong repository).

Like with issue links, when the user hovers the mouse cursor over a revision link, the hint box with the commit message is shown.

In addition to revisions, you may need to reference a particular source file and even its line, for example, to show where you think the problem lies. In such cases, use the following syntax:

source:Repository|Path@X#LY

Here, `Path` is the path to the file in the repository, `x` is the optional revision ID (numeric or not), `y` is the optional line number, and `Repository` should be used if this is not the default repository in the project. Here are some examples:

```
source:trunk/lib/redcloth3.rb
source:redmine|trunk/lib/redcloth3.rb
source:trunk/app/helpers/application_helper.rb@7248
source:trunk/app/helpers/application_helper.rb#L779
```

You can also use a repository link to let users download a file from the repository. In this case, use the following syntax:

```
export:Repository|Path
```

Also, all of these links (revision, source, and download) can be prepended with the project identifier if you want to reference a revision or a file from a different project.

Code

Redmine would not be a good project hosting and issue tracking tool without the ability to embed code in Wiki content. Furthermore, Redmine also allows you to highlight the syntax of embedded code.

Sometimes, for example, when you describe a class or a function, you may need to place a piece of code inline. There are two syntax rules that you can use in such cases.

First, you can enclose the code in the `@` marker, as follows:

```
@Redmine::WikiFormatting@
```

 In Markdown, you should enclose the inline code in ` (grave accent).

Alternatively, you can use the HTML `<code>` tag for this, as follows:

```
<code>Redmine::WikiFormatting</code>
```

Both these rules produce the same result, but the `<code>` tag additionally allows you to specify which programming language is used by the code:

```
<code class="Lang">...</code>
```

Here, `Lang` should be replaced with the language name. The currently supported values of this parameter are `C`, `CPlusPlus` (C++), `CSS`, `Clojure`, `Delphi` (Object Pascal), `Diff` (used to view differences in Redmine), `ERB` (eRuby), `Groovy`, `HAML`, `HTML`, `JSON`, `Java`, `JavaScript`, `PHP`, `Python`, `Ruby`, `SQL`, `XML`, and `YAML`.

Besides inline code, it is often necessary to embed blocks of code. This also can be done in several ways in Redmine.

First, it is enough just to add more spaces before each line of code, as follows:

```
The code block:
    module Test
       class Klass
       end
    end
```

 For Textile, a single space is enough, but for Markdown you will need to add at least four spaces.

Note, however, that, as with most other block rules, such a block must be separated from other paragraphs by an empty line.

Alternatively, you can use the HTML `<pre>` tag:

```
<pre>
module Test
   class Klass
   end
end
</pre>
```

 For Markdown, you can use ~~~ as the first line and the last line of the code block.

Both of these methods produce the block of code, but the latter can also be modified to use syntax highlighting. Thus, to make the syntax of the code inside the `<pre>` tag highlighted, you can add the `<code>` tag, which has been described earlier, as follows:

```
<pre><code class="ruby">
    def self.included(base)
```

```
    base.send(:include, InstanceMethods)
    base.class_eval do
        unloadable

        alias_method_chain :repository_field_tags,  :add
        alias_method_chain :subversion_field_tags,  :add
        alias_method_chain :mercurial_field_tags,   :add
        alias_method_chain :git_field_tags,         :add
        alias_method_chain :bazaar_field_tags,      :add
    end
end
</code></pre>
```

This markup will be rendered as shown in the following screenshot:

```
def self.included(base)
    base.send(:include, InstanceMethods)
    base.class_eval do
        unloadable

        alias_method_chain :repository_field_tags,  :add
        alias_method_chain :subversion_field_tags,  :add
        alias_method_chain :mercurial_field_tags,   :add
        alias_method_chain :git_field_tags,         :add
        alias_method_chain :bazaar_field_tags,      :add
    end
end
```

 To enable syntax highlighting in Markdown, just add the language name after the ~~~ marker in the first line of the code block, like this:

```
~~~ ruby
```

Tables

The idea behind lightweight markup languages such as Textile and Markdown is to keep the source text readable. This is the reason the | (the vertical bar) marker was chosen for tables. Thus, you can create a table using this code:

```
|               |Heading 1|Heading 2|Heading 3|
|Row heading 1|    ?    |    ?    |    ?    |
|Row heading 2|    ?    |    ?    |    ?    |
|Row heading 3|    ?    |    ?    |    ?    |
```

It will be formatted as follows:

	Heading 1	Heading 2	Heading 3
Row heading 1	?	?	?
Row heading 2	?	?	?
Row heading 3	?	?	?

The code looks very natural, doesn't it? In practice, however, users usually omit spaces, so the source text looks less readable.

Many Textile syntax rules support **options** (we will speak about this feature in detail later), and the table rule is among them. Thus, the _ option can be used to format the cell as a header. So, suppose we change the code to this:

```
|_.                     |_.Heading 1|_.Heading 2|_.Heading 3|
|_.Row heading 1|      ?      |      ?      |      ?      |
|_.Row heading 2|      ?      |      ?      |      ?      |
|_.Row heading 3|      ?      |      ?      |      ?      |
```

Then, it will be formatted as seen in the following screenshot:

	Heading 1	**Heading 2**	**Heading 3**
Row heading 1	?	?	?
Row heading 2	?	?	?
Row heading 3	?	?	?

Unfortunately — as you can see — the more complex the code, the less readable the source text.

However, I personally can't imagine good table support without support for merged cells. In Textile, cells can be merged horizontally using the \x option, where x is the number of cells to merge, and vertically using the /y option, where y is the number of cells as well. Let's see how it works, using the following code:

```
|_/2\2.                      |_\2. Common heading    |
                             |_.Heading 1|_.Heading 2|
|_/3.Common row|_.Row heading 1|      ?      |      ?      |
               |_.Row heading 2|      ?      |      ?      |
               |_.Row heading 3|      ?      |      ?      |
```

Here is the result:

		Common heading	
		Heading 1	Heading 2
	Row heading 1	?	?
Common row	Row heading 2	?	?
	Row heading 3	?	?

You might think that the table rule still misses some important options, for example, for aligning the content. But don't rush to a conclusion—wait for the advanced syntax that we will cover later in this chapter.

In Markdown, the syntax for tables is similar in some ways:

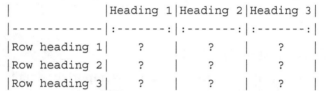

```
                |Heading 1|Heading 2|Heading 3|
|--------------|:-------:|:-------:|:-------:|
|Row heading 1|    ?    |    ?    |    ?    |
|Row heading 2|    ?    |    ?    |    ?    |
|Row heading 3|    ?    |    ?    |    ?    |
```

However, its table support is much more limited. Thus, it's not possible to merge cells. To align the content of a column , you can use a colon (:), as can be seen in the preceding example (if it was on the left side only, the content would be aligned to the left, and so on).

Macros

Everything that we have discussed so far cannot be altered or extended (or, at least, it's not easy—I mean, the Redmine API does not allow you to do this). However, Redmine also supports Wiki **macros** that are intended to be extended. This means that third-party plugins can bring in their own macros into Redmine.

The syntax of a Wiki macro looks like this:

```
{{MacroName(Arguments)}}
```

So, let's review those macros that are introduced by the Redmine core.

The Table of contents macro

Actually, Table of contents is not a macro, technically. However, it's reviewed here as its syntax resembles macros:

```
{{toc}}
```

This rule—if it's the only one on a line and is separated by empty lines from other paragraphs—generates the table of contents, as seen in the following screenshot:

```
First heading
    Second heading
        Third heading
            Fourth heading
```

The table of contents that is generated by the {{toc}} rule can also be aligned. Thus, to align it to the right, use {{>toc}}, and to align it to the left of the text, use {{<toc}}.

The Collapse macro

Sometimes, you may need to publish some less important details. The problem is that such information is going to occupy some space on the page and, probably, take attention away from the more important things. This is when the {{collapse}} macro comes in handy:

```
{{collapse(hint)
text
}}
```

This macro makes text invisible and shows only hint by default. Also, hint is rendered as a link; clicking on it unhides text:

```
▶ hint
```

The Thumbnail macro

What if you want to embed an attached image in a different size? Of course, you can have a separate attachment for each size. You can also use the advanced options (see the appropriate subsection later) to resize the image in the browser using CSS, but in this case it is going to be resized each time the user loads the Wiki content. Therefore, for such cases, Redmine provides the {{thumbnail}} macro, which has the following syntax:

```
{{thumbnail(image.png, size=100, title=Title)}}
```

Here, `image.png` must be attached to the current resource, `size` specifies the size of the thumbnail, and `Title` is its title.

Thumbnails not shown?
To generate thumbnails, Redmine uses ImageMagick's `convert` tool, which is probably missing on your installation. Check out *Chapter 2, Installing Redmine*, to learn how to install it.

The Include macro

If you need to copy some common text—such as a disclaimer or rules—into multiple Wiki pages, you can create a separate page with the common content and then include it in other pages using the `{{include}}` macro. The syntax of this macro is as follows:

```
{{include(Project:Name)}}
```

Here, `Project` is the project identifier and is optional. It is needed only if you are going to include a Wiki page from another project. `Name` is the name of the Wiki page to be included.

The Child pages macro

The Wiki navigation is built by Wiki writers through an extensive use of Wiki links. That's how Wiki systems work. However, nothing prevents Redmine from assisting with this by introducing the `{{child_pages}}` macro, which has the following syntax:

```
{{child_pages(Name, parent=1, depth=2)}}
```

Here, `Name` is the name of the Wiki page whose child pages are to be listed. If `Name` is omitted, Redmine will use the current Wiki page (and if the macro is not executed within a Wiki page, an error will be raised). If the `parent` option is enabled (that is, set to 1), the list will include the current page as well. The `depth` option controls the depth up to which child pages should be listed.

The following screenshot shows a sample output:

The Hello world macro

This macro was created for educational and testing purposes. It just outputs the given arguments and text, if any:

```
{{hello_world(argument=1)
Text
}}
```

So, you can play with this macro to learn the syntax of macros.

The Macro list macro

If a plugin ships with a macro, how do you know that it is available? That's where `{{macro_list}}` can help. This macro outputs short information about the macros that are available in the current Redmine installation.

The syntax is simple:

```
{{macro_list}}
```

 If you are using plugins that provide custom macros, it can be a good idea to create a special Wiki page named, for example, *Help*, with a list of all available macros.

The advanced syntax

This subsection is about Textile only.

In fact, Textile is much more powerful than it may seem to be at first glance. Its power lies in its advanced options, which are supported by most of its syntax rules. While you won't usually need to resort to these options, you may find some of them essential for getting the result that you need.

Advanced options are usually specified between the marker and the dot (.) that marks the end of the options. Thus, the following syntax can be used for table cells and some block rules:

```
|(Options). ...|
p(Options). ...
```

For some markers, such as the ones that are used to format lists, the options should be specified right after the marker and before the space (without the dot):

```
*(Options) ...
```

Images and normal links can use advanced options as well:

```
!(Options)image.png!
"(Options)Anchor":http://www.example.com
```

Alignment options

Some alignment options have already been mentioned, but those were options specific to certain rules. In addition to them, Redmine supports common alignment options, which are the following:

- <: Align to the left
- =: Align centrally
- <>: Justify
- >: Align to the right

Here are some examples of using these options:

```
p<>. This paragraph will be justified.
bq>. This quote will be aligned to the right.
```

Some elements, such as table cells, also support options for vertical alignment:

- ^: Align to the top
- -: Align to middle
- ~: Align to the bottom

Here is an example of using ^:

```
|/3^. Cell value aligned to the top|
```

Padding options

Block elements, such as paragraphs and cells, can be padded using the (and) options. These options control how many ems (typography units) of padding should be added to the left side [(] and the right side [)] of the block. The quantity is specified using a suitable number of parentheses. An example of using these options:

```
p(((). This paragraph will use padding.
```

For this paragraph, the left padding will be set to 3 ems and the right padding will be set to 1 em.

Custom styles and language

We can do even more with Textile. Thus, we can specify the name of the CSS class for an element, as follows (the class name is in parentheses):

```
p(info). This paragraphs will use <p class="info">.
"(redmine-link)Redmine":http://www.redmine.org
```

Of course, such CSS classes should have previously been defined in CSS files (for example, in the theme; see *Chapter 11, Customizing Redmine*).

However, if the style that you need is not specified in CSS, you can write some CSS rules directly in Textile, as follows (use curly brackets):

```
"{color:red}Redmine":http://www.redmine.org
*{font-family:Tahoma} Tahoma font
```

Unfortunately, not all CSS rules can be specified in this way. Thus, CSS properties that are supported by Textile include `color`, `width`, `height`, `border`, `background`, `padding`, `margin`, `font`, `text`, and those that start with `border-`, `background-`, `padding-`, `margin-`, `font-`, and `text-`.

Additionally, you can specify the (human) language of the element, as follows:

```
*[en] English
bq[en]. English quote.
```

The Textile span

If you are familiar with HTML and CSS, you should be aware of the magic `<span>` tag. I call this tag magic because it is intended to be used to style a part of the text if no other HTML tag fits better. This element is supported in Textile as well. Thus, it can be created using the `%` marker, as follows:

```
Let's make %{color:red}this text red% and %{color:yellow}this one
yellow%.
```

The *span* element supports most of the advanced options that were described earlier.

Disabling an element

What if you don't want the #1 text to be rendered as an issue link? Almost every marker or rule in Textile can be disabled using the special `!` marker.

Check out the following examples:

```
!#1
!r128
![[Wiki]]
!{{macro_list}}
```

All of these rules will be rendered as is (but without the exclamation mark).

Advanced table syntax

The table syntax is the most complex syntax in Textile, so it may become a headache to style all cells of a table properly using advanced options. For such cases, Textile supports batch styling.

So, to style an entire table, you can use the special `table.` rule (including the dot), which should be specified on its own line right before the table markers. Thus, to add a red border to a table, you can do the following:

```
table{border:2px solid red}.
|_.Heading 1|_.Heading 2|
|     ?     |     ?     |
```

A similar batch mode is also supported for table rows. Thus, to change the background color of the heading row to gray, you can write this:

```
{background-color:gray}. |_.Heading 1|_.Heading 2|
                         |     ?     |     ?     |
```

Summary

I hope you did not get the feeling that Redmine Wiki formatting is too complicated. Even if you did, believe me, this is only a first impression. As you practice more, you will find it flexible and entertaining.

I'm quite sure that, having read this chapter, you will not only be able to astonish your Redmine mates, but you will also be more intelligible in your posts, will emphasize more important information, and so on.

In the next chapter, you will learn how to improve the issue workflow, adapt it to your methodology, and control access to your Redmine installation.

7
Access Control and Workflow

You might expect to see the most major part of the administration menu being discussed in a single chapter, but that's not going to happen. In this book, I'm trying to review Redmine by its functional parts and not by sections of its web interface. Anyway, this chapter discusses the largest number of pages of this menu, as they are related to the access control and workflow.

On the other hand, you might wonder why the access control and workflow are reviewed in a single chapter. In Redmine, the workflow is a set of rules for the issue life cycle that consider trackers (issue types) and member roles. And it's actually member roles that define access permissions.

Also, this chapter is intended mostly for administrators as the administration menu is visible only to this type of user. However, it should also be interesting for project managers as it explains how to configure Redmine to ease and optimize the development process, in particular the issue life cycle. Other users might find this chapter useful as well, because here they can learn what permissions they need to gain access to certain types of functionality.

In this chapter, we will cover the following topics:

- The Roles and permissions page
- The Trackers page
- The Issue statuses page
- The Workflow page
- Modifying the workflow
- A practical example

The Roles and permissions page

As you already know, users are added to projects as **members**. To add a member, you need to select a user and a role. So in this context, a role is a kind of membership type. That's why roles in Redmine are often called member roles. However, the actual meaning of role is slightly broader than just a membership type for a project, as some role permissions affect not only the project of the user.

Roles are defined for the entire system. This can be done from the **Roles and permissions** page of the **Administration** menu, which is shown in the following screenshot:

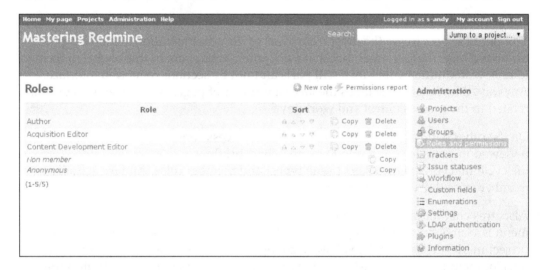

As you can see, the order of roles can be changed here using the arrows in the **Sort** column. The same order is used in the forms, with which users select roles for project members. Normally, you will want it to be from the most privileged at the top to the least privileged at the bottom.

However, the order can't be changed for the italicized **Non member** and **Anonymous** roles. They are always the last here. These are virtual roles, what means that they do not really exist in the database and thus cannot be edited. The **Non member** role is for users who are not members of the project, and the **Anonymous** role is for unauthorized (not logged in) users.

The **Copy** link can be used to copy a role's configuration, including the permissions and the associated workflow, to a new role. You should use this feature if the role which you are about to create is in some way similar to an existing one. Finally, the **Delete** link can be used to remove a role.

A role can be edited by clicking on its name in the list. When you do this, you get the following form:

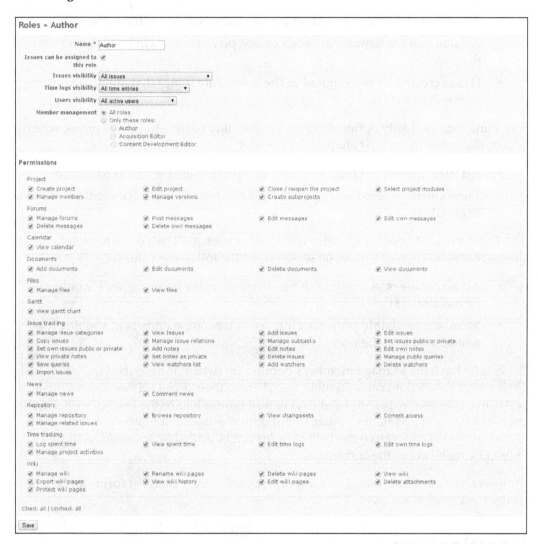

The **Issues can be assigned to this role** option determines whether members of the particular role will be available for the **Assignee** field of the issue form. Thus, this option can be disabled for a reporter or customer role, the members of which you will not likely want to make assignable.

The **Issues visibility** option specifies which issues are going to be visible to the project members of this role. It accepts the following values:

- **All issues**: All issues, including private ones, will be visible to the user
- **All non private issues**: All issues except private ones will be visible to the user
- **Issues created by or assigned to the user**: Only issues that are owned by the user will be visible

The **Time logs visibility** option controls the visibility of time tracking entries, which will be discussed in the next chapter. Its possible values are the following:

- **All time entries**: All time entries of all visible users (see the next option)
- **Time entries created by the user**: Only their own time entries will be visible to members of this role

The **Users visibility** option specifies which other users will be visible to members of the current role. This option can be set to one of the following values:

- **All active users**: All users will be visible (inactive users are visible only to administrators)
- **Members of visible projects**: Only users who are members of visible projects will be visible to the user

Users who have the **Manage members** permission (which is described in *The Project block* subsection) can add other members to their project. Thus, users with a restrictive role may appear to be able to re-add themselves to the project with a more privileged one. The **Member management** option was added to prevent such cases. With this option, you can control which roles can be added or removed from the project by members of the current role.

However, the most interesting and important part of the discussed form can be seen under the **Permissions** label.

Permissions

Generally, Redmine access control is built on permissions. All such permissions (if they are editable) can be found in this form. Thereby, when a plugin adds a permission, it appears here as well.

As you can see in the previous screenshot, the list of permissions is split into blocks — **Project**, **Forums**, and so on. Each such block, except **Project**, corresponds to the appropriate project module. Thus, when a plugin adds a project module with some permissions, you see a new block with new permissions here. An exception is the **Project** block, which is not related to any project module and includes permissions for the projects themselves.

In Redmine, users can be divided into three types: unauthorized or not logged in users, who are represented by the **Anonymous** role; authorized users but not members of the project, who are represented by the **Non member** role; and project members, who are represented by other roles. Generally, permissions are defined for these three types and not all permissions are available for all of them. For example, Redmine cannot allow unauthorized users to create projects. Many permissions can be enabled for project members only. And all permissions are implicitly granted to administrators.

So let's discuss the permissions of each block now.

The Project block

The **Project** block, as mentioned earlier, contains permissions for projects. However, if a plugin introduces any system permission (that is, the one that controls access to something that is not related to projects), such a permission will be added to this block as well.

Let's check out the permissions in this block:

- **Create project**: This is the only permission of this block that is available for all registered users. It decides whether the user is allowed to create new projects.

  As you know, the user should be associated with a role in order to get permissions, and to be associated with a role, the user should be added to a project. Then how can users get the **Create project** permission if they have not been added to any project yet? The first project in the system should always be created by an administrator. Normally, this will be a general project of the organization, which can even be named after the organization. You can add users whom you want to grant this permission to such a project. Alternatively, you may want to grant the **Create project** permission to the **Non member** role, but note that in this case, any registered user will be able to create projects.

- **Edit project**: This permission controls whether or not the project member can change the properties of the project, which can be found under the **Information** tab of the project's **Settings** page.

- **Close / reopen the project**: This permission determines whether the project member is able to close or reopen the project, what can be done from the project's **Overview** page.

- **Select project modules**: This permission controls whether the project member can enable or disable the project modules under the **Modules** tab of the project's **Settings** page.

- **Manage members**: This permission specifies whether the project member is allowed to manage project membership under the **Members** tab of the project's **Settings** page.

- **Manage versions**: This permission determines whether the project member is able to add, edit, and delete project versions. This can be done under the **Versions** tab of the project's **Settings** page.

- **Create subprojects**: This permission determines whether the project member is able to add subprojects to the project. However, to be able to do this, the project member must also have the **Create project** permission.

The Forums block

The **Forums** block contains permissions for message boards. These boards are provided by the Forums project module and can be found under the **Forums** tab in the project menu.

So, here are the permissions of this block:

- **Manage forums**: This permission controls whether the project member has access to the **Forums** tab of the project's **Settings** page, where message boards can be added, edited, or removed.

- **Post messages**: This permission specifies whether the user can add messages to the message boards of the project. This also includes whether the user can reply to messages. The permission is available for all users, including not logged in ones.

- **Edit messages**: This permission controls whether the project member can modify forum messages, including those that were added by other users. It is suitable for forum moderators.

- **Edit own messages**: This permission controls whether users can modify their own messages. When granting this permission you should remember that the original text can be copied by other users into their replies as a quote. So generally, the **Edit own messages** permission should be used only to correct typos. Certainly, it is available only for logged in users.

- **Delete messages**: This permission determines whether the project member can delete forum messages, including those that were created by other users. Thus, this permission can be used for spam moderation.

- **Delete own messages**: This permission determines whether users can delete their own forum messages. As with the **Edit own messages** permission, when granting this one, you should consider that the message text can be copied into replies or replies can be based on the message. This permission is available only for registered users as well.

The Calendar block

The **Calendar** block contains permissions that provide access control to the calendar, which can be found under the appropriate tab of the project, if the Calendar project module is enabled:

- **View calendar**: This permission is the only permission in this block. It specifies whether the user has access to the **Calendar** tab of the project menu. It can be specified for all users, including not logged in ones.

The Documents block

The **Documents** block contains permissions for access to the **Documents** tab of the project menu, which is provided by the Documents project module.

Let's check them out:

- **Add documents**: This permission controls whether the user can add documents to the project. It is available for all registered users.

- **Edit documents**: This permission, which is available for all registered users too, specifies whether the user may modify existing documents. Users with this permission will also be able to attach files to documents and remove such attachments.

- **Delete documents**: This permission determines whether the user can delete documents. It is available for all registered users.

- **View documents**: This permission determines whether the user can see documents and download their attachments. It can be granted to any user, including not logged in ones.

The Files block

The **Files** block contains permissions for access to the **Files** tab of the project menu. This tab is available only if the Files project module is enabled.

The permissions in this block are the following:

- **Manage files**: This permission determines whether the user is able to add and remove project files.

- **View files**: This permission is needed for the user to be able to download project files. It can be granted to any user, including not logged in ones. But note that project files still won't be accessible for non-members if the project is private.

The Gantt block

The **Gantt** block comes with permissions for access to the **Gantt** tab of the project menu, which contains the Gantt chart. This tab is available only if the Gantt project module is enabled.

- **The View gantt chart**: This permission controls whether the user has access to the **Gantt** tab of the project menu. It can be specified for all users, including those who are not logged in.

The Issue tracking block

The **Issue tracking** block contains permissions for issue tracking. This is the largest and perhaps the most important block. Its permissions affect not only the functionality that can be found under the **Issues** tab of the project menu, but also many other pages that provide some functionality related to issues. Moreover, these are almost all project pages, including the overview page, roadmap, calendar, and Gantt. Certainly, these permissions take effect only if the Issue tracking project module is enabled.

So, here they go:

- **Manage issue categories**: This permission controls whether the project member can add, edit, or delete issue categories, what can be done under the **Issue categories** tab of the project's **Settings** page (or within the issue form).

- **View issues**: This permission controls whether the user can see issues. Without this permission the user won't be able to access any issue in the project. So, in most cases, you will want it to be set. It is available for all users, including not logged in ones.

- **Add issues**: This permission determines whether the user is able to add new issues. It is available for users who are not logged in as well.

- **Edit issues**: This permission controls whether the user is able to edit issues, what includes adding attachments. It is available for all users, including not logged in ones.

- **Copy issues**: This permission is used to determine, whether the user is allowed to copy issues. It is available for all users, including not logged in ones.

- **Manage issue relations**: This permission controls whether the user can add or remove related issues, what can be done on the issue page. This permission is available for users who are not logged in as well.

- **Manage subtasks**: This permission determines whether the user is able to add subtasks to the issue, what can be done on the issue page. But note that such users should also have the **Add issues** permission. Like the latter, this permission is available for not logged in users as well.

- **Set issues public or private:** This permission specifies whether the user is able to modify the **Private** flag of the issue or not. If this permission or the **Set own issues public or private** permission is set, the user will also be able to see the value of this flag in the issue list (by enabling the appropriate column) and filter this list by its value. The permission is also available for users who are not logged in (and can be used if an anonymous user reports a critical security issue).

- **Set own issues public or private**: This permission specifies whether users are able to modify the **Private** flag of the issue which was created by them. Users with this permission will also be able to see the value of this flag in the issue list and filter the list by its value. The permission is available for all registered users.

- **Add notes**: This permission controls whether the user can comment on issues. Moreover, it allows users to add attachments to issues (though as sometimes, users may need to show files in their comments). This permission is available for all users, including not logged in ones.

- **Edit notes**: This permission controls whether the user can edit issue comments. However, it does not allow users to remove files that were attached to the issue along with a comment. It is available for all registered users and is suitable for moderation.

- **Edit own notes**: This permission allows the user to modify comments that were created by that user. However, it doesn't allow the user to remove files that were attached along with such comments. Also, permissions like this one should be used only to correct typos, as the original text from the comment can be used in replies as a quote. The permission is available for all registered users.

- **View private notes**: This permission controls whether private comments of issues are visible to the user. Certainly, it's available only to project members.

- **Set notes as private**: This permission controls whether the user can add private comments to issues. But note that without the **View private notes** permission, users won't be able to see their own private comments. This permission is available for project members only.

- **Delete issues**: This permission controls whether issues can be deleted by the project member.

> I believe that issues should never be deleted. Each issue is assigned a unique ID and can be referenced by this ID from other objects and pages. So if you delete an issue, its ID becomes unused. While most related objects are removed or unlinked by Redmine automatically, Wiki links to this issue will still remain and will become dead links. Therefore, issues can and should be closed instead.

- **Manage public queries**: This permission specifies whether the project member can add, modify, or delete public custom queries. Custom queries are a very powerful feature, and public custom queries can make a project more customer friendly. However, too many public queries per project can make this feature inefficient. So, this permission should be granted to users who really know what to do with it.

- **Save queries**: This permission determines whether the user can save custom queries. Custom queries are available for all users, including not logged in ones, but only registered users can save queries (if this permission is set).

- **View watchers list**: This permission controls whether or not the user can see who is watching the issue. It is available for all users, including those who are not logged in.

- **Add watchers**: This permission is available for all users as well. It specifies who is able to add watchers to the issue. (Anonymous users can be allowed to do this because, for example, they may know who will likely be interested in the issue.) However, while granting this permission, you should remember that watchers are going to receive email notifications. So, it may be not a very good idea to allow users, especially anonymous ones, to "configure" Redmine to send emails to other users.

- **Delete watchers**: This permission determines who will be able to remove watchers from the issue. It is available for all users, including not logged in ones, but you will most likely not want to grant this permission to anyone besides project managers. Also, the user who is watching the issue will expect to be notified about changes in the issue, so I don't think that it's good if someone besides this user removes him/her from the watchers.

- **Import issues**: This permission determines whether the user is able to import issues from a CSV file. It is available for all users, including not logged in ones. However, I would not recommend enabling it for users who are not members of the project.

The News block

The **News** block contains permissions for access to project news. They can be found under the **News** tab of the project menu if the News project module is enabled. The **News** tab is visible to everyone, including not logged in users, and there is no permission to change this (but you can still make the entire project private).

Here are the permissions:

- **Manage news**: This permission determines whether the project member is able to post, edit, and delete news in the project. A user with this permission will also be able to remove news comments (which makes it suitable for spam moderation).
- **Comment news**: This permission controls who can comment on news. It is available for all users, including not logged in ones. But I would not recommend granting this permission to anonymous users because, as I know from practice, this is where the spam goes most often.

The Repository block

The **Repository** block contains permissions that control access to repositories. Some of these permissions apply not only to Redmine (directly) but also to SCM servers if advanced repository integration has been configured (see *Chapter 3, Configuring Redmine*). Repositories are available under the **Repository** tab of the project menu if the Repository project module is enabled.

So, let's see what we have in this block:

- **Manage repository**: This permission allows the project member to add, edit, and delete repositories. Additionally, it allows the user to modify committer associations, what can be done under the **Repositories** tab of the project's **Settings** page.

- **Browse repository**: This permission determines whether the user can browse the content of the repository. If advanced integration has been configured for the SCM server, this permission also controls access to the repository on the SCM side. The permission can be set for all users, including those who are not logged in. Thus, if advanced repository integration has been configured in your Redmine and you want anonymous users of your SCM server to have read-only access to the repository, you should grant this permission to the **Anonymous** role.

- **View changesets**: This permission determines whether the user has access to the repository revision list and revision pages. To provide users with full read access to the repository, you need to grant this permission along with the **Browse repository** one. The permission is available for all users, including not logged in ones.

- **Commit access**: This permission has nothing to do with Redmine itself. It is used by the SCM server, if advanced integration has been configured, to determine whether write access to the repository should be given to the user. It is available for all users, including those who are not logged in.

- **Manage related issues**: This permission specifies whether the user should be able to add or remove issues that are related to the revision, what can be done on the revision page. It is available for all users, including not logged in ones.

The Time tracking block

The **Time tracking** block contains permissions that are used to control time tracking for the project. Time tracking will be reviewed in detail in the next chapter.

For the moment, let's check out the permissions that are available:

- **Log spent time**: This permission specifies whether the user should be able to add time entries to the project or not. Note that this also applies to time entries that are added via commit messages. The permission is available for all registered users.

- **View spent time**: This permission determines whether the user can see time entries in the project. This applies, not only to the time report, but also to the total hours on the project overview page, the spent hours on the issue page, and so on. The permission can be set for not logged in users.

- **Edit time logs**: This permission allows users to modify time entries of any user in the project. Certainly, it can be granted only to project members. Anyway, I doubt whether it's good to allow a user to modify the time entries of another user.

- **Edit own time logs**: This permission allows users to modify their own time entries. It is available for all registered users.

- **Manage project activities**: This permission determines whether the project member can enable or disable time tracking activities for the project, what can be done under the **Activities (time tracking)** tab of the project's **Settings** page.

The Wiki block

The **Wiki** block includes permissions for access to Wiki pages, which can be found under the **Wiki** tab of the project menu (if the Wiki project module is enabled). These permissions, however, do not apply to other Wiki-syntax-enabled contents (such as issue description):

- **Manage wiki**: This permission controls whether the project member has access to the **Wiki** tab of the project's **Settings** page (which allows you to specify the name of the starting Wiki page).

- **Rename wiki pages**: This permission determines whether the project member is able to move the Wiki page to a different parent page and/or change its name.

- **Delete wiki pages**: This permission specifies whether the project member is able to remove the Wiki page.

- **View wiki**: This permission determines whether the Wiki page is visible to the user. So, you can unset it if you want to hide the Wiki for particular roles. It is available for all users, including those who are not logged in.

- **Export wiki pages**: This permission determines whether the user is able to export the Wiki page in PDF, HTML, or TXT format. Unsetting this permission actually makes no sense, as users can always save the Wiki page using the browser (if they have the **View wiki** permission, of course). It is available for all users.

- **View wiki history**: This permission is also available for all users, including not logged in ones. As you know, the Wiki page stores the history of changes. But sometimes, some sensitive data can get there, so it may be necessary to hide previous versions. This permission allows the user to see not only the change history but also previous versions of the page, differences between versions, and who authored each line of the page.

- **Edit wiki pages**: This permission specifies whether the user should be allowed to edit Wiki pages of the project. Additionally, it allows users to add attachments to Wiki pages. The Wiki system stores the complete history of changes and allows rolling back to a previous version, if needed. So, it's quite safe to grant this permission even to the **Anonymous** role.

- **Delete attachments**: This permission allows the user to remove attachments from Wiki pages of the project. While Wiki stores the history of changes of the Wiki text, it does not store the history of attachments, so this permission can be used to prevent removal of important files by untrusted users. The permission is available for all roles.

- **Protect wiki pages**: This permission determines whether the project member can lock or unlock the Wiki page. Having all of the project's Wiki system editable by anyone, you can make some pages editable only by trusted users by granting this permission to them. (Yes, a page that was protected by one user can be edited by another user who has this permission as well.)

The Permissions report page

Member roles are used to differentiate users with the help of permissions. In other words, the purpose of a role is often not only to hold permissions, but also to make sure that only one role has some specific permissions. Therefore, the role name does not have to replicate the real-life position—it is better to represent the granted permissions. In this case, it will be easier to manage Redmine, to determine which role should be given to a particular user, and so on. Thus, access to project settings may be granted to *Project manager* or *Project administrator*, editing permissions to *Moderator* or *Content editor*, and so on. Also remember that it's okay to assign several roles to a single project member.

However, in such cases, it can be hard to keep all the role names and their purposes in mind while editing permissions using the role page that has just been described. For this reason, many Redmine administrators prefer to use the **Permissions report** page, which can be accessed through the link with the same name on the **Roles and permissions** page. Check it out in the following screenshot:

Roles » Permissions report

Permissions	Author ✔	Acquisition Editor ✔	Content Development Editor ✔	Non member ✔	Anonymous ✔
✔ Create project	✔				
✔ Edit project	✔				
✔ Close / reopen the project	✔				
✔ Select project modules	✔				
✔ Manage members	✔				
✔ Manage versions	✔				
✔ Create subprojects	✔				
Forums	Author	Acquisition Editor	Content Development Editor	Non member	Anonymous
✔ Manage forums	✔				
✔ Post messages	✔	✔	✔	✔	
✔ Edit messages	✔				
✔ Edit own messages	✔				
✔ Delete messages	✔				
✔ Delete own messages	✔				
Calendar	Author	Acquisition Editor	Content Development Editor	Non member	Anonymous
✔ View calendar	✔	✔	✔	✔	✔
Documents	Author	Acquisition Editor	Content Development Editor	Non member	Anonymous
✔ Add documents	✔				
✔ Edit documents	✔				
✔ Delete documents	✔	✔	✔		
✔ View documents	✔	✔			
Files	Author	Acquisition Editor	Content Development Editor	Non member	Anonymous
✔ Manage files	✔	✔	✔		
✔ View files	✔	✔			
Gantt	Author	Acquisition Editor	Content Development Editor	Non member	Anonymous
✔ View gantt chart	✔	✔	✔	✔	✔
Issue tracking	Author	Acquisition Editor	Content Development Editor	Non member	Anonymous
✔ Manage issue categories	✔				
✔ View Issues	✔	✔	✔	✔	✔
✔ Add issues	✔	✔	✔	✔	
✔ Edit issues	✔	✔	✔		
✔ Copy issues	✔				
✔ Manage issue relations	✔	✔	✔		
✔ Manage subtasks	✔	✔	✔		
✔ Set issues public or private	✔	✔	✔		
✔ Set own issues public or private	✔	✔	✔		
✔ Add notes	✔	✔	✔	✔	
✔ Edit notes	✔	✔	✔		
✔ Edit own notes	✔	✔	✔		
✔ View private notes	✔	✔	✔		
✔ Set notes as private	✔	✔	✔		
✔ Delete issues	✔				
✔ Manage public queries	✔				
✔ Save queries	✔			✔	
✔ View watchers list	✔	✔	✔		
✔ Add watchers	✔	✔			
✔ Delete watchers	✔	✔			
✔ Import issues	✔				
News	Author	Acquisition Editor	Content Development Editor	Non member	Anonymous
✔ Manage news	✔	✔	✔		
✔ Comment news	✔	✔	✔	✔	
Repository	Author	Acquisition Editor	Content Development Editor	Non member	Anonymous
✔ Manage repository	✔				
✔ Browse repository	✔	✔	✔	✔	✔
✔ View changesets	✔	✔	✔	✔	✔
✔ Commit access	✔				
✔ Manage related issues	✔	✔			
Time tracking	Author	Acquisition Editor	Content Development Editor	Non member	Anonymous
✔ Log spent time	✔				
✔ View spent time	✔	✔	✔	✔	
✔ Edit time logs	✔				
✔ Edit own time logs	✔				
✔ Manage project activities	✔				
Wiki	Author	Acquisition Editor	Content Development Editor	Non member	Anonymous
✔ Manage wiki	✔	✔	✔		
✔ Rename wiki pages	✔	✔	✔		
✔ Delete wiki pages	✔	✔	✔		
✔ View wiki	✔	✔	✔	✔	✔
✔ Export wiki pages	✔	✔	✔		
✔ View wiki history	✔	✔	✔		
✔ Edit wiki pages	✔	✔	✔		
✔ Delete attachments	✔	✔	✔		
✔ Protect wiki pages	✔	✔	✔		

Check all | Uncheck all

Save

This page allows you to quickly check which permissions are assigned to which roles. It also allows you to modify them. The green check marks (✔) in the column and row titles can be used to check or uncheck all the permissions in the column or row correspondingly. Like the role editing page, this page is divided into blocks by project modules, where each block can be collapsed or expanded by clicking on the minus ▣ or plus ▣ icon to the left-hand side of the block title correspondingly.

On this page, you can also clearly see that some permissions are not available for all types of user.

The Trackers page

In any issue tracking application, an issue has a type, such as bug, feature, or support (the default types in Redmine). In Redmine, such issue types are called **trackers**.

Trackers play an essential role in issue tracking, as they define issue properties, conditions for issue status transitions, field availability, and so on. Thus, a feature should not have the status *Fixed* and a bug should not have the status *Planned*.

Trackers can be managed — that is, created, edited, or removed — on the **Trackers** page of the **Administration** menu. You can see this page in the following screenshot:

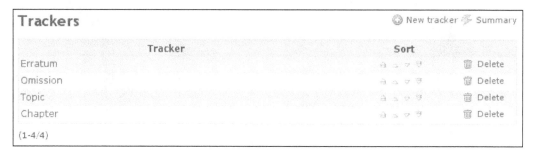

The order of trackers is not insignificant here. The same order is used when listing trackers in application forms. So, the most frequently used trackers or those that you want to be used most often should be on top. To change the order, you can use the green arrow icons: ⬈ ⬈ ⬇ ⬇.

The **Summary** link in the top-right corner opens this page:

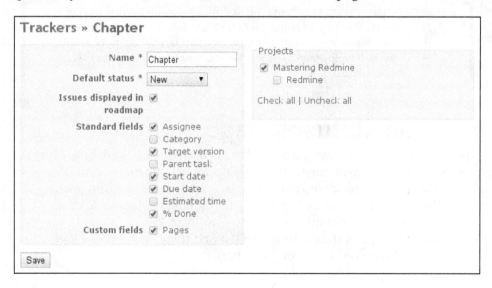

On this page, you can select which issue fields should be available for each tracker. The green check mark icon ✔ can be used to toggle all checkboxes in a row or a column.

The availability of issue fields can also be configured on the tracker page, which can be opened if you click on a tracker name on the **Trackers** page.

Here, the **Default status** option should be used to specify the initial issue status for the tracker. In the web form for a new issue, the initial issue status can be changed without any problems, but this possibility does not always exist in other cases. For example, the initial status can be omitted in email messages that are used to create new issues. So, it's extremely important to specify the right initial status for each tracker using the tracker page.

The **Issues displayed in roadmap** option determines whether the issues of this tracker should be displayed in the roadmap by default. The roadmap was reviewed in detail in *Chapter 5, Managing Projects*.

Keep your roadmap short and clear

Usually, in the roadmap, people list features. They don't list bug fixes, as those are less important for end users (and are important only for those users who have faced the corresponding bug).

In the fifth chapter, which is *Managing Projects*, we also reviewed the **Information** tab of the project's **Settings** page. If you remember, there you could also choose trackers that should be available for the project. In the right-hand side column of the tracker page, we have just another way of doing the same — we can choose projects for which the tracker should be available.

You may want to rename the Redmine's default *Feature* tracker to something more common that better describes your work. Thus, the development of a system's core is unlikely to be named feature development. For such cases, you may prefer the *Task* name instead.

The Issue statuses page

We can say with confidence that issue tracking is useless without the use of issue statuses. Moreover, the more detailed the issue statuses, the more accurate the workflow. On the other hand, too many details can make the working process annoying. Therefore, I believe that choosing the right issue statuses for your processes is extremely important in order for your users to have a good experience with Redmine. In fact, this should be one of the first things that you configure after having deployed Redmine in your organization.

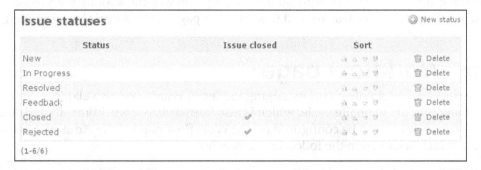

Generally, an issue can be open or closed. Therefore, each issue status has a property that determines whether this status makes an issue closed. In the list that is shown in the preceding screenshot, such issue statuses are marked with a check mark ✔ under the **Issue closed** column. Also, as you can see, Redmine can have several statuses that mark the issue as closed. For example, they can be **Closed** or **Rejected**, as in the screenshot, or *Won't Fix, Obsolete, Not Confirmed, Fixed*, and so on.

Again, the order of issue statuses on this page is important and can be modified using the green arrows under the **Sort** column. The same order is used in issue forms. Ideally this order should reflect the completeness of the issue from the very initial state (such as **New**) to the final state (such as **Closed**).

Issue statuses can be edited by clicking on their names. A new issue status can be added by clicking on the **New status** link. In both cases, the following form is opened:

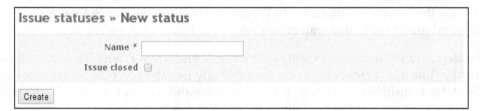

 As mentioned in *Chapter 4, Issue Tracking*, if the **Calculate the issue done ratio with** setting is set to **Use the issue status** under the **Issue tracking** tab of the global **Settings** page, this form also contains the **% Done** field and the issue statuses list includes the **% Done** column.

Generally, that's all regarding the **Issue statuses** page, despite the fact that issue statuses are actually what defines the life cycle of the issue and builds the workflow. However, it would be too complicated to manage the workflow along with issue statuses. Therefore, this was moved to a separate page of the **Administration** menu.

The Workflow page

Issue tracking is not only about managing the list of issues, but also about implementing the issue life cycle, which is also known as the **workflow**. In Redmine, the issue workflow can be configured on the **Workflow** page of the **Administration** menu, which is shown in the following screenshot:

So let's review each tab of this page.

The Status transitions tab

The main purpose of the workflow is to control which issue status can be set for the issue in certain conditions. Thus, instead of using the **Open** status after **In Progress** (for example, if the issue was returned), you may want to use the special *Reopened* status. For this, you can allow the **Open** status to be set only after the **New** one and allow the *Reopened* status after **In Progress**. These are the things that can be configured under the **Status transitions** tab.

Issue status transitions can be configured per role and tracker, which are to be chosen using the **Role** and **Tracker** fields correspondingly (see the preceding screenshot). If the status transitions are similar for several roles and/or trackers, you can use the plus icon ( ) to convert the field into a multiselect mode.

Some issue statuses may be not used by certain trackers (for example, the *Fixed* status would not be needed for the **Feature** tracker), so to simplify the form, Redmine skips such issue statuses by default. However, we still need a way to configure new statuses, which of course won't be used by any tracker yet. So, to show all the available issue statuses, you can uncheck the **Only display statuses that are used by this tracker** checkbox.

After clicking the **Edit** button, we get the following form:

✔ Current status	New statuses allowed					
	✔ New	✔ In Progress	✔ Resolved	✔ Feedback	✔ Closed	✔ Rejected
✔ New	☐	✔	✔	✔	✔	✔
✔ In Progress	✔	☐	✔	✔	✔	✔
✔ Resolved	✔	✔	☐	✔	✔	✔
✔ Feedback	✔	✔	✔	☐	✔	✔
✔ Closed	✔	✔	✔	✔	☐	✔
✔ Rejected	✔	✔	✔	✔	✔	☐

▸ Additional transitions allowed when the user is the author
▸ Additional transitions allowed when the user is the assignee

Save

In the left-hand side column, you can see the initial issue status, and in the rows, you can see possible target statuses. In other words, this table allows you to decide whether the status in the left-hand side column can be changed to other statuses in the row. If the checkbox is checked, the change can be made.

For user convenience, the background color of the cell, the checkbox of which was initially selected, is green here. In this way, you can check what was modified before submitting your changes.

If several roles or trackers are selected and the issue transition is not the same for all the combinations of them, Redmine will use the select box instead, as shown in this screenshot:

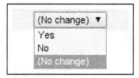

The form for issue transitions is divided into three blocks. The top block contains the common configuration, while the other two blocks, which are collapsed by default, can optionally contain modifications to the common configuration. The common configuration applies to all users of the current role and to all issues of the tracker. The next block is for cases when the user is the author of the issue (that is, the issue was created by this particular user). And the last one applies to cases when the issue is or was previously assigned to the user.

There is no need to copy the common configuration into other blocks, as other blocks can only enable issue status transitions. Disabled transitions are just ignored there.

The Fields permissions tab

The **Fields permissions** tab can be used to make certain issue fields read-only or to require them for some trackers. This tab uses the same form as **Status transitions**.

 Switching between the **Status transitions** and **Fields permissions** tabs preserves the configuration of the form.

Clicking on the **Edit** button opens the form shown in the following screenshot:

Each select box in this form allows you to choose the **Read-only** option. If this option is chosen for a field, a user of the corresponding role won't be able to change the value of this field, provided the issue is of the corresponding tracker.

Issue fields that are required by default are marked with a red asterisk (*) in this table. Fields that are not required have the additional **Required** option. If this option is selected for a field, it will become required for users of the corresponding role, provided the issue is of the corresponding tracker.

Normally, when you mark a field as read-only or required, you want it to remain the same for all subsequent issue statuses in the particular row. If this is the case, you can use the » link to copy the option to the columns on the right-hand side.

Also, as with issue status transitions, if fields permissions were set before, they are loaded with the backgrounds of the corresponding cells changed to the appropriate colors, as shown here:

Here, the gray stands for the **Read-only** option, and the red stands for the **Required** option.

Copying the workflow

The workflow page also has the contextual menu with links in the top-right corner, which we did not review. I skipped this menu because at that moment you did not know enough to understand what they are for.

The **Copy** link of this menu can be used to quickly copy a configuration from one role and tracker pair to another. This feature can be used if, for example, you have mistakenly changed a wrong pair. Anyway, as you have seen, the workflow configuration is quite complex and utilizes many checkboxes and select boxes, so many of you may find this feature useful for different purposes. This link opens the page that is shown in the following screenshot:

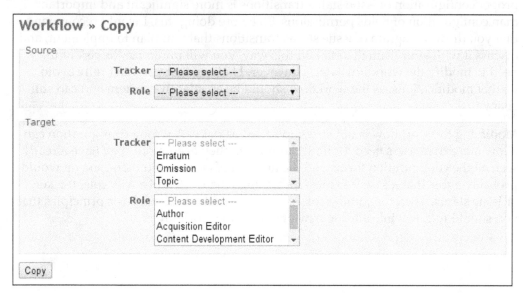

As you can see, for user convenience, this form allows the selection of several target trackers and roles at a time.

Checking the workflow summary

The **Summary** link redirects to a page that contains the aggregate data. This page is shown in the following screenshot:

Workflow » Summary				
	Author	**Acquisition Editor**	**Content Development Editor**	*Non member*
Erratum	26	13	13	✖
Omission	30	13	13	✖
Topic	30	13	13	✖
Chapter	30	13	13	✖

These numbers represent the number of enabled issue transitions per role and tracker, and the cross icon ✖ means that no transitions are enabled. While these numbers are generally useless, each number and cross icon is a link that redirects to the corresponding form. So, the summary page can be used for quick access to transitions editing.

Modifying the workflow

Configuring the workflow is one of the most complicated tasks in Redmine. Also, proper configuration of issue status transitions is more significant and important than configuration of fields permissions. So before doing this, I would recommend that you draw a diagram of issue status transitions that you plan to implement, and discuss it with your team in detail. In this way, you will minimize the risk of the need to modify the workflow later. However, I believe that you can't fully avoid further modifications, as the workflow should be an adaptive system and can still change.

Modifying the workflow is not so complicated as risky. A wrong configuration can allow more than users need, or limit them when they need more. You have already seen all the configuration forms and the amount of elements in them, so you would probably agree that it's easy to miss something when you add a new role, tracker, or issue status. Therefore, under this section, we will talk about basic principles that you should follow while adding new objects to the workflow.

Adding a role

Member roles can be added using the **New role** link, which can be found in the contextual menu in the top-right corner of the **Roles and permissions** page. Clicking on this link opens the following form:

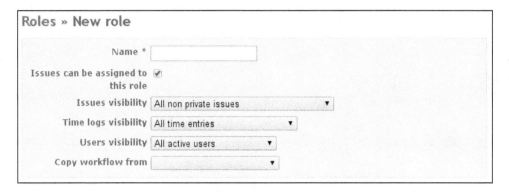

This form also contains **Permissions**, which I did not include in the screenshot. The same form can be invoked with the **Copy** link which is located in the rightmost column of the role list.

As you can see, the new role form is very much like the role edit form that was discussed earlier, but with a new **Copy workflow from** option. This new option allows you to choose the role, the workflow configuration for all trackers (that is, issue status transitions and fields permissions, but not role permissions) of which will be copied into the newly created one.

So, let's compile a list of actions that you should do when creating a new role, to make this process easy and flawless:

1. Choose an existing role which has the permissions that are closest to the permissions that the new role should have.

2. Click on the **Copy** link, which can be found in the rightmost column of the chosen role's row, to open the new role form.

3. For the **Copy workflow from** option, choose an existing role, issue status transitions and fields permissions of which are closest to the configuration that you want to have in the new role.

4. Use the green arrow icons to move the new role to the appropriate position in the role list.

5. Use **Permissions report** to adjust permissions for the new role.

6. Use the **Workflow** page to adjust workflows for the newly created role (if needed).

Adding a tracker

A new tracker can be added using the **New tracker** link. This link is located in the top-right contextual menu of the tracker list that can be found on the **Trackers** page. It opens the following form:

This form is almost identical to the one which is used for editing trackers. Like the new role form, this form also has the **Copy workflow from** option, which has exactly the same meaning—if a tracker is selected for this option, the workflow configuration for all roles and the selected tracker will be copied into the new tracker.

So, to avoid mistakes and misconfiguration, try to follow these principles while creating new tracker:

1. Using the **Copy workflow from** option, select the tracker whose configuration is closest to the configuration that you want to have for the new tracker.

2. Uncheck the fields that you want to disable for the new tracker.

3. Choose the projects for which you want to activate the new tracker.

4. Using the green arrow icons in the tracker list, move the new tracker to the appropriate position.

5. Using the **Workflow** page, adjust workflows for the newly created tracker (if needed).

Adding an issue status

A new issue status can be added using the **New status** link, which can be found on the **Issue statuses** page. This link opens the following form:

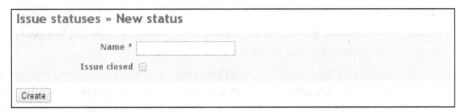

This form is exactly the same as the one that is used to edit issue statuses. As you can see, no **Copy workflow from** option is available this time. Adding an issue status is not going to be so easy.

The workflow for issue statuses cannot be just copied, as new statuses are usually placed somewhere between existing ones (for example, **New** — *New status* — **In Progress**). This means that new issue statuses definitely need to be configured manually. In practice, however, users often forget about the need to add the new status to the workflow, which ends up in confusion and a lack of understanding as to why the new issue status is not visible in the issue forms and the workflow. Unfortunately, Redmine's interface and approach to this problem do not help much.

So let's try to define some principles that can help make this process easier:

1. Create the new issue status.
2. Using the green arrow icons in the issue status list, move the new status to the appropriate position (keep closed statuses at the bottom).
3. Print, write down numbers, or take a screenshot of the content of the summary page, which can be accessed using the **Summary** link on the **Workflow** page.
4. On the **Workflow** page, select any role and any tracker.
5. Uncheck the **Only display statuses that are used by this tracker** option. Otherwise, the workflow won't show the newly added status.
6. Reconfigure the workflow, taking the new status into account. Do this for authors and assignees as well, if applicable. And don't forget about fields permissions.

7. Using the **Copy** link on the **Workflow** page, copy the workflow that was just configured to other role-tracker pairs, but only to those ones that are going to have similar workflows.

8. Adjust the workflows to which you have just copied the configuration (if needed).

9. Repeat the previous five steps (4-8) for every group of role-tracker pairs that are going to have a similar workflow configuration.

10. Use the **Summary** link on the **Workflow** page and the data saved earlier to check whether all relevant numbers have changed. These are just numbers of the allowed status transitions, but in this case, they can help you determine whether changes have been made to all the necessary role-tracker pairs.

A practical example

I can't think of any better way to demonstrate the configuration of the workflow than reviewing a real-life practical example. As the Kanban agile methodology is very popular nowadays, let's see how to configure the workflow to satisfy Kanban task rotation practices.

 Before configuring the workflow, it is always helpful to draw a diagram of the issue life cycle.

Kanban does not have any strict requirements for the board and column names, so here we'll use the following issue statuses, which should correspond to column names on the Kanban board (except the **New** status, which is to be set on issue creation and means *to be reviewed*):

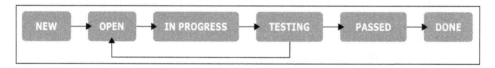

NEW → OPEN → IN PROGRESS → TESTING → PASSED → DONE

It is assumed that there is only one tracker and there are three roles: **Project manager** (who reviews new issues and closes completed ones), **Developer**, and **Tester**. The following minimal configuration should be applied in Redmine:

	NEW	ACCEPTED	IN PROGRESS	TESTING	PASSED	DONE
Project manager						
NEW		✓				✓
PASSED						✓
Developer						
ACCEPTED			✓			
IN PROGRESS				✓		
Tester						
TESTING		✓			✓	

Of course, this is a very basic example, but you can use it as a starting point.

The Redmine Backlogs plugin

If you are using agile development in your team, you may find the Backlogs plugin useful. Go to `http://www.redminebacklogs.net`.

Summary

In practice, users rarely configure the workflow and just use the default configuration that comes with Redmine. Some users add new roles, trackers, and issue statuses, but do not utilize the full power of the workflow. Instead, they just allow all trusted users to change all statuses to any other status. My guess is that this is due to the complexity of that part of the Redmine interface which is responsible for managing the workflow. Therefore, I hope that in this chapter I've succeeded in clarifying how to embrace this important feature. Nevertheless, I'm quite sure that project managers who have read this chapter will feel more comfortable with Redmine now and will be able to transform it into a very helpful assistant.

In the next chapter, we are going to review another interesting feature of Redmine. In fact, it can be considered one of the main features of this application. We'll discuss how you can track your work time using Redmine. In particular, you will learn how you can add time entries from SCM commit messages.

8
Time Tracking

Considering the fact that time tracking functionality is provided by a project module, why didn't we review it along with other modules in *Chapter 5, Managing Projects*? Other project modules do not provide enough functionality to make users install Redmine for them, or they just have a much better competitor (for example, MediaWiki or DocuWiki is much better than the Wiki module, Invision Power Board or phpBB is better than the Forums module, and so on). On the contrary, the Time tracking module is complete and competitive (considering the functionality that is provided by the Redmine core and its other project modules,), and often enough it becomes one of the main reasons for using Redmine. Thus, I first used Redmine as a time tracking application.

But why is this chapter so late in the book? Despite its functionality, time tracking cannot be considered a primary feature of Redmine. Moreover, in practice, it is disabled in the majority of Redmine installations. In other words, it's less important to know than the functionalities that were reviewed in previous chapters. Therefore, this is also the first (and the only) chapter that you don't need to master (if you don't plan to use time tracking, of course). If, however, you decide to continue reading it, you will learn how to submit your time entries, how to generate time reports and what third-party tools you can use to improve your time tracking experience. Certainly, in this chapter, we will also mention some other functionality, especially issue tracking, as time tracking is generally based on issues.

So, in this chapter, we will cover the following topics:

- Time tracking in Redmine
- Activities
- Tracking your time
- Checking out the spent time
- Time reports

Time tracking in Redmine

Why should Redmine be chosen over other time tracking alternatives? The answer is, because of the inclusion of other features (not only issue tracking). Generally, time tracking applications rarely come alone, as this is a simple task that is unlikely to have many features. Thus, it is available as an additional feature in Trac, OrangeHRM, and so on.

So, let's check out the benefits of time tracking with Redmine:

- In Redmine, time entries are associated with issues. And issues have a detailed description of what should be done. They can be shown on the Gantt chart, and much more.

- Issues can also have an estimated time. This time can be used to evaluate the speed of development, determine problematic tasks, and so on.

- Users can specify what they have been doing using the **Comment** field of the time entry.

- With the help of the **Activity** field, administrators and project managers can categorize time entries.

- Redmine allows users to add time entries through SCM commit messages (we'll discuss how to do this in detail later).

- A report on the spent time is available.

- Whether it's a benefit or not, Redmine supports only the hour value (which can be a float though) and does not care about the start and end times.

In order to be able to use the Time tracking module in the project, make sure that the **Time tracking** checkbox is checked under the **Modules** tab of the project's **Settings** page.

Also, to enable the Time tracking module for all new projects by default, do the same under the **Projects** tab of the **Settings** page in the **Administration** menu.

Activities

In order to be completed, a task may need different types of work to be done. Thus, a software feature can be designed, developed, and tested. Sometimes, information about the time that was spent on such types of work is very important, as it helps determine which work is more time-consuming and therefore allows optimization of the workflow. Also, such information is especially needful if different types of work involve different hourly payment rates. So, that's what the **Activity** field of the time entry should be used for.

Certainly, activities for time entries should not be defined by end users—their names and usage should be controlled by managers. Therefore, in Redmine, they can be managed only by administrators and only project managers (users who have the **Manage project activities** permission) can choose which activities apply to the project.

Administrators can manage activities using the **Activities (time tracking)** table, which can be found on the **Enumerations** page of the **Administration** menu. It is shown in the following screenshot:

Activities (time tracking)				
Name	Default value	Active	Sort	
Design		✓	⬆ ⬗ ⬇ ⬆	🗑 Delete
Development		✓	⬆ ⬗ ⬇ ⬆	🗑 Delete
New value				

Here, activities are in the same order as they appear on the time entry form. This order can be changed using the green arrow icons in the **Sort** column. The activity will be enabled for a project by default if the **Active** option is set, and will be selected by default in the time entry form if the **Default value** option is set.

A new activity can be added using the **New value** link. An existing activity can be modified by clicking on its name in the list. Both these actions open the form that is shown in this screenshot:

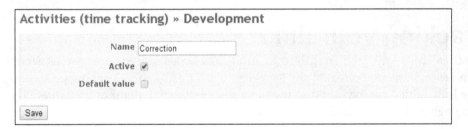

As it has been mentioned, activities that are listed on the **Enumerations** page also appear in the **Activities (time tracking)** tab of the project's **Settings** page, as shown here:

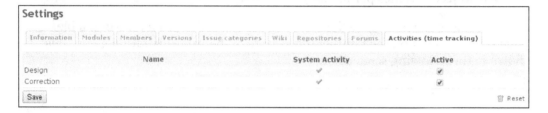

This is the page where project managers can select activities (using checkboxes in the **Active** column) that will be available for the project.

If you click on the **Reset** link, which can be seen in the bottom-right corner, only those activities that are also active on the system's **Enumerations** page will remain checked here.

The **System Activity** column can be a source of confusion. Check marks that are shown in this column indicate whether the state of the checkbox in the **Active** column is taken from the **Active** option on the **Enumerations** page. Thus, if you modify the value of the **Active** column here, the check mark for the corresponding activity will disappear (even if you uncheck it first and then check it back). This would mean that the state of the activity is stored separately in this project.

Tracking your time

The time entry form, which is used to add time entries to Redmine, can be accessed from several places. For example, users can open this form by clicking on the **Log time** link, which can be found in the top-right contextual menu of the issue page. This page is shown in the following screenshot:

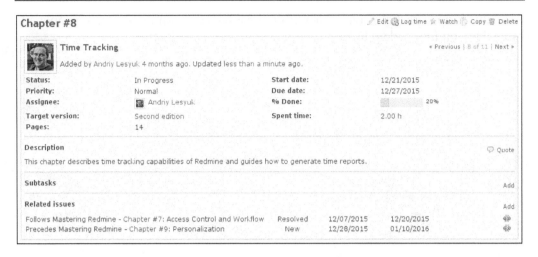

Similar **Log time** links can be found on the project overview page (on the sidebar) and on the time report page, which will be reviewed later in this chapter.

 To be able to log time, the user must have the **Log spent time** permission.

The time entry form can also be opened by selecting the **Log time** item in the drop-down menu that can be invoked by right-clicking on an issue in the issue list. Here is a screenshot of this menu:

But note that the **Log time** item does not appear in this menu if you selected more than one issue.

Also, this form is partially available within the issue edit form, which can be opened by clicking on the **Update** link on the issue page. It looks like this:

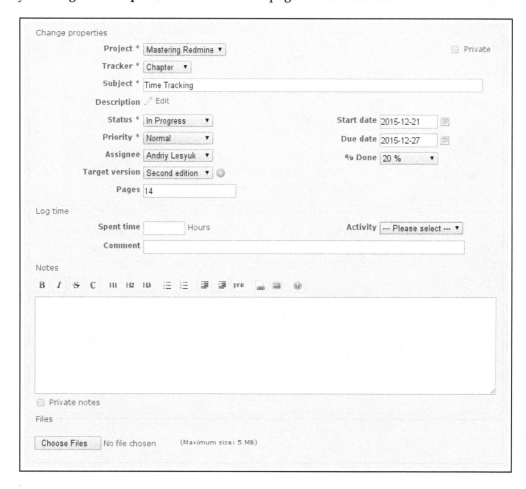

Note the **Log time** block, which is available only if the Time tracking module is enabled for the project.

> **The Bulk Time Entry plugin**
>
> You can install the Bulk Time Entry plugin, which was originally authored by Eric Davis, to make it possible to add several time entries at a time. This plugin adds the **Bulk time entries** item to the top-left menu that is shown on every page. Check it out at:
>
> ```
> https://github.com/Warecorp/redmine-bulk_time_
> entry_plugin
> ```

The complete time entry form can be invoked using the **Log time** link on the system time report, which can be opened using the **Overall spent time** link on the **Projects** page. It looks like this:

As you can see, the **Project** and **Issue** fields are optional. That is, you can add time entries that are not associated with an issue and even a project. This can be useful if, for example, you need to track time that was spent on company meetings.

The **Date** field of this form should be set to the date when you spent the time. By default, this field is set to today's date.

The **Hours** field should contain the number of hours that you spent. The value of this field can be a decimal or a time in a human-readable format, for example, *30m*, *30min*, *1h30*, *1h30m* or *1:30*.

 If you decide to specify a decimal value in the **Hours** field, please note that it should contain decimals after the point, not minutes, that is, *.00* to *.99* and not *.00* to *.59*. Thus, to specify *1:30* (one hour and thirty minutes) you should enter *1.50* in this field.

While the **Comment** field is optional, it's recommended you use this field to briefly describe what exactly you have been doing. Generally, this comment is for your managers, so if they do not need such details, you can leave it empty.

 Avoid using general comments such as, *Worked* or *Tested*. Good examples are *Investigated, why did the issue come up*, *Implemented GetSomething() function*, and *Was writing the Time Tracking section*.

The **Activity** field of this form should be set to the type of work that you were doing. If you were doing various jobs, you should create separate time entries for each type.

The Time Tracker plugin

The Time Tracker plugin, which was originally authored by Jérémie Delaitre, can simplify the process of logging time by adding **Start** and **Stop** links to the account menu (which is located in the top-right corner). Check it out at `https://github.com/hicknhack-software/redmine_time_tracker`.

Once you have filled in the form, you can click on either the **Create** button to be redirected to the page from which you came to this form, or the **Create and continue** button to get this form again and add another time entry.

Tracking time from a mobile device

To track time from an iPhone or Android device, you can use RedminePM, which can be found at `http://redminepm.com`. This is a full-featured Redmine client that supports time logging in addition to many other functions.

Tracking time through commit messages

When we were reviewing the **Repositories** tab of the **Settings** page, which can be found in the **Administration** menu (we did it twice, in *Chapter 3, Configuring Redmine*, and *Chapter 4, Issue Tracking*), we skipped the part of the form that is shown in the following screenshot:

In this form, we skipped the **Enable time logging** and **Activity for logged time** settings as you knew nothing about time logging at that time. So let's now see what we can do with these settings.

If the **Enable time logging** setting is enabled, users will be able to add time entries through SCM commit messages. Thus, suppose a user commits changes to a repository using this command:

```
$ svn commit -m 'Finished controller, refs #1554 @4:30'
```

This will tell Redmine to add a time entry for issue #1554 with the **Hours** attribute set to 4 hours and 30 minutes. This time entry will use the activity that has been selected in the **Activity for logged time** setting. Its comment will be *Applied in changeset R*, where *R* is the revision ID. The date on which the commit has been made will be used for the **Date** attribute of the added time entry.

So, to add a time entry through an SCM, a user should make sure that the commit message contains a string that follows this format:

```
refs #N @HM
```

Let's discuss what it means:

- refs: This is any of the keywords that are specified in the **Referencing keywords** setting (however, it's not needed if **Referencing keywords** are set to *).

- #N: This is an issue number, for example, #1554.

- @HM: This specifies the time that was spent. HM can be in a variety of formats, for example, *1h30m, 5hours, 1hour5min, 20min, 1:30, 1.5h, 2*, or *8h* (all without spaces).

Checking out the spent time

The Time tracking module is one of the most deeply integrated project modules in Redmine. Therefore, you can see overall time values in many places in its interface. That's also why we will use this section to review how time entries are used and where they can be found.

> To be able to check time entries, the user must have the **View spent time** permission. So, if you want to hide time entries from your customers, make sure that the corresponding roles do not have this permission (as well as the **Non member** and **Anonymous** roles).

This section will be of interest mainly to managers, but other users who track their time using Redmine should find some interesting information here as well.

> **The Invoices plugin**
>
> The Invoices plugin by Kirill Bezrukov can be used to generate invoices using hours specified in time entries. Note, however, that you need the commercial PRO version for this. Check out the plugin at: http://redminecrm.com/projects/invoices.

Time spent on issues

If an issue has time entries, the grand total of all hours of all time entries for the issue will be displayed on the issue page in the **Spent time** attribute, as shown in the following screenshot:

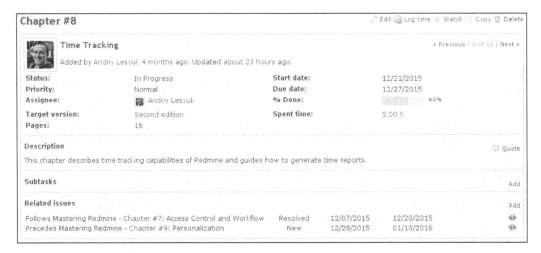

Here, the number of hours (that is, **5.00 h**) is a link. If you click on it, you will be redirected to the time report for the issue (we will discuss time reports later in this chapter).

Time spent on versions

If a version has issues associated with it (through the **Target version** attribute of the issues), the grand total of all hours of all time entries for these issues will be displayed on the version page, as shown in this screenshot:

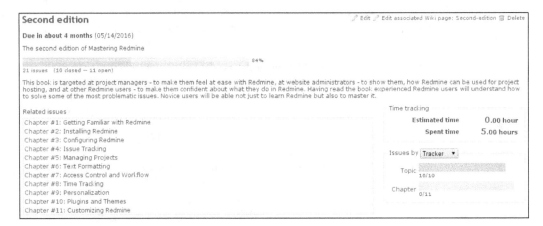

Here, **5.00 hours** is just text and not a link. Also note **Estimated time**, which is the grand total of all estimated hours for these issues. In this way, you can easily compare the estimated and the spent times of the version using this page.

Time spent on projects

The grand total of all hours ever entered for the project is shown in the sidebar of the project overview page, as follows:

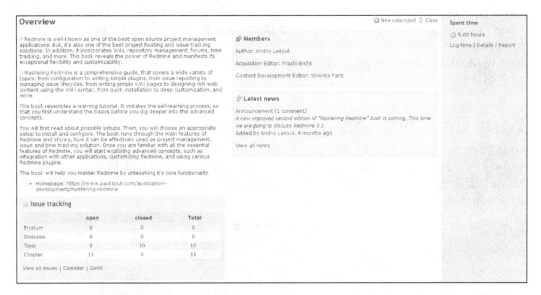

I'm not sure whether anyone needs this value, but you can find really useful links below it. Thus, the **Details** and **Report** links point to the time report that will be reviewed in the next section. The **Log time** link has been mentioned earlier—it opens the form used to add time entries.

Activity of users

Time entries that were entered for a project can also be seen on the project activity page, which is available under the project's **Activity** tab. Additionally, all time entries for all projects can be seen on the global activity page, which can be opened by clicking on the **Overall activity** link. This link can be found on the global **Projects** page (the top-left menu). But, to be able to see time entries on these pages, you need to enable the **Spent time** filter on their sidebars. Also, the user's personal activity feed can be found on the user's profile (this page is opened when you click on the user's name).

In all of these activity feeds, time entries are displayed as shown in the following screenshot:

If you click on the title of the event, that is, on **2.00 hours (Chapter #8 (In Progress): Time Tracking)**, you will be redirected to the time report for issue #8. Below the title, you can see the comment for the time entry. However, the date and time of the event refer to the date when the user added the time entry and not when the user worked on the issue.

Your time entries

Your latest time entries (sorted by the date on which you spent the time) can also be found in the **Spent time (last 7 days)** block of **My page** (if this block is enabled, of course). This page and its blocks are going to be discussed in the next chapter. For now, here is how it looks:

Activity	Project	Comment	Hours	
My page			Personalize this page	
Spent time (last 7 days)				
Total time: **2.00**			Log time	
Activity	Project	Comment	Hours	
Today			2.00	
Rewrite	Mastering Redmine - Chapter #8: Time Tracking	Updated the chapter for the rewrite phase	2.00	

Time reports

Redmine is known to lack reporting functionality, but not in the case of time tracking, as time tracking is generally useless without reporting.

In the previous section, you learned that Redmine provides many links to time reports. Let's list them here:

- **Overall spent time** on the project list page, which can be accessed through the **Projects** item in the top-left menu. This link opens a report that lists all visible time entries for all projects.
- The **Details** and **Report** links on the **project's Overview** page. The corresponding report lists all the time entries for the project.

- The number of hours on the issue page. This report lists all the time entries for the issue.

- The title of a time entry event on an activity page. The report that such a link points to lists all the time entries for the corresponding issue.

So, as you can see, time reports are generally available for three nesting levels: the global level (for all projects and issues), the project level (for all issues), and the issue level.

In this section, we will review the report for the issue level (for **Chapter #8**). Check it out in the following screenshot:

The breadcrumbs in the top-left corner can be used to switch between nesting levels. To the right-hand side of the breadcrumbs, you can see the **Log time** link, which can be used to add new time entries.

Below the **Spent time** title, you can see the **Filters** block. By default, only the **Date** filter is enabled here, but you can use the **Add filter** select box to add other filters.

Here are the filters that are supported by the time report:

The **Project** filter, however, is available only on the global level (for all projects). On other levels, it is enforced.

Below **Filters**, you can also see the **Options** block, which is shown in the next screenshot. It is collapsed by default.

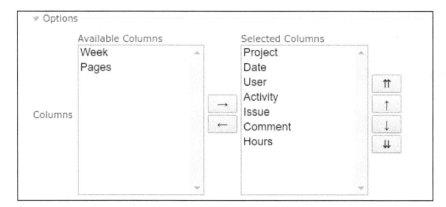

Using these options, you can choose which columns should be included in the report. Moreover, it can include custom fields as columns (**Pages** is a custom field).

Now let's review the **Details** and **Report** tabs, which contain different views of the report.

The Details tab

In this subsection, we continue to discuss the first screenshot of the *Time reports* section.

Under the **Details** tab, we get a list of time entries that match the specified filters. This list is shown in the table, most columns of which can be used for sorting (all except **Comment** and custom fields, actually). Above the list, you can see the grand total of all hours for all the time entries that are included in the report. The rightmost column (the untitled one) contains icon links that can be used to edit ( ) and delete ( ) time entries (of course, users should have the appropriate permissions to see and use these links). Below the list, you can see the **Atom** and **CSV** links. The former can be used to subscribe to time entries and the latter can be used to export the report.

As you might have noticed, rows of the list can be selected by either checking the checkboxes in the leftmost column, or clicking on the rows themselves (you can hold the *Ctrl* key to select more than one row). Additionally, you can click on the icon in the leftmost column to select all rows at once.

Right-clicking on the selected row (or rows) invokes the drop-down menu that is shown in the following screenshot:

Using this menu, you can delete selected time entries, change their activity, or invoke the bulk edit form. The latter can be used to change several time entries at a time. Check it out here:

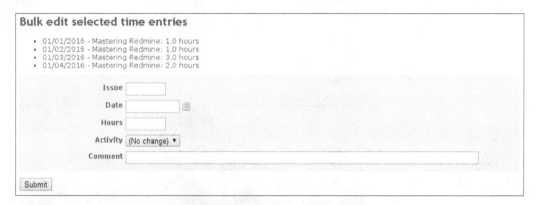

The Report tab

Under the **Report** tab, you can see the report builder, which is shown in the following screenshot:

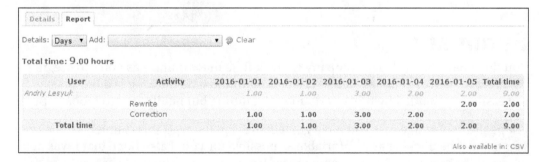

The **Details** field specifies what date-based columns the report will include. In my case, these are **Days** (**2016-01-01**, **2016-01-02**, and so on). The report supports **Years**, **Months**, **Weeks**, and **Days** values for this field.

The **Add** field is more interesting. It allows you to choose up to three grouping attributes that will be shown in the report as columns. Thus, in the previous screenshot, the first grouping attribute is **User** and the second one is **Activity**. Also, the grouping attributes are to be added in the same order in which they should appear in the report. Thus, to get the report that is shown in the preceding screenshot I first added the **User** group and then added **Activity**.

Possible values of the **Add** field are shown here:

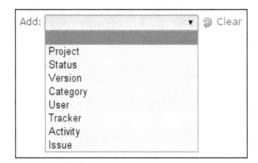

The **Clear** link can be used to reset the report's configuration.

The resulting report can be exported using the **CSV** link, which can be found in the bottom-right corner.

> **The Timesheet plugin**
>
> The Timesheet plugin, which was originally authored by Eric Davis, can be used to generate more flexible time reports. Check it out at `https://github.com/arkhitech/redmine_timesheet_plugin`.

Summary

You don't have to work in a company to track time in Redmine—as you can see, it fits great for personal use as well. Although Redmine time tracking is quite basic, it can easily be extended by third-party tools, including but not limited to mobile apps.

I hope the knowledge that you have gained after having read this chapter will help you make time tracking as comfortable as possible for you. I also hope that I was able to reveal the power of the time report to project managers. The next chapter is going to be useful for all types of Redmine users, as it describes how to make Redmine more personal.

9
Personalization

Some readers might want to start this book with this chapter, as it looks like an introduction to using Redmine. But it's not an introductory chapter. Usually people first get used to a new place and only then unpack their boxes. And unpacking your boxes and making Redmine your *home* application is actually what this chapter is about.

Also, this is the first time we will speak about Redmine from the user's perspective. Thus, this chapter will try to answer the following questions:

- What can users do to improve their experience with Redmine?
- How can users get quick access to the needed functionality?
- How can users be sure that they won't miss important updates?

And these are only some of the questions that we will address.

Like the previous chapter, this one is intended for all users. For project managers and site owners, it also gives an idea of what users might need to get a better experience with Redmine.

In this chapter, we will cover the following topics:

- Gravatar
- The personal page
- Getting updates
- Personalizing the issue list
- On-the-fly account creation

Gravatar

Gravatar is a very popular avatar image service (the name stands for **Globally Recognized AVATAR**). It uses a very simple algorithm to associate an image with a user email. Thus, a client application (Redmine in our case) sends a request with the hash of the user's email to this service and it returns the associated image. If no image is associated with the specified hash, Gravatar returns one of the default images (we reviewed them in *The Display tab* subsection of *The general settings* section in *Chapter 3, Configuring Redmine*).

> Using avatars helps to visually identify your data (issues, comments, activities, and so on) among other user data.

This simplicity caused Gravatar to be chosen as the source of profile pictures in WordPress and StackOverflow. With custom plugins, support for Gravatars can also be added to Drupal, Joomla, SugarCRM, and so on. This means that, if you configure a Gravatar for Redmine, you will also have it automatically in WordPress, StackOverflow, some Drupal sites, and more.

In practice, however, the majority of Redmine users do not make use of Gravatar. Maybe because Redmine comes with no information anywhere that would explain the possibility for adding a profile picture using this service? So let's review how to do this in this section.

Gravatar uses `https://wordpress.com/` user accounts. So, if you are registered on WordPress.com, you can use your existing credentials to sign in to Gravatar. You can do this by using `https://gravatar.com/connect` link.

If you don't have a WordPress.com account yet, you need to go to `https://en.gravatar.com/connect/?source=_signup` and register there using the email address that you have chosen or are going to choose for your Redmine account.

After a successful sign-in, you will be redirected to Gravatar's email addresses configuration page, which is shown in the following screenshot:

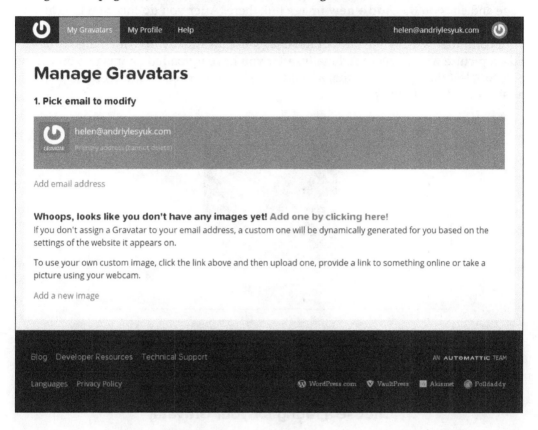

As you can see, Gravatar allows you to register and manage multiple email addresses under a single account. So, if you have used a different email address in Redmine, you can register it in your existing Gravatar account using this page.

To add a picture, you need to click on either the **Add one by clicking here!** link or the **Add a new image** link on this page. Alternatively, you can go to the **My Gravatar** page and click on the **Add a new image** link there. After you do this, you'll be given options for uploading images to Gravatar—you will be able to upload them from your computer, specify the URL of the image, use an already uploaded image, or take a picture with a webcam. Finally, after you have uploaded an image, you will be able to select the square area that should be used for the avatar and crop the picture, as shown in the following screenshot:

When you click on the **Crop and Finish!** button, you will be redirected to the last page of this wizard. On that page, you will be asked to choose a rating for the avatar image, as shown in this screenshot:

Normally, you will need to choose the **G** rating here (by clicking on the appropriate box). Anyway, you really should not use images with rude gestures, nudity, hard drug use, violence, or sexual content as your avatars in Redmine!

After you have selected a rating, the avatar becomes associated with the email address and is ready to use. So, when you come back to Redmine, you should see the new avatar near the name of the user, as shown in the following screenshot:

Henceforth, this avatar will be shown in almost every place where the link to the user's profile is rendered.

> **The Local Avatars plugin**
>
> In some cases, you may need to have avatars stored locally, for example, if your corporate network has a limited Internet connection. In such cases, you may use the Local Avatars plugin, which was originally authored by Andrew Chaika. It is available at `https://github.com/thorin/redmine_local_avatars`.

The personal page

Perhaps you have already visited **My page**—the page that is opened after successful authentication if Redmine fails to redirect you to the previous Redmine page (for example, if you first came right to the login page). You can open this page by clicking on the **My page** link in the top-left menu. It looks like this:

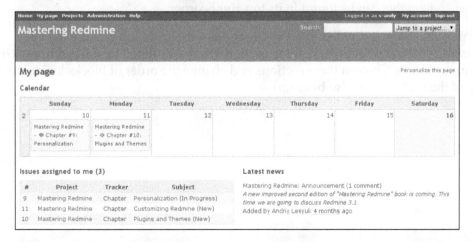

The idea of this page is to gather all of the information that is interesting to the user in one place so that he/she can quickly move to the page of interest. However, as you already know, there is a lot of information that the user can be interested in. Therefore, this page comes with the **Personalize this page** link. This link can be used to switch it into edit mode, which is shown in the following screenshot:

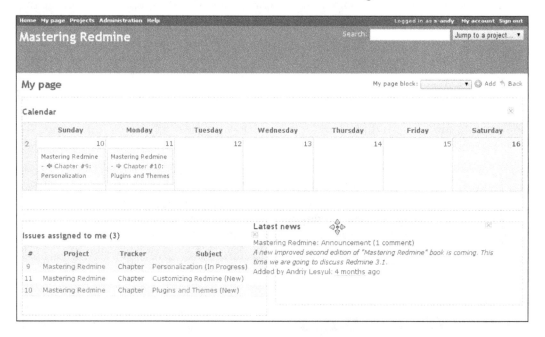

In this mode, each block of the personal page can be dragged or removed. To drag a block, you need to press the mouse button when the cursor is above its header, and move the mouse arrow while holding the button pressed (thus, in the preceding screenshot, I'm moving the **Latest news** block). To remove a block, you need to click on the ⊠ icon that can be found in its top-right corner.

The personal page is divided into three sections—the wide top section, the left column section, and the right column section. Each is outlined by dashed lines. You can move blocks between these sections and change the order of blocks inside them. Any of the sections can also be empty.

To add a new block, you can use the **My page block** drop-down list. Its content is shown in the following screenshot:

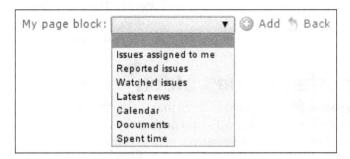

So, to add a block, you need to select it in this list and click on the **Add** link. After this, the block will appear in the wide top section, from where you will be able to move it to another section. Also note that you can add any of the listed blocks to your personal page only once.

The **Back** link should be used to switch the personal page into the normal non-editable mode.

Now let's review what information these blocks provide.

 Some plugins may come with additional **My page** blocks.

The Issues assigned to me block

The **Issues assigned to me** block contains the list of issues that are assigned to you. It looks like the following screenshot:

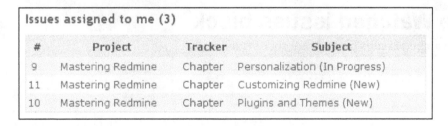

This list is limited to 10 items. However, the **Issues assigned to me** link (the header) can be used to go to the issue list with the issue filter set to the appropriate values, which will make the issue list include all such issues. The issues in this block are ordered by their priority and last update time. Also, the right mouse button can be used to invoke the issue contextual menu, which should already be familiar to you.

The Reported issues block

The **Reported issues** block contains issues that were created by you. In fact, this is the only place where you can quickly find such issues. Therefore, I personally use this block quite often (you can also use a custom query to list such issues, though).

Reported issues (21)

#	Project	Tracker	Subject
9	Mastering Redmine	Chapter	Personalization (In Progress)
8	Mastering Redmine	Chapter	Time Tracking (Resolved)
7	Mastering Redmine	Chapter	Access Control and Workflow (Resolved)
6	Mastering Redmine	Chapter	Text Formatting (Resolved)
11	Mastering Redmine	Chapter	Customizing Redmine (New)
10	Mastering Redmine	Chapter	Plugins and Themes (New)
5	Mastering Redmine	Chapter	Managing Projects (Resolved)
4	Mastering Redmine	Chapter	Issue Tracking (Resolved)
3	Mastering Redmine	Chapter	Configuring Redmine (Resolved)
2	Mastering Redmine	Chapter	Installing Redmine (Resolved)

The issues in this block are ordered by their update time. As with the previous block, you can use the right mouse button to invoke the contextual menu for selected issues (hold *Ctrl* to select several issues). The header of the block is a link that points to the issue list that will include all issues reported by you.

The Watched issues block

The **Watched issues** block is another issue list.

Watched issues (1)

#	Project	Tracker	Subject
9	Mastering Redmine	Chapter	Personalization (In Progress)

This block lists issues that are watched by you. They are sorted by their update time. The block also supports the contextual menu and its header is also a link to the full issue list.

The Latest news block

The **Latest news** block contains the 10 latest news items from projects that you are a member of. It looks like in this screenshot:

The Calendar block

The **Calendar** block is your personal calendar for the current week.

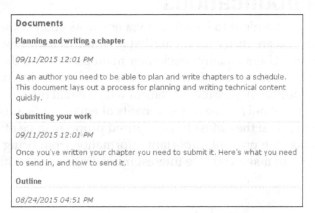

Like the **Calendar** tab of a project, this block contains important events on projects that you are a member of.

The Documents block

The **Documents** block lists up to 10 documents from projects that you are a member of. It looks like this:

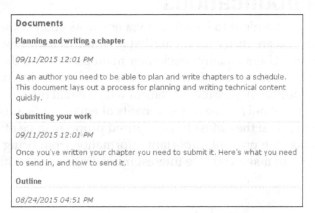

This list contains recently added documents.

The Spent time block

If you want to use Redmine for time tracking, you may find the **Spent time** block useful.

This block lists your time entries for the last seven days. As you can see, here they can be modified and removed. Also, here you can add new time entries using the **Log time** link. Moreover, clicking on the **Spent time** link (the header) opens the time report with the filter set to show only your time logs.

Getting updates

Unless you are checking out Redmine on a regular basis – that is, once a day or even more frequently – it's easy to miss some important information, such as a new issue that was assigned to you, new data on an issue, changes in Wiki documentation, a new reply in a forum topic, and so on. Unfortunately, not all of such data can be found on a single page (say **My page**), and such pages can contain too much information to examine (for example, the **Activity** tab of the project). Therefore, in this section, we will discuss how to make sure that you will be notified about changes that are made to the objects you are interested in.

The email notifications

Personally, I find it convenient to be notified via email, as you get these kinds of notifications when you are ready for them (that is, you check for new messages and expect them to come). Users usually check their mailboxes once a day or even more often. There are many different tools that can help users get their emails in time. In email clients, it is commonly possible to control which email messages you receive (using filters). These are only some of the benefits of email notifications. The only problem with them is that they must be configured properly to be effective – a too narrow configuration can prevent important information from being sent and a too wide configuration can make you lose interest in reading every notification message.

So, let's discuss how to configure email notifications. Click on the **My account** link in the top-right menu. This will open the account page. Find the **Email notifications** box, which looks as follows:

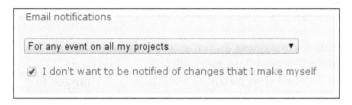

Let's review all the available notification options:

- **For any event on all my projects**: This option is selected by default. If you choose it, you will get all the notifications for all the events (for example, for changes in Wiki pages, replies on forums, comments in issues, and so on) on all projects that you are a member of. Practice shows that it's really too much! So, you will likely not want to leave this option selected.

- **For any event on the selected projects only...**: When you choose this option, the list of your projects will appear below the drop-down list. In that list, you will be able to select for which projects you want to receive notifications for all events. So, this is a kind of limited previous notification option. For other projects—that is, ones that are not selected—Redmine will use the following notification option:

- **Only for things I watch or I'm involved in**: If you choose this option, you will be notified about events in objects that you watch, or created, that are assigned to you, or were assigned to you. This is perhaps the best choice. But if you choose it, do not forget to watch objects that you are interested in but which were not created by you and are not/were not assigned to you.

- **Only for things I am assigned to**: If you select this option, you'll be notified about events on objects that you watch or that are assigned to you. In Redmine, only issues can be assigned to users. So, this means that only notifications that are related to issues will be sent to you (except, of course, notifications related to watched objects).

- **Only for things I am the owner of**: If you select this option, you'll be notified about events only on those objects that you watch or created.

- **No events**: This option disables notifications completely (including notifications related to any watched objects, what actually makes watching useless).

No notifications even when you enabled them?

Ask your Redmine administrators whether they configured email delivery for Redmine. Refer to *Chapter 3, Configuring Redmine*, for more details.

If, for example, you are watching an issue and add a comment to it, then by default you will get a notification that you have added that comment. This behavior can be disabled by checking the **I don't want to be notified of changes that I make myself** checkbox, which is unchecked by default. I believe that this is one of the first options that should be changed in your account right after registration.

Still no (or only some) notifications come?

For example, you are getting notifications for watched issues but not for watched topics. Most likely, this means that your Redmine administrators disabled the **Message added** action under the **Email notifications** tab on the **Settings** page, which can be found in the **Administration** menu. So, you need to ask them to check whether the appropriate actions are enabled.

Watching

In Redmine, the best way to ensure that you'll be notified about changes that are made to an object is to watch it. Watching an object is easy—just click on the **Watch** link in its contextual menu (which can be usually found in the top-right corner of its content area), as shown in the following screenshot:

After this, or if you are already watching the object, the title of the corresponding link turns to **Unwatch** and the star icon becomes yellow, like this:

Currently in Redmine, users can watch issues, news (including their index), Wiki pages and indexes, forums, and topics.

News feeds

The **Only for things I watch or I'm involved in** option for email notifications (which was discussed in *The email notifications* subsection earlier) is quite satisfactory, but what if you want to be notified about new issues? Yes, you can watch issues, but not new ones. Should you switch to the **For any event on all my projects** option in this case? No. Luckily, there is one more way to get such updates—news feeds.

If an object or a list has an **Atom** link similar to the one shown in the preceding screenshot, this means that you can subscribe to that object or list using a news feeds aggregator, such as iTunes or Safari. If this link is available, it can usually be found in the bottom-right corner of the page.

Atom is an XML-based language for web feeds. To be able to read them you need a special application called a **reader** or **aggregator**. The **Atom** link points to such a web feed.

> Currently, you can subscribe to the project list, news, Wiki indexes, the issue list, issue comments, activities, the forum list, the topic list, time entries, and revisions.

Personalizing the issue list

Having your issues organized is extremely important for good performance. So, that's when custom queries come in handy again.

Custom queries were described in detail in *Chapter 4, Issue Tracking*. Some samples of them can be found in the *Project maintenance best practices* section of *Chapter 5, Managing Projects*. This is the time to mention them again, what proves how useful they are.

So, in the following table, let's review some samples of custom queries that you can use to create specific issue lists for your own usage:

Name	Filters	
	Field/Option	Condition/Value
My open issues	Status	open
	Assigned to	"<<me>>"
Issues I work on	Status	In Progress
	Assigned to	"<<me>>"

Name	Filters	
	Field/Option	**Condition/Value**
My overdue issues	Status	open
	Assigned to	"<<me>>"
	Due date	more than days ago 0 days
My issues that are due soon	Status	open
	Assigned to	"<<me>>"
	Due date	in less than 0 days

Also remember that you can subscribe to a customized issue list using the **Atom** link. Moreover, you don't even need to save the custom query to be able to subscribe to it—just click on the **Apply** link and use the generated **Atom** link.

On-the-fly account creation

Under this section, we will review not user registration but automatic account creation that does not require filling in any form. So, this section is not intended solely for ordinary users but also for site owners and administrators. Ordinary users will learn how they can use their third-party accounts in Redmine, and site owners and administrators will learn how to make this possible.

Just in case you did not know, most users avoid registering on each new site. There are many reasons for this, among them the following:

- They don't trust the new site and therefore do not want to share their email addresses, passwords, and so on

- They do not want to remember another username and password combination and do not want to reuse the ones that they are already using in other systems

- They see no reasons weighty enough for creating an account on the new site

 The reason that is mentioned last hints at the solution—make sure that your potential users do know the benefits of registering on your website.

However, Redmine can liberate you from the need to remember a new username and password combination. It supports at least two technologies that allow it to do this— OpenID and LDAP.

OpenID

OpenID is an open standard for authentication that uses an OpenID identity provider as an authentication server. This way, users do not need to store their passwords in Redmine. Instead, OpenID users are redirected to the OpenID provider, where they authenticate, and are then returned to Redmine authenticated if the authentication is successful.

 Don't confuse OpenID with OpenID Connect, which is based on OAuth 2.0. OpenID Connect is used, for example, by Google.

The great thing is that the OpenID provider can be any Internet host, and this protocol is supported by industry giants such as Yahoo. This means that you can authorize in Redmine using, for example, your Yahoo account. The drawback of this authentication solution is that you need to specify the URL of the OpenID provider in the login form. Check it out in the following screenshot:

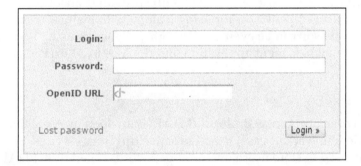

To log in using OpenID, the user needs to specify the appropriate URL in the **OpenID URL** field and then just click on the **Login** button (that is, if you are using OpenID you don't need to specify anything in the **Login** and **Password** fields). After this, the user will be redirected to the OpenID provider. The provider will usually ask for credentials that the user has in its system. After the user logs in there (or if the user is already logged in), the provider will ask for confirmation that the user really wants to grant Redmine access to his/her profile. In particular, to create a dedicated profile for the user, Redmine will need the full name and email address of the user. And it will fetch this data from the OpenID provider if the user has authorized it. Moreover, the newly created user will have the same username that he/she has in the OpenID provider's system.

 OpenID providers also usually allow you to revoke the authorization if, for example, you change your mind.

Depending on the Redmine configuration, after successful authorization in the OpenID provider, you will be:

- Asked to activate your account in Redmine using the URL that has been sent to you by email, if the **Self-registration** setting – which can be found under the **Authentication** tab of the **Settings** page in the **Administration** menu – is set to **account activation by email**.

- Asked to wait for your new account to be approved by an administrator if the **Self-registration** setting is set to **manual account activation**.

- Logged in to your new account if the **Self-registration** setting is set to **automatic account activation**.

- Asked to fill in some additional data for your new account, the password and username among them. This actually indicates that something went wrong in Redmine's OpenID stack, and it did not allow you to use the OpenID provider to authenticate.

The fact that any Internet host can be an OpenID provider can, of course, become a reason for not using OpenID (or for using it along with manual or email account activation). This reason can be even more weighty if you are using Redmine as a corporate project management application. But don't be in a hurry to get upset!

LDAP

Lightweight Directory Access Protocol (LDAP) is an open protocol that allows an application (Redmine in our case) to access active directory services. Such services are commonly used to store usernames and passwords. Therefore, LDAP can be used for authentication as well. Most known directory service servers are OpenLDAP and Microsoft Active Directory. So, yes! With LDAP, you can connect Redmine to the Microsoft AD domain.

Unlike OpenID, to support an LDAP server an administrator must register it first on the **LDAP authentication** page of the **Administration** menu (using the **New authentication mode** link, as described in *Chapter 3, Configuring Redmine*). If administrators have added several LDAP servers, Redmine will attempt to authenticate a new user against each of them (until one of them returns a successful response). Also, if the **On-the-fly user creation** option is enabled for the server, Redmine will create accounts for new users on their first successful logins.

Moreover, unlike OpenID, the login process of LDAP users does not differ from that of local users. That is, users specify their usernames and passwords in the login form as usual and are not redirected to any third-party websites.

User/group synchronization

Ricardo Santos created the LDAP Sync plugin, which can perform user and group synchronization between Redmine and LDAP servers. Visit the following GitHub page for more information:

`https://github.com/thorin/redmine_ldap_sync`

Summary

This chapter is one of the last chapters, as you are expected to already know Redmine. Thus, to customize the issue list, you need to know how to use custom queries. To configure and troubleshoot email notifications, you need to know which settings should be specified in the administration pages. To customize personal pages, you need to be familiar with the information that is shown in the blocks. And so on.

Perhaps this could be a good chapter to end the book with, but Redmine is not just a tool with a fixed list of features. It has a great special feature that makes its feature list nearly unlimited. This feature is the plugin API. There are a lot of plugins for Redmine with very different functionalities — from just adding a feature to turning Redmine into a different application. So, in the next chapter, we will review what plugins are, how to find the plugins that you need, and other related topics. Additionally, we will review some interesting plugins there.

10
Plugins and Themes

I have always liked playing with plugins—not only as a user but also as a developer. I was amazed by the power that plugin APIs of some applications (for example, Apache HTTP server) give to let a developer extend their functionality. But when I started to learn the Redmine plugin API, I was amazed even more. Honestly, I can't say that I love Ruby on Rails or am a fan of it, but Redmine's plugin API (which is based on Ruby and Rails) is definitely the thing! Unlike other plugin APIs that I've seen before, it's not a regular plugin API. Thus, it embraces the Redmine API and the Rails API. And, it is based on Ruby, which is a very powerful metaprogramming language and provides unsurpassed means for patching code at runtime. As a result, this makes the Redmine plugin API nearly limitless—in other words, you can do almost anything with it.

While Redmine is quite featureful without plugins, you will most likely encounter a couple of them that you will want to make use of. However, this is where the first problem appears—it's not easy to find a working plugin for a certain version of Redmine. Also, the official list of plugins misses some their recent versions. Therefore, in this chapter, you will learn how to find plugins. Additionally, we will review some of them. But besides plugins, we will also pay some attention to Redmine themes, as a theme is what can help make an application look different.

So, who is this chapter for? In spite of what you might think, it's not only for administrators (who can install plugins) but also for other users who can use them (and, for example, ask an administrator to install some plugins).

In this chapter, we will cover the following topics:

- Finding plugins
- Installing a plugin
- A review of some plugins
- Themes
- A review of some themes

Finding plugins

The official website of Redmine has a plugin directory, which you can use to find a plugin that you need (the directory, by the way, is implemented with another plugin that was written by Jean-Philippe Lang). However, many plugins on this list are not updated. For example, a plugin might be listed for an older Redmine, while its more recent version can actually be available. Also, more recent versions of some plugins can be available elsewhere, for example, on GitHub. (Sometimes, plugin authors, including me, fail to release updates for new versions of Redmine on time. So, volunteers can fork and update such plugins on GitHub.) Therefore, unfortunately, it is usually not enough to use the official directory to find a plugin for your version of Redmine.

A forum dedicated to plugins

In addition to the plugin directory, http://www.redmine.org/ has a forum that is dedicated to plugins. On it, you can discuss plugins, ask for help, request the development of a custom plugin, and so on. Check it out here:

http://www.redmine.org/projects/redmine/boards/3

The official directory

Anyway, the official Redmine plugin directory should be your primary source of information about Redmine plugins. Yes, it's not ideal and not all plugins or their versions are registered there, but it was designed to maintain the list of plugins. Therefore, it has a legible structure, supports Redmine versions, allows us to filter plugins by a Redmine version, has a rating system, and so on.

This plugin directory can be accessed using `http://www.redmine.org/plugins`. Its start page is shown in the following screenshot:

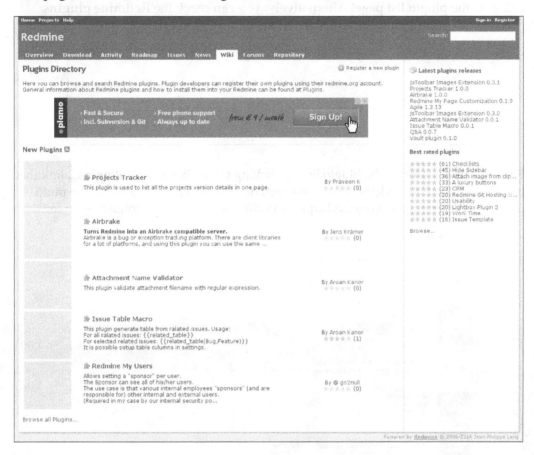

The page that is shown in the preceding screenshot contains five recently registered plugins. On its sidebar, you can also see ten recently released versions (which include versions of plugins that were recently registered).

 You can subscribe to new plugins using the icon near the **New Plugins** title and a feeds aggregator.

Below **Latest plugins releases** on the sidebar, you can see the top 10 best rated plugins. If you click on the **Browse...** link below it, you'll be redirected to a multi-page list of plugins (which we'll discuss later). This list will be sorted by ratings. In other words, using this link, you can quickly check out popular Redmine plugins.

You can also search for a plugin by entering related keywords in the **Search** box that is located in the top-right corner. However, it's important that you do this while being on the plugin list page! Alternatively, you can check the **Redmine plugins** checkbox in the search form, as shown in the following screenshot:

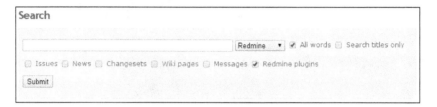

Finally, you can browse the plugin list by clicking on the **Browse all Plugins...** link that is located in the bottom-left corner. After you do so, you'll be redirected to the multi-page list where plugins are sorted alphabetically, as shown in the following screenshot:

Note this drop-down list in the top-right corner:

Show only plugins compatible with Redmine: `-- Any -- ▼`

This select box can be used to filter plugins by a specific Redmine version. But remember that some plugin versions may be not registered in the official directory yet (you can try checking out the home page of the plugin or finding its forked version on GitHub, what is described in the very next subsection).

Finally, let's see what a plugin page looks like:

In the preceding screenshot, you can see only the upper part of the page. Usually, plugin pages contain a description of the plugin, which may include a couple of screenshots (so such pages are usually quite long).

Below the description, there is the **Atom** link. It can be used to subscribe to new versions of the plugin (and you should really do this if you use it). Also, the page lists all versions of the plugin, as shown on the following screenshot:

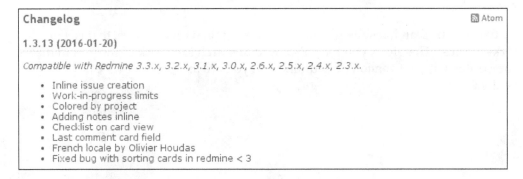

Below the **Changelog** section, you can find the **User ratings** section. It is shown in the following screenshot:

User ratings

★★★★★ by stella fredo 1 day ago
a must have one, works with redmine 3.2.0, ruby 2.3.0, apache2, centos7

★★★★★ by joey zhou 5 days ago

★★★★★ by Adam Szakacs about 1 month ago
Great plugin - provides a good alternative to the traditional table view of issues with the 'agile' feel...

GitHub

Redmine was written in Ruby on Rails, just like GitHub. GitHub is a project hosting and collaboration platform that is admired by open source developers mainly due to its social networking capabilities. Thus, even the code of Ruby on Rails is hosted there. For all these reasons, this great service is especially loved by "Rubists". Therefore, I guess it is not a surprise that most Redmine plugins can be found on GitHub.

In other words, GitHub can be a secondary source of information on Redmine plugins. So let's learn how we can find plugins there. To do this, we'll use the search form that is available at `https://github.com/search`

In this form, you should specify `language:Ruby` to make it search only for Ruby code and add keywords that describe the searched plugin along with the keyword `Redmine`.

By default, the search results will include only original repositories, that is, not forks (copies). Therefore, you may also need to search for a fork of the plugin that is compatible with the version of Redmine that you are using. So let's see how this can be done.

Limiting results by update date

You can restrict search results on GitHub by last push date using the `pushed` keyword. For example, use the `language:Ruby Redmine pushed:>2015-02-19 fork:true` query to find repositories that were modified after the release of Redmine 3.0.0, which happened on February 2, 2015. The `fork:true` condition is needed here as original repositories can remain unmodified for a longer time.

Thus, if you search for the Redmine Time Tracker plugin, which is believed to work only with Redmine 1.3.x according to the official plugin directory (at the time of writing this book), you will most likely find the repository of Fernando Kosh, as shown in this screenshot:

Unfortunately, the version of the plugin in this repository is for Redmine 2.4 and the last commit to it was made on April 11, 2014 (that's what I see at the time of writing this book). So, we need to find the most recently updated fork of this repository, that should theoretically support the most recent version of Redmine. To do this, we need to open the **network graph**, what can be done by clicking on the number of forks (**141**, as can be seen in the previous screenshot) on the search result page or the repository page. This is how this number is shown on the repository page:

Now, check out a sample of the network graph that is shown in the following screenshot:

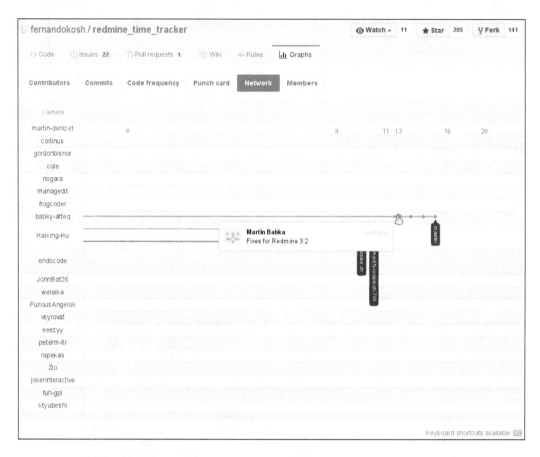

On this graph, the spots are commits (that is, code changes). As we need to find the latest commit that was made to any of the forks shown in this graph, we drag it to the left (by clicking on it and moving the mouse arrow to the left-hand side) until we find the very rightmost spot.

When you hover your mouse arrow over a spot, a small box with brief information about the commit will be shown, as can be seen in the previous screenshot. This information will include the name of the author, the hash, and the commit message. In our case, the shown commit was made to support Redmine 3.2, and this is exactly what we need. So, it looks as if the repository of **babky-atteq** (**Martin Babka**) contains the searched version of the plugin. To move to this repository, just click on the spot.

On GitHub, forks are created by volunteers, who can make changes that are required by them or their organizations. So, the most recent commits do not automatically mean support for recent versions of Redmine. Therefore, you should always read commit messages to get an idea of what the changes are for. Also note that authors of forks are not necessarily good at programming (and so are authors of plugins though), so their forks can be buggy. Additionally, it's always a good idea to read the README.md file of the repository, which is shown on its start page, as this file can contain some information about the state of the code and known issues.

Installing a plugin

The installation procedure may differ for different plugins, but it has some common steps, which we will review in this section. Before installing a plugin, you should always check out its documentation to ensure that you will be doing this properly.

This section is intended for administrators who have access to the filesystem of the server on which Redmine runs. Also, plugin installation may require root access.

Redmine plugins usually come in a directory, which should be copied to the `plugins` subdirectory of Redmine (that is, for example, into `/opt/redmine/redmine-3.2.0/plugins` if you have installed Redmine at `/opt/redmine/redmine-3.2.0`).

What if the plugin's directory is missing or has an invalid name?

The plugin should contain the init.rb file in its main directory. So, if this file is in the root, it means that the plugin's directory is missing. Also, the init.rb file should contain the following line:

```
Redmine::Plugin.register :plugin_name do
```

Here, plugin_name is the name of the plugin. The plugin's directory must have exactly the same name.

Most plugins require migration. This means that, in order for the plugin to work, some changes must be made to the Redmine database. To perform plugin migration, execute the following command on the Redmine server:

```
$ rake redmine:plugins:migrate RAILS_ENV=production
```

It is safe to execute this command even if the plugin does not require migration.

 Files for migration come in the db subdirectory of the plugin's directory. So, if such a directory exists and contains files, migration is necessary.

Finally, to activate the plugin, you need to restart Redmine using the following command:

```
$ sudo service apache2 reload
```

This is actually all you need to do to install an ordinary plugin for Redmine.

 If the installation is successful, the plugin will appear on the **Plugins** page of the **Administration** menu.

Upgrading plugins

Often, new versions of plugins are released to support newer versions of Redmine. Therefore, when a new version of a plugin arrives, you need to make sure that it still supports the version of Redmine that you are using. Otherwise, upgrading to such a version may break your installation. But how can you check for supported versions?

The first source where you should check this is the page from which you got the plugin. Thus, if it was GitHub, check in the README.md file (if it's missing there, look for similar files, for example, README.txt).

You can also check the page of the plugin in the official Redmine plugin directory at http://www.redmine.org/plugins. Check out a sample page, shown in the following screenshot:

The versions of Redmine that are supported by the latest version of the plugin are listed in the **Compatible with** field (you can also check which versions of Redmine were supported by older versions of the plugin in the **Changelog** section of the page). Unfortunately, this information can be outdated in the official directory (because, for example, the latest version was not registered yet).

Alternatively, you can try checking the home page of the plugin, which should be shown in the installed plugins list, if specified. To check this list, open the **Plugins** page in the **Administration** menu. Certainly, for this information to be reflected on the home page, the new version should be authored by the same person as the version that you are already using (in other words, it should not be a fork).

Now, let's speak about the upgrade procedure. In general, it is the same as the installation one. That is, to upgrade a plugin, you usually need to perform the same three steps:

1. Update the code (it would be a great idea to back up the old code).
2. Run the migration.
3. Restart Redmine.

Uninstalling a plugin

I assume that you will want to try several plugins to decide which one best fits your needs (unfortunately, some plugins do not provide enough information to make a decision without trying them). So, in this case, you will need to know how to uninstall them correctly.

 Don't play with plugins on the production server! Set up a test server (it can be a virtual machine) for this purpose.

To uninstall a plugin, you first need to roll back the database changes that were made during the migration phase of the installation. Thus, if you want to remove the plugin_name plugin, you need to execute this:

```
$ rake redmine:plugins:migrate NAME=plugin_name VERSION=0 RAILS_
ENV=production
```

Note VERSION=0, which means that the plugin should be migrated to the "zero" (that is, none) version. Also note that it is safe to execute this command even if the plugin does not include migration scripts.

After that, you can remove the plugin's directory (which is named after it) from the `plugins` subdirectory of the Redmine root directory (that is, `/opt/redmine/redmine-3.2.0` if you installed Redmine there).

Finally, you need to restart Redmine:

```
$ sudo service apache2 reload
```

A review of some plugins

Can Redmine be used without plugins? Surely it can. Is Redmine thorough without plugins? I'm not sure whether it is—I haven't seen a Redmine installation that does not use any plugins. Anyway, if you can extend your installation with features that you need, why not do this?

Of course, we won't be able to review all the available plugins in this chapter. Therefore, we'll start with the ones that I believe are essential for any Redmine installation. Then we'll check a plugin that implements a highly anticipated feature that is missing in the Redmine core. Finally, we'll review plugins that are discussed by experienced Redmine users most often.

So, let's check out what amazing things can be done with some plugins. Under this section, we will review:

- The Exception Handler plugin
- The jsToolbar CodeRay Extension
- The Monitoring and Controlling plugin
- The Git Hosting plugin
- The Agile plugin

The Exception Handler plugin

There is no perfect software—any application can throw an error. By error here, I mean an exception that occurs when an application cannot handle an emergency situation. Yes, such cases can't be avoided, but that's not even the main problem. The main problem is that an exception can happen silently and you may never know that it has happened, because you can't be sure that the user who faces it will report it to you.

This becomes especially important if you are using:

- The most recent version of Redmine
- Badly tested third-party plugins or their most recent versions
- Custom plugins that were developed for this particular Redmine installation

Luckily, Redmine writes all such exceptions to its log files or the log files of the HTTP server. But if your Redmine installation is heavily loaded and/or server administrators do not check all log files regularly (that is, at least once a day), you can still easily miss them.

The solution comes from the now-former Redmine core developer Eric Davis, who developed the Exception Handler plugin. This plugin catches unhandled exceptions, generates reports, and sends them to the specified email addresses.

 You can find the up-to-date fork of this plugin, which is maintained by Ricardo Santos, at `https://github.com/thorin/redmine_exception_handler`.

To install the plugin, you need to copy its code into the `redmine_exception_handler` subdirectory of the `plugins` directory, install the `tinder` and `exception_notification` gems (using `gem install`, possibly with the `-v` option), and run `bundle install`.

This plugin requires Ruby 2.0.

The very first thing that needs to be done after installation of this plugin is specifying the email addresses at which you want to receive information about exceptions. To do this, go to the **Plugins** page of the **Administration** menu and click on the **Configure** link that is located to the right-hand side of the plugin's row. You should get the form which is shown in the following screenshot:

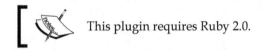

After completing this form, you can check whether notifications can be sent to the specified email addresses using the **Test Settings by triggering a fake exception** link.

Now, you will always know when your Redmine fails. So, unless you are able to check Redmine log files regularly and carefully, I believe that installing this plugin is essential.

The jsToolbar CodeRay extension

As described in *Chapter 6*, *Text Formatting*, to make a code in a Wiki content formatted appropriately, you need to embed it in the `<pre>` and `<code>` tags (for Textile). Moreover, you need to do this manually! Also, to have the code highlighted properly, you need to specify the correct programming language in the `class` attribute of the starting `<code>` tag. As practice shows, this is a problem for new Redmine users. Therefore, they often embed the code without syntax highlighting.

So, to make the lives of your users easier, you can install the jsToolbar CodeRay Extension. This plugin adds a new button to the Wiki toolbar, as shown here:

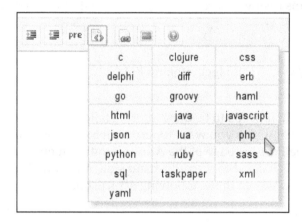

With this button, you just select the code, or place the cursor at the position where you want to write it, and click on the corresponding language in the drop-down box. As simple as this!

 This plugin consists of two parts, which are available at: `https://github.com/tleish/redmine_jstoolbar_ext_coderay` and `https://github.com/tleish/redmine_jstoolbar_ext`

As this plugin solves one of the issues that are common to many Redmine users, I believe it's essential to have it installed on your Redmine installation.

 This plugin does not work with the Markdown formatter.

The Monitoring & Controlling plugin

As it has been mentioned, Redmine lacks reporting and statistics. This is a well-known issue, so no wonder there exist several plugins that implement these missing features for Redmine. One of these plugins is Redmine Monitoring & Controlling (which is also known as M&C).

The Monitoring & Controlling plugin implements its functionality as a project module, so to be able to use it you need to enable this module for your project. This can be done under the **Modules** tab of the project's **Settings** page (remember that you can also enable it by default for all new projects on the global **Settings** page). Here is this tab:

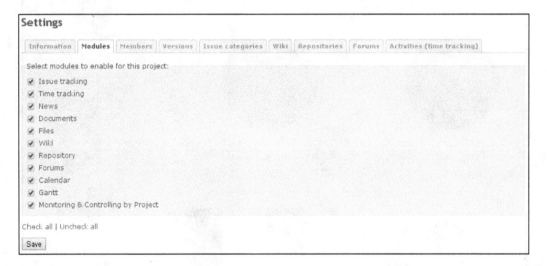

After you have enabled the **Monitoring & Controlling by Project** module here, you will see in your project menu the following new tab:

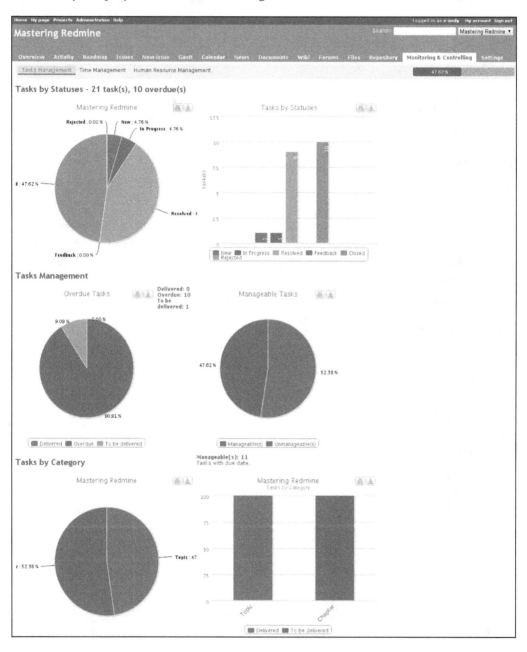

Each of the charts that are shown on this page can be printed or downloaded using the icons:

As you might have noticed, this page has its own tabs and the previous screenshot shows just one of them: **Tasks Management**. The other tabs are: **Time Management**, which contains charts for due and spent hours, and **Human Resource Management**, which contains a chart that displays the number of issues per project member.

 An up-to-date fork of the plugin is available at `https://github.com/benoitlm/Redmine-Monitoring-Controlling`.

The Git Hosting plugin

The most popular protocols for accessing Git repositories are HTTPS and SSH. In particular, these two protocols are used by GitHub. In *Chapter 3*, *Configuring Redmine*, I mentioned that the Git server can be configured to use Redmine users through the `Redmine.pm` tool. Such a configuration allows Redmine users to access Git repositories via the HTTP/HTTPS protocol. However, Git alone does not implement an HTTP server—it needs a separate application for this, which is Apache in our case (due to `Redmine.pm`, which is an Apache Perl module). In the same way, Git alone does not implement an SSH server—it needs a separate application to implement SSH access as well.

So, to provide SSH access to your repositories, you need an SSH server. But additionally, you need something like `Redmine.pm` that will support Redmine users. One such tool is **Gitolite**. It's a kind of shell that is opened when the user logs in to the SSH server using a special SSH account. Usually, the name of such an account is just `git` (it can also be `gitolite` or `gitolite3`). That's why the URL for SSH access usually looks like `git@hostname.com` (`git` is the username here). In other words, Gitolite uses a single system account for its operations. And, for Git users, it provides virtual accounts, much like `Redmine.pm`.

However, Gitolite cannot work with Redmine directly, as it knows nothing about this application. So, to integrate it with Redmine, you need the Redmine Git Hosting plugin. This plugin makes sure that Gitolite will be able to recognize Redmine users and authorize them according to their roles and permissions. In addition to this, the plugin turns Redmine into a feature-rich Git hosting application. That's why the authors of the plugin chose such a name for it.

As the plugin dramatically extends the capabilities of the Git SCM, for its own Git repositories it introduces the special virtual Gitolite/Xitolite SCM. Therefore, for the plugin to be activated, this SCM must be enabled under the **Repositories** tab of the **Settings** page in the **Administration** menu, as shown in this screenshot:

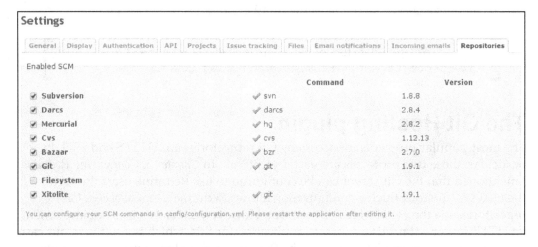

If the **Xitolite** SCM is enabled here, you will see the new **Gitolite** SCM in the new repository form (this form can be opened by clicking on the **New repository** link under the **Repositories** tab of the project's **Settings** page), as shown in the following screenshot:

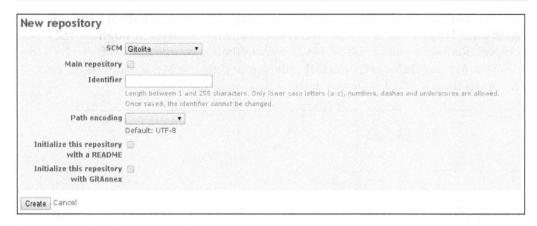

The difference between normal repositories and **Gitolite** ones can be seen right after a Gitolite repository is added to the project. Thus, it obviously has many more capabilities.

The settings page of such a repository, which can be opened by clicking on the **Edit** link, reveals what these capabilities are.

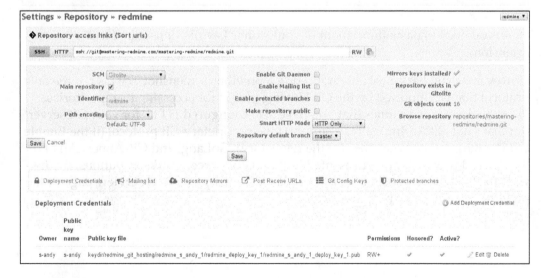

The **Deployment Credentials** section on this page reminds us that SSH access is based on SSH keys. So, to be able to access Gitolite repositories through the SSH protocol, Redmine users must add such keys to their accounts first. This can be done using the **My public keys** link, which can be found on the **My account** page. This link opens the page that is shown in the following screenshot:

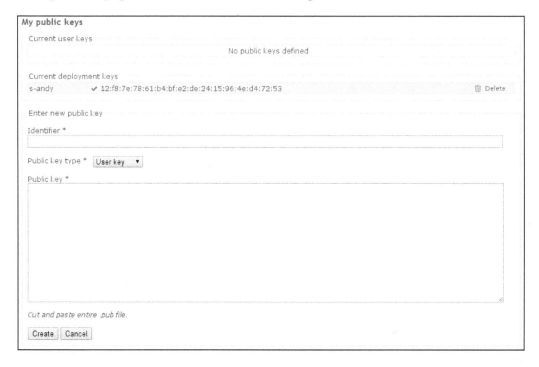

Here, you need to paste the content of your public key file (it usually has a `.pub` extension).

However, as you have probably noticed in a previous screenshot, SSH is not the only protocol that is supported by the Git Hosting plugin for accessing its repositories. Thus, by default, it assumes that you have also configured HTTP for your Git server. But that's not all! Additionally, it supports the proprietary Git protocol (if the **Enable Git Daemon** option is enabled for the repository), GoLang, and Git-Annex. All of the enabled protocols are represented in **Repository access links** as buttons. By the way, the box with these links is also displayed on the project's **Overview** page (if the project has a Gitolite repository, of course).

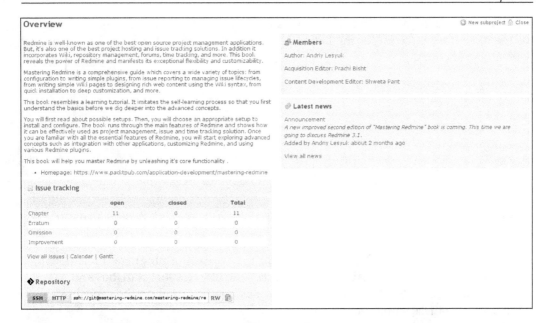

These access links (**SSH, HTTP**) can also be seen on the repository page, which also has some other improvements that are provided by the Git Hosting plugin. For example, the sidebar of this page looks like in the following screenshot:

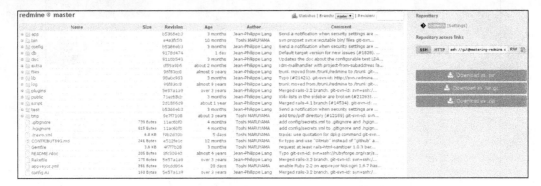

Another improvement is support for the GitHub-style README, which is shown on the repository page under the **Latest revisions** block (if such a file exists in the repository, of course):

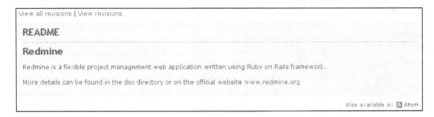

As on GitHub, this README file uses the Markdown formatter, even if you are using Textile for the rest of the system.

Another really cool and important feature of the Git Hosting plugin is the comprehensive repository statistics that replace the native short statistics and become available under the **Statistics** link, which can be found on the repository page. Here are these statistics:

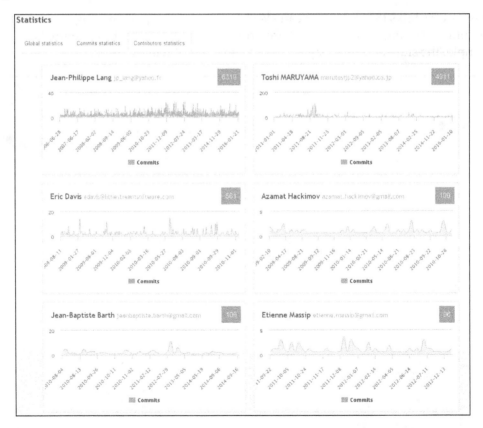

In this screenshot, you see just one of the tabs. It looks much like the statistics on GitHub, right?

Among other features that are provided by this amazing plugin are the following:

- Automatic creation of repositories on the Gitolite server. In this way, the plugin does the same job as the `reposman.rb` tool (this tool was described in *Chapter 3, Configuring Redmine*) but, unlike the latter, it does this job on-the-fly. Additionally, it can automatically create repositories for new projects.
- Support for GitHub-style post-receive URLs. In this way, Redmine will be able to notify third-party applications about new changes that have been made to the repository.
- The plugin can automatically mirror the repository to third-party Git servers, for example, to GitHub.
- The plugin can also restrict some branches to specific Redmine users and groups.

As you can see, it's a powerful and complex plugin that depends on third-party systems, such as SSH server and Gitolite. Therefore, its installation procedure is, unfortunately, quite complicated.

 This plugin also requires the Redmine Bootstrap Kit plugin to be installed. Detailed installation instructions for these two plugins are available at `http://redmine-git-hosting.io/get_started`.

The Agile plugin

Agile methodologies are intended to make software development processes adaptive, iterative, and evolutionary. While Agile is in fact more about project planning and collaboration between team members, it may also need certain features to be present in the project management tools that are used by the team. Unfortunately, the Redmine core does not come with any special agile-specific functionality, but luckily such a functionality can be found in some plugins for Redmine.

The Agile plugin by Kirill Bezrukov is the most popular Redmine plugin that is intended to assist in agile software development. Thus, it is so popular that it's even pre-installed by some hosting providers that offer Redmine in images or as SaaS (for example, BitNami, Plan.io, and so on; see also *Chapter 2, Installing Redmine*). But unfortunately, it's not completely free—there is the light free version and the PRO commercial one.

The agile-related functionality is provided by this plugin as a project module. So it must be enabled for the project, what can be done under the **Modules** tab of the project's **Settings** page, as shown here:

Here, this plugin is listed as the **Agile** project module. Alternatively, you can enable it for all new projects under the **Projects** tab of the system **Settings** page, which can be found in the **Administration** menu.

When the project module is enabled, the new **Agile** tab is added to the project menu, like this:

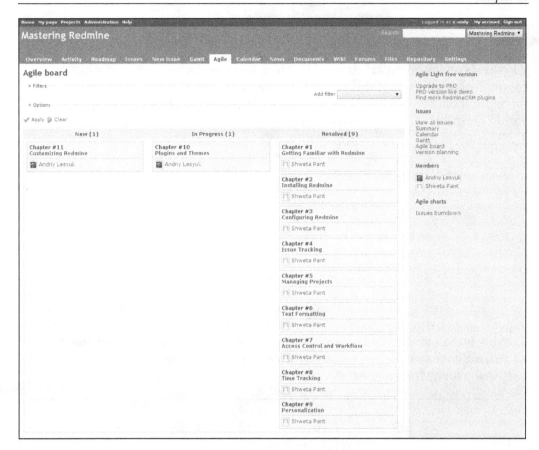

What you see in this screenshot is known as an agile task board. The main purpose of such boards is to visualize the development process and, therefore, to help detect any problems that are related to it. That's also the reason why such boards are usually used in the real world (that is, not in an electronic form) and are kept in a location where most team members can see them. Nevertheless, the virtual board may also be needed sometimes—for such cases, you can use Redmine with the Agile plugin.

Filters, which you can see at the top of this page, are in fact the same as on the issue list. However, **Options** are specific to the Agile board. Here they are:

Here, **Board columns** are issues statuses which should be used as the columns of the board. And, **Card fields** are issue fields that should be shown in **cards** on the board.

Also cards on the board are draggable. Thus, you can change their order in the column, what can be useful if you believe that some cards are more important and therefore should be on top. But you can also drag them to other columns, what would mean changing their issue status.

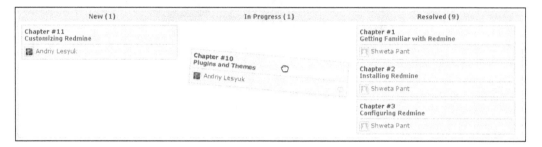

By the way, when you hover the mouse arrow over a card, the comment 💬 icon appears in its bottom-right corner—this can also be seen in the previous screenshot. Clicking on this icon allows you to quickly add a comment to the card/issue. When added, the comment is shown within the card until you refresh the page. This can be seen in the following screenshots:

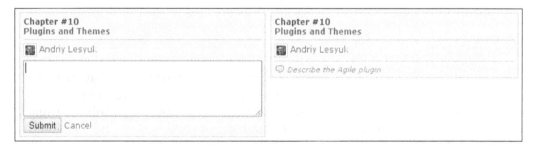

This is, in fact, an ordinary issue note and it will also be shown on the issue page.

But this is not the only board that is provided by the plugin. In the **Issues** section on the sidebar of an issue page, you can see the new **Version planning** link (for example, in the second screenshot of this subsection). If you open this link, another board will be opened. On that board, you can drag issues between versions, in this way assigning the issue to a different version (much like the way you would change the issue status using the previous board).

Additionally, the Agile plugin comes with the **burn-down chart**. This chart can be opened if you click on the **Issues burndown** link under the **Agile charts** label on the sidebar. Here is a sample of the chart:

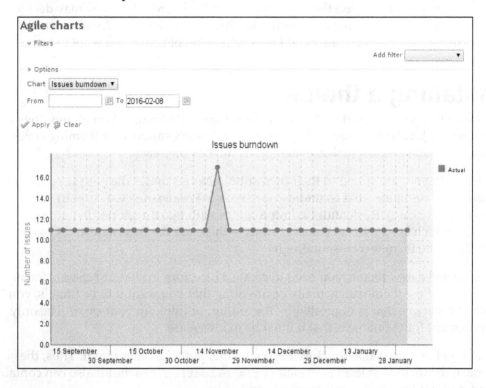

This chart is another well-known Agile tool that shows how much work is left to do. Moreover, it can be considered to be essential for issue tracking applications such as Redmine.

 The Agile plugin can be obtained from:
http://www.redminecrm.com/projects/agile

This is the only functionality that is available in the light free version of this amazing plugin. The PRO version (which unfortunately costs a lot at the time of writing) comes with many more features, such as the ability to configure and save boards, the ability to group cards on the board, different colors for cards based on issue fields, and more charts.

You can play with the PRO version of the plugin online using this URL:
http://demo.redminecrm.com/projects/agile/agile/board

For a good agile experience, your task board should not just reflect the issue statuses. Instead, if you want to use the agile methodology and its task board practice with the help of the Agile plugin, you should adjust the issue statuses so that they better reflect your processes and then use them as columns on the board. Thus, you may decide that you want to use it as a more specific Kanban or scrum board. In other words, before using this plugin, you should know what kind of board you want to have.

Installing a theme

Redmine themes are based on CSS and often come with images. Sometimes, they can also include JavaScript code. But, generally, Redmine's support for theming is very basic. Nevertheless, this makes installing its themes very easy.

Redmine themes are stored in their own subdirectories under the `public/themes` directory of Redmine (that is, under `/opt/redmine/redmine-3.2.0/public/themes` in my case). By default Redmine comes with two directories in `public/themes`, which are `alternate` and `classic` — these are the **Alternate** and **Classic** core Redmine themes correspondingly.

So, to install a new theme, you need to create a directory in `public/themes` for it. The name of the theme can actually be anything that you want it to be (that is, you can use the name that is suggested by the author, or think up your own). The only requirement for the name is that it must be in lowercase.

After you have created a directory for the theme, put all its files into it. Thus, the theme must include at least `stylesheets/application.css`, but it also can contain images under the `images` subdirectory, and so on.

When finished, you need to restart Redmine in order to load the new themes:

```
$ sudo service apache2 reload
```

Finally, to switch to a new theme, navigate to the **Administration | Settings | Display** tab, and select its name from the drop-down list of the **Theme** field. Then click on **Save**.

That's it! Enjoy!

 Uninstalling a theme is even easier. Just remove its directory and restart Redmine.

A review of some themes

Now let's review some of the most beautiful themes for Redmine (in my personal opinion).

Remember, however, that by selecting a theme, you actually choose which existing site you want your Redmine to look like. Public themes, especially nice-looking ones, are used widely and often. So, if you can afford it, order a unique theme for your website.

The Basecamp theme

The Basecamp theme was created by Peter Theill. It is a port of 37signals' Basecamp theme for Redmine:

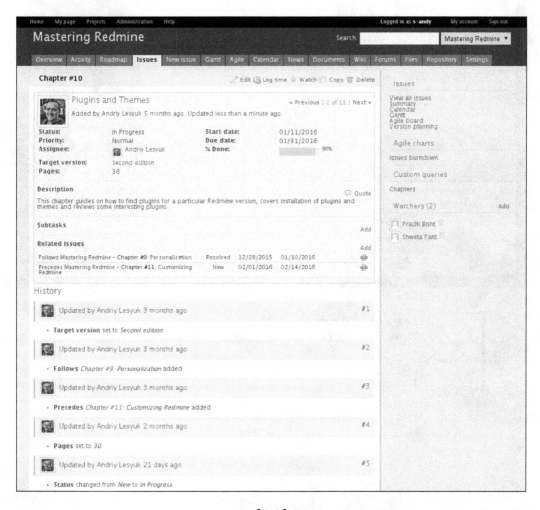

This theme can be downloaded from `https://github.com/theill/redmine-basecamp-theme`.

The Modula Mojito theme

This theme was originally authored by Eero Louhenperä from Modula.

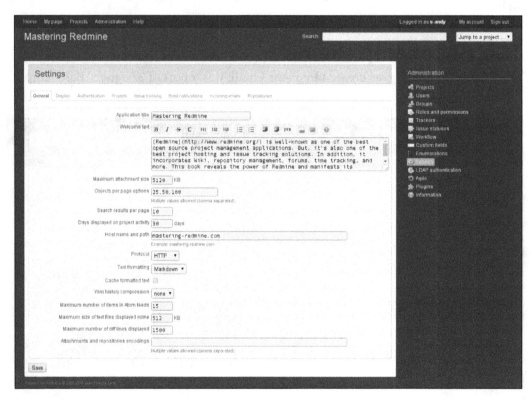

 Later, the maintenance of this theme was taken over by Steven Jones from Computer minds, so now it can be found at `https://github.com/computerminds/modula-mojito`. Unfortunately, it has not been updated for a long time (3 years).

The A1 theme

This theme was created by Kirill Bezrukov. It is based on Ronin's theme (a time tracking application).

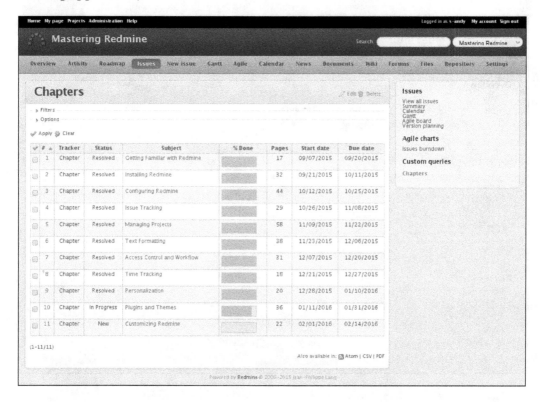

 This theme can be downloaded from http://www. redminecrm.com/pages/a1-theme.

The Highrise theme

This theme was also created by Kirill Bezrukov. It is based on 37signals' Highrise CRM theme.

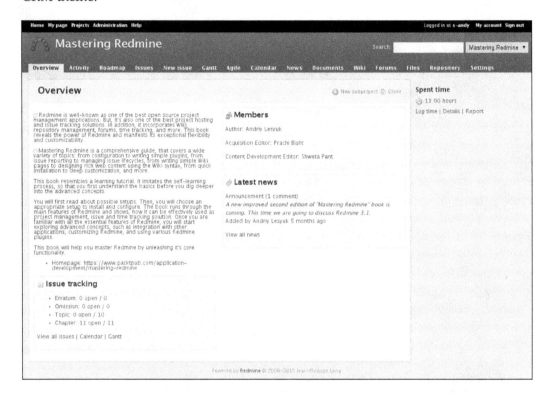

 This one can be downloaded from `http://www.redminecrm.com/pages/highrise-theme`.

Summary

In this chapter, I wanted to share my experience of searching for functional Redmine plugins, as I personally find this process quite complicated and, most likely, you won't be able to avoid using plugins. In other words, I wanted you to feel easy about finding and installing the plugins that you'll need.

To demonstrate what can be done with plugins, we reviewed some of them. Of course, we have still ignored many interesting, useful, and popular ones, but the goal of this chapter was not to review all of them (as this chapter would be too huge). I wanted to draw your attention to some of the plugins to show what interesting things can be done with them.

I assume that you have searched for and found plugins that you will use, and you have already chosen and installed a theme that will become the face of your Redmine installation. If you have done this, you have just done the basic customization that gets done by everyone who uses Redmine. The next chapter is about advanced customization—it describes how to turn Redmine into a unique website. Therefore, the next chapter is for project managers, site owners, Redmine administrators, and server administrators.

11
Customizing Redmine

The previous two chapters were about what could be called **customization**. And that's natural, because after we have learned the application, we will want to make it fit our needs better. Thus, personalization is a customization that is made by users, using the permissions that they have. Installing plugins is a customization that can be done by server administrators (don't confuse them with Redmine administrators). However, those chapters describe common things that are done by everyone who installs Redmine. There are also advanced things that you may want to do, for example, if you use Redmine for a public forge website.

In such cases, people usually seek to customize the look and feel (for example, the theme), add some custom content to a few pages, and so on. During this customization step, people also usually ask experts for help. Thus, they sometimes ask them to develop plugins to implement different ideas, though plugins are not always needed. Also, during this step, people often customize Redmine by themselves and often do it wrong. So, what is the right way to customize Redmine, and what can you do without developing custom plugins? These are the topics that we will discuss now.

So, in this chapter, we will cover the following topics:

- Custom fields
- Customizing with Textile
- Customizing the theme
- Customizing with a plugin
- Helping Redmine

Custom fields

I believe that support for custom fields is essential for any issue tracker, and luckily Redmine implements this feature very well. Thus, in Redmine, custom fields can be defined for issues, projects, versions, users, groups, time entries, and so on (even for some objects that are provided by third-party plugins). Custom fields enrich these objects by allowing you to add properties that are missing. Additionally, they can be used, for example, in search filters. In other words, to a great extent, custom fields let you change the way Redmine looks and behaves. So, this makes them a tool for advanced customization (and that's why they are reviewed in this chapter).

> Be sure to plan the use of custom fields. Thus, avoid adding custom fields that are going to be rarely used, as too many custom fields can confuse your users.

Custom fields can be managed on the **Custom fields** page, which can be found in the **Administration** menu. Check out the following screenshot:

This page has tabs that correspond to different customized objects, which have custom fields defined (currently, I have a custom field for issues only, as can be seen in the screenshot). So, each tab contains the list of custom fields for the particular object.

The **New custom field** link can be used to create custom fields. So, let's see what happens if we click on it:

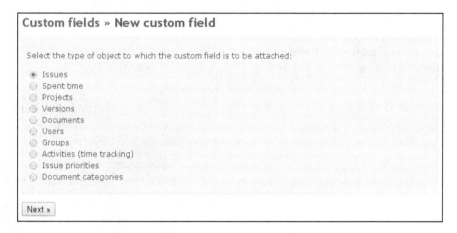

As you can see, Redmine uses a wizard type of dialog for the creation of a custom field. The first page of this wizard asks you to select the type of object for which you want to create it. When you click on the **Next »** button, you see the following form:

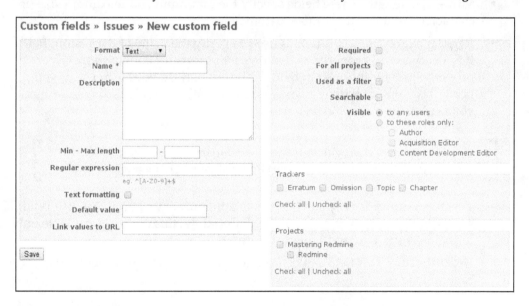

This form is for issue custom fields. Forms for other objects can differ, but most elements remain the same (actually, the form for issue custom fields is the most complete one). The same form is also used for editing a custom field when you click on its name in the list, which is shown on the **Custom fields** page (see the first screenshot of this section).

The block in the left-hand side column contains properties of the custom field and does not differ for different customized objects, but it does differ for different formats of custom fields (they will be reviewed later). The following are the explanations of these properties:

- **Format**: This field allows you to select the format of the custom field. As each format has its own set of available properties, we will review the supported formats separately in a subsection a little later.

- **Name**: This is the only required property, and it should contain an easy-to-understand and intelligible name for the custom field. This name will be shown in forms and on some pages of the customized objects.

- **Description**: This field can be used to add a subtitle to the name. The subtitle will be shown when the user hovers the mouse arrow over the name of the custom field, as can be seen in the following screenshot:

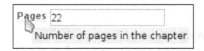

- **Min – Max length**: These fields specify the minimum and maximum size (in characters) of the value for the custom field.

- **Regular expression**: This field is used to verify the value of the custom field. It is a very useful property, as it allows you to ensure that users specify proper values for the custom field. Unfortunately, to be able to use it, you need to be familiar with regular expressions. Still, I highly recommend that you learn them.

 You can learn regular expressions using interactive tutorials and practical examples that can be found at: http://regexone.com/.

- **Text formatting**: This option decides whether users will be able to use Wiki syntax in the value of the custom field. Certainly, this option is available only for fields of the **Text** and **Long text** formats.

- **Default value**: This field can be used to specify the default value for the custom field.

Changing the way values of custom fields are displayed

in The Extended Fields plugin can be used to define custom template files for certain custom fields (by format or by name). In this way, you can render **Boolean** values as check marks, Twitter usernames as Follow buttons, and so on. To learn more about the Extended Fields plugin, check out `http://projects.andriylesyuk.com/projects/extended-fields/wiki/Custom-fields-view-customization`.

There are also more specific properties that are available only for certain formats of custom fields. Thus, the **Link values to URL** property, which allows you to convert the value into a link, when rendered, is available for all formats except **Link**, **Long text**, **User**, and **Version**. For this property, you need to specify a URL that can optionally contain the following variables:

- `%value%`: This will be replaced by the value of the custom field.

- `%id%`: This will be replaced by the ID of the customized object, for example, by the issue ID, if the custom field was added for issues.

- `%project_id%`: This will be replaced by the numeric ID of the project the customized object is associated with (if any). As such numeric project IDs are used internally only, it is not likely that you'll need to use this variable.

- `%project_identifier%`: This will be replaced by the identifier of the project that the customized object is associated with (if any).

- `%m1%`, `%m2%`, and so on (that is, `%mX%`): These will be replaced by capture group matches. These variables are available only if you have specified a regular expression for the custom field and if the specified expression contains capture groups. **Capture groups** are parts of the regular expression, that are in parentheses. For example, the regular expression `^([A-Z]+)-([0-9]+)$` contains two capture groups: `([A-Z]+)` and `([0-9]+)`. If the value of the custom field is `ABC-123` (which matches our regular expression), then `%m1%` will be replaced by `ABC` and `%m2%` – by `123`.

Suppose you want to have an issue custom field, that will contain the ID of the issue in the JIRA tracker and the value of which should be rendered as a link to the external issue page. In this case, you can specify something like the following in the **Link values to URL** field: `https://company.atlassian.net/browse/%value%`.

Custom fields of **Boolean**, **Key/value list**, **List**, **User**, and **Version** formats additionally have the **Display** property, which controls how the custom field is rendered in forms. Here it is:

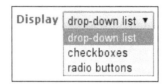

The **radio buttons** option is available only for **Boolean** custom fields though.

Finally, custom fields of **Key/value list**, **List**, **User**, and **Version** formats come with the **Multiple values** option. If this option is enabled, users will be able to select several values for the custom field.

These are still not all the possible properties for custom fields. But the rest are specific to certain formats, and therefore, they will be reviewed along with those formats later.

Custom field options

The upper box in the right-hand side column of the custom field form, which was shown earlier, contains custom field options. The following table shows the availability of these options for different customized objects:

Customized object	Required	Editable	For all projects	Used as a filter	Searchable	Visible
Issues	✓		✓	✓	✓	✓
Time entries	✓			✓		
Projects	✓			✓	✓	✓
Versions	✓			✓		
Documents	✓					
Users	✓	✓		✓		✓
Groups	✓			✓		
Activities	✓					
Issue priorities	✓					
Document categories	✓					

Now let's discuss each of them.

The Required option

The **Required** option, which is available for all customized objects, decides whether or not the value of the custom field is required.

 For issues, you can have more flexible control over whether the custom field should be required using the **Fields permissions** tab of the **Workflow** page. This tab and page were reviewed in *Chapter 7, Access Control and Workflow*.

The Editable option

The **Editable** option specifies whether users should be able to see and edit the value of the custom field. This option is currently available only for the **User** object. So, user custom fields that have this option disabled will be seen only by administrators (via the **Users** page, which can be found in the **Administration** menu).

The For all projects option

The **For all projects** option, which is currently used only by issue custom fields, determines whether the custom field will be available for all projects automatically. If this option is not enabled, project managers will still be able to enable the custom field for the particular project in the project's settings (using the **Custom fields** block under the **Information** tab of the project's **Settings** page).

Additionally, the custom field form includes the **Projects** block for issues. In this block, administrators can select projects for which the custom field should be enabled. This is an alternative way to do what can be done in the project's settings. Certainly, this is possible only if the **For all projects** option is disabled.

 Do not forget to additionally enable the custom field for trackers that are available in the selected projects.

The Used as a filter option

The **Used as a filter** option allows the custom field to be used as a filter, in, for example, issue custom queries. It's available for issues, time entries, projects, versions, users, and groups. Take a look at the following screenshots:

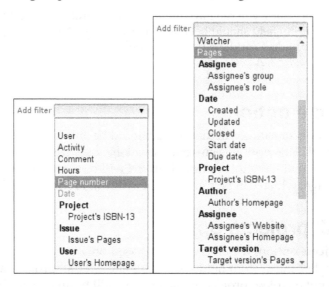

To the left, you can see the available filters for issue custom queries that are used under the **Issues**, **Gantt**, and **Calendar** tabs of the project. In this list, the selected **Pager** is an issue custom field. But this list also includes project, user, version, and group custom fields, under appropriate labels and with appropriate prefixes. Thus, **Project's ISBN-13** is a project custom field (which has the name **ISBN-13**), **Author's Homepage** and **Assignee's Homepage** are user custom fields (which have the name **Homepage**), **Assignee's Website** is a group custom field, and **Target version's Pages** is a version custom field. Certainly, the **Used as a filter** option is enabled for these fields and that's why they are here.

To the right of the previous screenshots, you can see the available filters for the time report (this report can be opened, for example, by clicking on the **Report** link on the sidebar of the project's **Overview** page, if the Time tracking module is enabled). In this list, the selected **Page number** is a time entry custom field. Additionally, as you can see, the list can include **Project**, **Issue**, and **User** custom fields if the **Used as a filter** option is enabled for them.

The Searchable option

The **Searchable** option determines whether the value of the custom field will be inspected when Redmine performs a search in customized objects. This option is available only for projects and issues, as they can be searched using the Redmine search form. Here is this form:

This search form can be accessed via the **Search** link, which can be found in the top-right corner of the Redmine interface (near the search bar).

The Visible option

The **Visible** option controls whether the value of the custom field will be displayed on open pages of the customized object (for example, on the project's **Overview** page or the user profile). In other words, if this option is disabled, the value of the custom field will be visible only in edit mode of the customized object (for example, on the project's **Settings** page or in the user account, which is seen only by administrators).

Also, for project and user custom fields, this option is available as a checkbox, while for issue custom fields, it allows you to select either all users or only certain user roles (as can be seen in the third screenshot of this section).

Custom field formats

Sometimes, you may need to store a string in a custom field. At other times, you may want to store a date or a boolean value. Such a data type of the custom field is controlled by the **Format** property. So, let's check out what options it has.

> **The Computed Custom Field plugin**
>
> Sometimes, it may be necessary to have a custom field with a value, that is calculated from other fields. This can be done with the Computed Custom Field format, which is provided by the plugin, that can be found at: https://github.com/annikoff/redmine_plugin_computed_custom_field.

The Boolean format

The **Boolean** format should be used if the custom field has to accept only *Yes* or *No*. When this format is selected, the properties block looks like what is shown in the following screenshot:

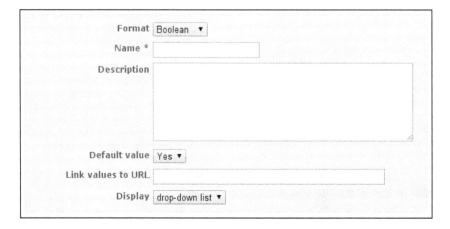

Using the **Display** property, you can have a custom field of this type rendered in forms as a drop-down list, checkboxes, or radio buttons.

The Date format

The **Date** format can be used to store a date in a custom field. The input element for such custom fields is rendered with the calendar 📅 icon, clicking on which opens the calendar dialog. This small dialog is intended to help users select a proper date value, as shown in the following screenshot:

The properties block for custom fields of the **Date** format also differs. Thus, the **Default value** property comes with the icon that opens the calendar dialog as well.

The Float format

The **Float** format of custom fields was designed to store floating-point numbers. Such custom fields additionally support the **Min – Max length** property, which can be used to limit the number of digits in the value, and the **Regular expression** property, which can be used, for example, to allow only positive numbers.

The Integer format

The **Integer** format of custom fields allows you to store integer values. It uses the same properties block as the **Float** format.

The Key/value list format

In many cases, custom fields are needed to ask users to select a value from a set of options, for example, a project license — from the list of available licenses, a resolution type from the list of resolution types, and so on. This is what can be done with the **Key/value list** format.

An unusual thing about this format is that the initial form for it does not include any field for specifying possible values for the custom field. Such a field appears only after you have created the custom field of this format, as shown in the following screenshot:

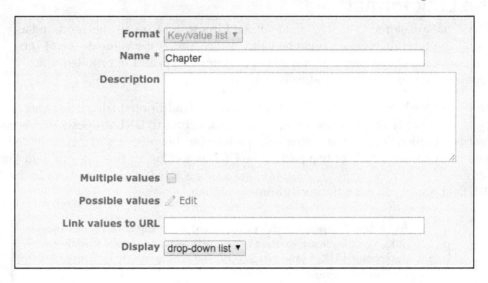

So, right after creating a custom field of this format, you should click on the **Edit** link of the **Possible values** field to add possible values for it. This link will open the following form:

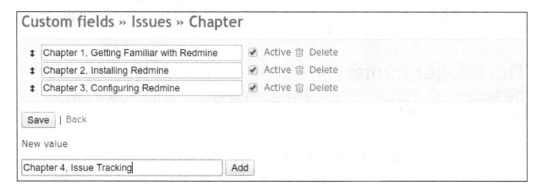

Using this page, you can manage the value list of this particular custom field. The same order of values will be used in forms where users will select them. So, you can change it by dragging values using their arrow ✴ icons to the left. The **Active** checkbox controls whether it will be possible to select the particular value in forms.

The Link format

Values that are stored in custom fields of the **Link** format are always rendered as links. Therefore, such values must be valid URLs. Also, if the value does not start with `protocol://` (where `protocol` is `http`, `https`, `ftp`, and so on), Redmine prepends `http://` to it automatically.

The properties block for the **Link** format includes an additional **URL** field. This field in fact, has exactly the same meaning as the **Link values to URL** property that was described earlier. So, if you define a URL pattern for this property of a custom field, users will need to specify only a part of the URL as a value for that custom field (for example, if you enter `https://company.atlassian.net/browse/%value%` in the **URL** field, users will need to specify something like `ABC-123`).

As values of custom fields of this format are going to be rendered as links, you may want to use a regular expression to make sure that the specified URLs (and rendered links) are correct. Thus, you can use this expression:

`^(https?:\/\/)?([\da-z-]+\.)+[a-z]{2,6}[\/\w\.-]*$`

The List format

The **List** format very much resembles **Key/value list**. The difference between these two formats is in how their possible values are specified. Thus, for the **List** format, the **Possible values** field is rendered as a text area, where you just enter options from which users will need to select a value for the custom field. Each such option should be on its own line. And, yes, the **Possible values** field is present in the initial form for this format, so you can specify possible values while creating a custom field.

To avoid typos, copy and paste a value for the **Default value** property from the **Possible values** text area.

The Long text format

The **Long text** format should be used when you want to allow users to enter a large volume of free text. In forms, custom fields of this format are rendered as text areas, like the one which is used for the **Default value** property in this screenshot:

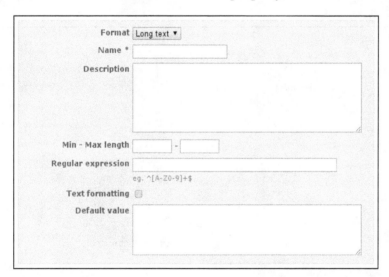

As it was mentioned at the beginning of this section, if the **Text formatting** option is enabled, users will be able to use Wiki syntax for the custom field.

Unfortunately, text areas for custom fields for which you have enabled the **Text formatting** option won't include the Wiki toolbar. So, you also need to let users know somehow that they can use Wiki syntax for such custom field. For example, you can write this in **Description**.

The Text format

The **Text** format is very much like **Long text**, except that it accepts shorter values and is therefore rendered in forms as a textbox. The properties block for this format is also similar to the one that is used for **Long text**, but additionally, contains the **Link values to URL** property (besides, the **Default value** property is rendered as a textbox too—of course).

The User format

The **User** format can be used to allow choosing a project member as a value for the custom field (for example, it can be used for a second assignee, QA, or code reviewer).

 This format is available only for issues, time entries, versions, documents, and projects.

The properties block for this format looks like what is shown in the following screenshot:

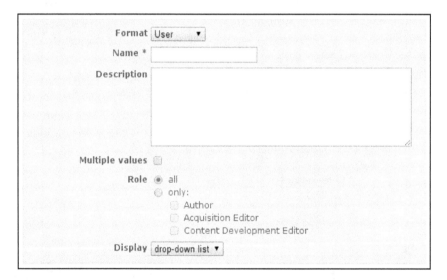

As you can see, the list of project members which can be chosen as values for the custom field can be limited to specific roles.

The Version format

The **Version** format allows you to select a project version as a value for the custom field (for example, it can be used to specify a stable version for the project).

This format is available only for issues, time entries, versions, documents, and projects.

The properties block for this format is very similar to the one for the **User** format, except that instead of the **Role** property, it includes the **Status** property, as shown in this screenshot:

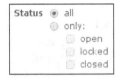

Customized objects

Each customized object uses custom fields in its own way. That's what we are going to discuss in this subsection.

- **Issues**: Redmine is an issue tracker. Therefore, it's no wonder that its support for custom fields is most advanced for issues. Thus, in addition to the custom field page (that is, **Custom fields** in the **Administration** menu), issue custom fields can be managed on the **Workflow** page (in the same **Administration** menu). There, you can make them read-only or required depending on the issue status (see also *Chapter 7, Access Control and Workflow*).

  Values for issue custom fields can be specified in the issue form, but it's not that they can be seen only on the issue page. You can also show them in the issue list and, use them in custom queries and even in time reports.

   If you want to create a **Resolution** custom field, make it read-only for all issue statuses except closed ones.

- **Spent time**: Custom fields can also be added to time entries. The values of such custom fields can be edited in the log time form and used in the time report.

- **Projects**: Project custom fields can be used to collect more details about the project. The values for such custom fields can be specified under the **Information** tab of the project's **Settings** page. If the **Visible** option is enabled for a custom field, its value will be displayed on the project's **Overview** page (under the description in the left-hand column). Also, the values of project custom fields can be used in issue custom queries.

- **Versions**: Project versions can have custom fields as well. The values for such custom fields can be specified in the version form and viewed on the roadmap and individual version pages. Additionally, such custom fields can be used in issue custom queries.

- **Documents**: Document custom fields can be edited in the document form and viewed on the document page.

- **Users**: In my opinion, the default Redmine user profile is too scant, as it provides too little information that can be useful to other Redmine users. Thus, you may want it to include Facebook and Twitter accounts, a phone number, a phone extension, a company, a position, and much more. Luckily, such data can be added to the user profile with the help of custom fields.

  The values of user custom fields can be edited in the user account (via the **Users** page of the **Administration** menu) by administrators, or in the user profile (via the **My account** link in the top-right corner) by users. The latter is possible only if the **Editable** option is enabled for such custom fields. If the **Visible** option is enabled, the value will also be shown on the user page. Additionally, a user custom field can be referred to by issue custom queries.

- **Groups**: User groups can have custom fields as well. The values for such custom fields can be specified in the group edit form (which can be accessed via the **Groups** page of the **Administration** menu). Unfortunately, such custom fields are not shown anywhere else. However, they can be used by issue custom queries (if the **Used as a filter** option is enabled).

- **Activities (time tracking)**: Time tracking activities are **enumerations** that, like other enumerations, can be managed on the **Enumerations** page of the **Administration** menu. Enumerations are simple objects that allow you to store list-style values. These objects also support custom fields.

  Custom fields for time tracking activities can be managed in the enumeration edit form. This form can be opened from the **Enumerations** page, or under the **Activities (time tracking)** tab of the project's **Settings** page.

 Remember that by editing an activity in the project settings, you make a copy of the corresponding system activity.

- **Issue priorities**: Issue priorities is another enumeration that supports custom fields. The values of such custom fields can be managed only in the enumeration edit form, that is, on the **Enumerations** page of the **Administration** menu.

- **Document categories**: Document categories is an enumeration too, and like the other enumerations, it supports custom fields. The values of such custom fields can be managed in the enumeration edit form, which can be opened from the **Enumerations** page of the **Administration** menu.

Customizing with Textile

Once, I was asked to create a custom plugin for Redmine to improve the look and feel of its start page (which can be opened by clicking on the **Home** link) by adding buttons, links, sections, and other similar stuff. My answer was, *You don't need a plugin to do that.*

Textile is very simplified HTML. Therefore, it can't be used to create full-featured HTML pages, but for some things, it may appear to be sufficient. However, to achieve the necessary results, you will most likely need to use the most advanced features of Textile. Also, like for HTML, you can't learn how to create a good look and feel with Textile—you may only understand the concept. You will need to inject your own creativity to get what you need. Therefore, in this section, we will review some interesting customization examples that should help you understand the technique.

> **Wiki pages as tabs in the project menu**
>
> The Wiki Extensions plugin, which was created by Haruyuki Iida, allows you to add Wiki pages to the project menu as tabs (configured per project). You can find more information about this plugin at `http://www.r-labs.org/projects/r-labs/wiki/Wiki_Extensions_en`.

The things that we'll discuss here will look tricky, so you may wonder why they should be preferred over writing a plugin. The answer is: because Textile formatting will survive upgrades of Redmine, whereas a plugin will most likely need to be updated.

> As Markdown is less powerful at the time of writing this book, many things that are discussed in this section, are not possible to implement using it. For this reason, Markdown is not reviewed here.

Styled boxes

CSS classes that are used for the Redmine interface can also be used to create information boxes inside the Wiki content. For example, check out the following code:

```
p(conflict). A warning message.
p(box). Rendered as a box.
```

It will be rendered into this:

⚠ A warning message.

Rendered as a box.

 You can also add custom CSS rules to the Redmine theme, specifically to use them in the Wiki content. We'll talk about this in the *Customizing the theme* section.

Using icons

You can also put an icon before the text, for example:

```
You can insert "(icon icon-fav)a link with an icon":http://www.
andriylesyuk.com or even %(icon icon-checked)not a link%...
```

This Textile code will be rendered as follows:

You can insert ☆ a link with an icon or even ✓ not a link...

Here, we used icon CSS classes of the Redmine interface and the magic % marker.

Table-based layout

In modern web design, everyone prefers to build the page layout using divs instead of tables (the old-style approach). But in Textile, we don't have enough control over divs. Nevertheless, we can still use tables:

```
table{border:none}.
|{border:none}.eBook: %{color:#bbb}£18.99%|{border:none;padding:1em}.%
{font-size:1.5em}£15.19%
```

```
save 20%|{border:none}.!http://www.packtpub.com/sites/all/themes/
packt_new/images/addtocart.gif!:https://www.packtpub.com/application-
development/mastering-redmine|
|{border:none}.Print + free eBook + free PacktLib access to the
book: %{color:#bbb}£49.98%|{border:none;padding:1em}.%{font-
size:1.5em}£27.89%
save 44%|{border:none}.!http://www.packtpub.com/sites/all/themes/
packt_new/images/addtocart.gif!:https://www.packtpub.com/application-
development/mastering-redmine|
```

This tricky code produces the following result:

In this example, we defined the CSS style for the table (`table{border:none}.`) and its cells (for example, `|{border:none;padding:1em}.`). Also, we used the magic `%` marker (for example, `%{color:#bbb}£49.98%`).

Customizing the theme

A common scenario of customization is when users first choose a theme for Redmine and then slightly modify it to make it fit their needs. As a result, such users lose the possibility to upgrade that theme in the future (this is because it henceforth contains their changes, which are going to be overridden during an upgrade).

Suppose you want to customize the default Redmine theme. Instead of modifying its files under the `public/stylesheets` directory, let's create a new theme based on it. To do this, let's create the `mastering-redmine` subdirectory for our theme (this will be its name) in the `public/themes` directory. In the newly created directory, create the `stylesheets` subdirectory, and the `application.css` file in it.

Now add the following code to that CSS file:

```
@import url(../../../stylesheets/application.css);

#top-menu { background: #373c40; }
#header { background-color: #e7692c; }
#main-menu li a:hover { background-color: #d92238; }
```

Here, the first line imports CSS rules from the **Default** theme. So, in my customized version of the theme, I needed to include only the difference (thus, I changed the background colors of the page header and its menus).

 If you want to customize a theme other than Default, for example, **Alternate**, you need to change the first line to the following:

```
@import url(../../../themes/alternate/stylesheets/
application.css);
```

To apply your customized theme, don't forget to select it under the **Display** tab of the system **Settings** page and reload Redmine.

Customizing with a plugin

The most advanced customization can be accomplished by writing a custom plugin. With a plugin, you can customize anything in Redmine. Of course, to write a full-featured plugin, you need to be familiar with Ruby, Rails, the Redmine API, JavaScript, HTML, CSS, the concept of web development, and so on. But who said that you need a full-featured plugin?

As you already know, the files of a plugin are kept in a separate directory that is named after the plugin and located under the `plugins` directory of Redmine. So, when Redmine is upgraded, such files remain untouched. On the other side, many users put their customizations into the Redmine core files that are overridden on upgrades. So why not use a special plugin for this instead?

The Redmine plugin API is quite flexible. In particular, it allows you to:

- Override any core view file without touching the original one
- Add custom content to some views
- Load additional CSS style sheets, JavaScript files, and so on

This makes it possible to use a plugin as a tool for customization. And for this, you do not need to write any complicated Ruby code—you can simply use small code snippets to activate different capabilities of the plugin. That's what you'll learn in this section.

Of course, to be able to customize the look and feel, you need to be familiar with HTML at least. Familiarity with CSS is optional, but it will be very useful.

Writing a simple plugin

Before creating a plugin, you need to choose a name for it. I'll use the name `mastering_redmine`.

 Name your customization plugin after your organization or website. Use alphanumeric characters and underscores.

Next, you need to create a subdirectory for the plugin in the `plugins` directory of Redmine. The created subdirectory must have the name of the plugin. In other words, the full path for my plugin will be `/opt/redmine/redmine-3.2.0/plugins/mastering_redmine`.

After this, in the newly created directory, you need to create the `init.rb` file (the entry point for the plugin) and put the following code into it:

```
require 'redmine'

Rails.logger.info 'Starting Mastering Redmine Plugin for Redmine'

Redmine::Plugin.register :mastering_redmine do
    name 'Mastering Redmine customization'
    author 'Andriy Lesyuk'
    author_url 'http://www.andriylesyuk.com'
    description 'Website customization using the plugin.'
    url 'http://mastering-redmine.com'
    version '2.0.0'
end
```

Of course, you need to use your plugin name instead of `:mastering_redmine` (but keep the colon at the beginning). What should be changed in the rest of the code, I believe, is quite clear.

When you're done, restart Redmine. Now you should see your plugin listed on the **Plugins** page of the **Administration** menu, as shown in the following screenshot:

Plugins		
Mastering Redmine customization		
Website customization using the plugin. http://mastering-redmine.com	Andriy Lesyuk	2.0.0

At the moment, this plugin does nothing (besides putting itself into the plugin list), but that's only for now.

Customizing view files

Redmine uses the **Model-View-Controller** (**MVC**) architecture, in which view files store the interface information. Most of the content of these files is just HTML code (the rest of the content is eRuby, JavaScript, and so on). All such files are located under the app/views directory of Redmine. Moreover, any such file can be overridden just by copying it to the corresponding path under the plugin's app/views directory (in this case, the original file remains unchanged). So, let's see how this works by reviewing one of the most common customization tasks—adding a logo to the Redmine interface.

First, you need to create a directory for images in your plugin. Its path has to be assets/images. After you have done this, put the logo image into this directory.

Next, create the app/views/layouts directory in the plugin and copy the app/views/layouts/base.html.erb file from Redmine there (thus, the full target path in my case is plugins/mastering_redmine/app/views/layouts/base.html.erb).

Now, open your copy of the base.html.erb file and find this line of code (it's line 44 currently):

```
<h1><%= page_header_title %></h1>
```

This code renders the title of the page. Now, add the following line of code before that line:

```
<%= image_tag('mastering-redmine.png', :plugin => :mastering_redmine,
:style => 'float: left; padding-right: 1em;') %>
```

Here, mastering-redmine.png is the name of the logo image and :mastering_redmine (the colon is important) is the name of the plugin.

 Alternatively, the logo can be added using CSS (for example, by creating a custom theme). Thus, it can be specified as a background image for the #header block. However, if the #header area already has a background image (such an image can be set, for example, by a theme), the logo will override it. Anyway, the advantage of this method is that this customization most likely won't need to be updated after an upgrade of Redmine.

After saving the changes, you need to restart Redmine to apply them. Now, if you reload any Redmine page, you should see something like this:

 Always track the changes that you make to the copies of the Redmine core files, as you may need to make them again if those Redmine files are modified in an upgrade.

Using hooks

Redmine comes with support for **hooks**. Hooks are **callbacks** that can be used to inject custom content into some predefined places of certain Redmine views. If possible, it is better to use a hook to add a content to the view instead of making a copy of the view file. This is because, for hooks, you need to provide only the content itself and they are not affected by upgrades. So, let's check out how this works through another real-life example – let's add a message to the login page (for example, it can contain login instructions).

To be able to use hooks, you need to add a hook listener to the plugin. To do this, create the `lib` directory in the plugin and put the `mastering_redmine_hook.rb` file into it (actually, you can use any filename). Now, add the following code into the newly created file:

```
class MasteringRedmineHook < Redmine::Hook::ViewListener
    render_on :view_account_login_top,
              :partial => 'mastering_redmine/login'
end
```

Here, the name of the class, that is, `MasteringRedmineHook`, reflects the filename (your class name should reflect your filename too), `:view_account_login_top` is the name of the hook that is called on the login form, and the `:partial` option is set to the path to the view file that contains the custom content.

Now, you need to create the view file with the custom content that has to be added to the login form. First, you need to create the `mastering_redmine` directory in `app/views`, and then create the `_login.html.erb` file in it (note the `_` character at the beginning of the filename – it is required). Here, the name of the directory, `mastering_redmine`, and the name of file, `_login.html.erb`, are what forms the value of the `:partial` option. Now put your custom content, which can be just HTML, into this newly created file.

The Hooks Manager plugin

This plugin provides a nice interface for specifying custom content for many Redmine hooks (no need to write a plugin). Check it out at `http://projects.andriylesyuk.com/project/redmine/hooks-manager`.

Finally, you need to register the hook listener. To do this, just add the following line of code into the `init.rb` file (below `require 'redmine'`):

```
require_dependency 'mastering_redmine_hook'
```

Here, `mastering_redmine_hook` is the filename of the hook listener without extension.

Now, if you restart Redmine and go to the login page, you should see something like this:

Let's quickly check out what other hooks are provided by Redmine. The following table lists some of them:

Hook	Location
`:view_welcome_index_left`	Bottom of the left column, on the welcome page
`:view_welcome_index_right`	Bottom of the right column, on the welcome page
`:view_account_login_bottom`	Below the login form
`:view_layouts_base_content`	Below the content, on each page
`:view_projects_show_left`	Bottom of the left column, on the project overview page
`:view_projects_show_right`	Bottom of the right column, on the project overview page
`:view_issues_new_top`	Above the form, on the new issue page

A complete list of hooks that are provided by Redmine can be found at `http://www.redmine.org/projects/redmine/wiki/Hooks_List#View-hooks`.

Helping Redmine

There is one more way to customize Redmine—to modify Redmine itself, thus sharing your customization with other users. Any contribution is very important for free and open source projects, such as Redmine. An active and passionate community is what makes such projects good.

When most people hear about contribution to a free and open source project, they assume contribution in the form of some development, but in fact, there are many more areas where people can help. For example, this book helps Redmine by spreading information about it, teaching how to use it, and demonstrating its capabilities. Also, you have already helped Redmine by purchasing this book, not only because you can become a potential fan of this project, but also because Packt Publishing—the company that publishes this book—will pay a royalty to the Redmine team.

So let's discuss how else you can help Redmine:

- As it has already been mentioned, let's start with development. If you are a developer, you can help by contributing code or patches to Redmine. To be able to do this, you should be familiar with Ruby and Rails. But even if you are familiar with Perl, you can still help by improving `Redmine.pm`. You can help even more if you know HTML/CSS and/or JavaScript because these technologies are intensively used by Redmine and may need improvements. If you are familiar with neither of the aforementioned technologies, you can still help by, for example, developing a REST API client library for Redmine using the technologies that you are familiar with.

  Here are some links regarding development for Redmine:

  - General information: `http://www.redmine.org/projects/redmine/wiki/Contribute`
  - Subversion repository: `https://svn.redmine.org/redmine`
  - Git repository: `https://github.com/redmine/redmine`

- If you are a designer, you can make new themes for Redmine. This is an extremely important area, as good themes attract more users.

  - See also `http://www.redmine.org/projects/redmine/wiki/HowTo_create_a_custom_Redmine_theme`.

- You can write articles, blog posts, tutorials, and books, improve the source code documentation (it uses RDoc), and more. You can do this in English or any other language.

- Regarding other languages. You can also translate Redmine, its official or unofficial tutorials, and so on, into other languages.

  ○ See also `http://www.redmine.org/projects/redmine/wiki/ HowTo_translate_Redmine_in_your_own_language`.

- If you are just a user or are going to become a user of Redmine, do not hesitate to report bugs or suggest new features. If you are not sure whether something is a bug, you are still advised to open a discussion in the Redmine forum and ask the community. Many bugs are hard to find and not many people report them.

  ○ See also `http://www.redmine.org/projects/redmine/boards`.

- Finally, you can show your support for Redmine by making a donation.

  ○ See also `http://www.redmine.org/projects/redmine/wiki/ Donors`.

In a very similar way, you can help many free and open source plugins for Redmine.

Summary

If a Redmine installation is not customized, it's a demo. Even Redmine.org is customized (the ad on the sidebar, the plugins directory, and so on). All users prefer to customize applications that they are using. Many users of Redmine install some third-party plugins and a theme, but this can be considered a part of the installation and configuration. The real customization is what we discussed in this chapter.

Probably, some of you will never need the things that were described here (though I hope that the chapter was still interesting to you). But those of you who will will be able to save time and money by performing customization properly.

Quick Syntax Reference

Here are the syntax rules that are provided by the Textile markup language:

Block rules		List rules	
p.	Starts a paragraph	#	Numbered list item
h1.	First-level heading	##	Nested numbered list item
h2.	Second-level heading	*	Bulleted list item
h3.	Third-level heading	**	Nested bulleted list item
h4.	Fourth-level heading	#*	Nested mixed list item
h5.	Fifth-level heading	**Phrase rules**	
h6.	Sixth-level heading	*...*	Strong text
bq.	Quote block	**...**	Bold text
>	Quote	??...??	Citation
>>	Second-level quote	+...+	Inserted text
fn**N**. ...	Footnote text (see also [N])	-...-	Removed text

Inline rules		_···_	Emphasized text
`...[N]`	Footnote index	`_ _···_ _`	Italicized text
`ABC(...)`	Acronym	`^...^`	Superscript
Textile links		`~...~`	Subscript
`http://...`	HTTP link	**Image rule**	
`www....`	HTTP link	`!url!`	Image
`ftp://...`	FTP link	`!url(title)!`	Image with title
`mailto:...`	Email link	`!url!:http://...`	Image link
`"text":http://...`	Link with anchor	**Code**	
`"text(...)":http://...`	Link with title	`@...@`	Inline code
Tables		`<code>...</code>`	Inline code
`| ...	... |`	Cells	`<pre>...</pre>`	Code block
`|_. ... |_. ... |`	Heading cells	`<code class="lang">...</code>`	
`|\N. ... |`	Cell merged horizontally	`<pre><code class="lang">` `...` `</code></pre>`	
`|/N. ... |`	Cell merged vertically	`!rule`	Disabling rule
Horizontal line markers		**Disabling formatting**	
`---` or `***` or `_ _ _`		`<notextile>...</notextile>`	

The syntax rules that are provided by Redmine itself are the following:

Wiki links		Issue links	
`[[...]]`	Link to a Wiki page	`#N`	Link to an issue
`[[...#section]]`	Link to a section	`#N-X`	Link to a note
`[[...|text]]`	Link with an anchor	`#N#note-X`	Link to a note

`[[project:...]]`	Link to another project	**Repository links**	
`[[project:...#section|text]]`		`rN`	Link to a revision
Version links		`commit:id`	Link to a revision
`version#N`	Link by ID	`source:path`	Link to a file
`version:...`	Link by name	`source:path@rev`	Link to a file in revision
`project:version:...`	Link to another project	`source:path#LN`	Link to a line
Attachment links		`source:path@rev#LN`	Link to a line in a revision
`attachment:file`	Link to an attachment	`export:path`	File download
Project links		`repo|rN`	Link to a revision
`project:project`	Link to a project	`commit:repo|id`	Link to a revision
`project:"..."`	Link by name	`source:"repo|path"`	Link to a file
News links		`export:repo|path`	File download
`news#N`	Link by ID	`project:rN`	Revision in a project
`news:"..."`	Link by title	`project:commit:id`	Revision in a project
`project:news:"..."`	Link to another project	`project:source:path`	File in a project
Forum links		`project:export:path`	Download from a project
`forum#N`	Link by ID	**Document links**	
`forum:"..."`	Link by name	`document#N`	Link by ID
`message#N`	Link by ID	`document:"..."`	Link by title
`project:forum:"..."`	Link to another project	`project:document:"..."`	Link to another project
Macros			
`{{toc}}`	Table of contents	`{{collapse(hint)` `...` `}}`	Collapsed block
`{{thumbnail(image.png)}}`			
`{{thumbnail(image.png, size=100)}}`		`{{child_pages(page)}}`	Child pages index
`{{thumbnail(image.png, title=...)}}`		`{{child_pages(depth=N)}}`	
`{{include(page)}}`	Include a Wiki page	`{{child_pages(parent=1)}}`	

`{{include(project:page)}}`	`{{macro_list}}`	List of macros

The following are advanced style options that are provided by the Textile markup language:

Advanced options (used inside syntax rules)			
Alignment		**Padding**	
`<`	Align to left	`(`	Left padding
`=`	Align centrally	`)`	Right padding
`<>`	Justify	`(())`	Both paddings
`>`	Align to right	**CSS**	
`^`	Align to top	`(css classes)`	CSS class names
`-`	Align to middle	`{css-rule}`	CSS style rules
`~`	Align to bottom	`[lang]`	Language
Special rules (intended for the use of advanced options)			
`%options...%`	Phrase options	`table<options>.`	Table options

Finally, here are the syntax rules that are provided by the Markdown markup language:

Block rules		List rules	
`#`	First-level heading	`1.`	Numbered list item
`##`	Second-level heading	`1.`	Nested numbered list item
`###`	Third-level heading	`*`	Bulleted list item
`####`	Fourth-level heading	`*`	Nested bulleted list item
`#####`	Fifth-level heading	**Phrase rules**	
`######`	Sixth-level heading	`**...**`	Strong text
`>`	Quote	`~~...~~`	Removed text
`>>`	Second-level quote	`*...*`	Emphasized text
Footnotes		`^...`	Superscript
`[^X]: ...`	Footnote text	`***...***`	Strong emphasize text
`[^X]`	Inline footnote index	**Image rule**	

Markdown links		`![] (url)`	Image
`http://...`	HTTP link	`![title] (url)`	Image with title
www....	HTTP link	**Code**	
`ftp://...`	FTP link	`` `...` ``	Inline code
`user@host`	Email link	`~~~ lang`	
`[text] (http://...)`	Link with anchor	`...`	
Tables		`~~~`	
`| ... | ...|`	Cells	**Table column alignment**	
`|---|---|`	Line between heading and body	`|:---|`	Align to the left
Horizontal line marker		`|:---:|`	Align centrally
`---`		`|---:|`	Align to the right

Index

callbacks 327
Child pages macro 201
code
 syntax 195-197
Collapse macro 200
commit messages
 time, tracking through 244, 245
commits
 fetching 80, 81
Computed Custom Field plugin
 about 313
 URL 313
configuration options, issue tracking
 issue tracking module 115
 issue tracking tab 116-119
 Repositories tab 119-121
configuration.yml file 64
cron
 using 81
custom field formats
 about 313
 Boolean format 314
 Date format 314
 Float format 315
 Integer format 315
 Key/value list format 315, 316
 Link format 316
 List format 317
 Long text format 317
 Text format 318
 User format 318
 Version format 318, 319
custom field options
 about 310
 Editable option 311
 For all projects option 311
 Required option 311
 Searchable option 313
 Used as a filter option 312
 Visible option 313
custom fields
 about 306
 creating 307-310
 properties 308
customization
 about 305

with plugin 324
with Textile 321
customized objects 319
customized objects, custom fields
 activities (time tracking) 320
 document categories 321
 documents 320
 groups 320
 issue priorities 320
 issues 319
 projects 319
 spent time 319
 users 320
 versions 320
custom queries
 about 171
 examples 171
 issue list, customizing 107, 108
custom style 204

D

database
 configuring 37
 setting up 41
dependencies
 Apache, installing 40
 installing 39, 40
 MySQL server, installing 40
 Passenger, installing 40
Details tab
 used, for viewing time reports 250, 251
Display tab
 about 55, 56
 Default Gravatar image setting 56-58
 Display attachment thumbnails setting 58
 Gravatar user icons setting 56
DMSF plugin
 about 131
 URL 131
Docker
 image, URL 50
 using 49, 50
Docker Machine 50
document links 192
documents
 versus files 132

Documents block
permission options 213
Documents module 130, 131

E

EasyRedmine
URL 46
email integration
about 63
configuration.yml file 64, 65
email delivery 64
email notifications tab 66-68
email retrieval 70
emails, fetching from IMAP/POP3 75-77
emails, forwarding from mail server 73-75
incoming emails, handling 70-72
reminder emails 68, 69
Exception Handler plugin
about 282, 283
URL 283
Extended Fields plugin
about 309
URL 309

F

FastCGI 17
feature development 224
Feature tracker 224
Fields permissions tab 228
files
versus documents 132
Files block
permission options 213, 214
Files module 132
Files tab 59, 60
footnote 184
forum links 192, 193
Forums block
permission options 212, 213
Forums module 144-147

G

Gantt block
permission options 214
Gantt module 149, 150

general settings
about 53
API tab 58, 59
Display tab 55
Files tab 59, 60
General tab 54
General tab
about 54
cache formatted text setting 54
settings, tips 55
Git Hosting plugin
about 287-293
URL 293
GitHub
about 276
plugins, searching 276-279
GitHub Hook plugin
URL 83
Git repository 139
global configuration 151-153
Globally Recognized AVATAR (Gravatar)
about 56, 254
URL, for signing up 254
using 255-257

H

headings 182
Hello world macro 202
Highrise theme
about 302
URL 302
hooks
about 81-83, 327
URL 329
using 327, 328
Hooks Manager plugin
about 328
URL 328

I

icons
using 322
ICS Export plugin
about 149
URL 149

text formatting 176, 177
Textile
    advanced style options 334
    advanced syntax 202
    advanced table syntax 205
    alignment options 203
    custom style 204
    element, disabling 204
    icons, using 322
    language 204
    padding options 203
    styled boxes, creating 322
    syntax rules 331, 332
    table-based layout, creating 322
    used, for customization 321
    versus Markdown 12, 13
Textile span 204
themes
    A1 theme 301
    about 298
    Basecamp theme 299
    customizing 323
    Highrise theme 302
    installing 298
    Modula Mojito theme 300
    reference link 329
    reviewing 299
    uninstalling 298
Thumbnail macro 200, 201
time entries
    tracking 248
time reports
    about 248-250
    Details tab 250, 251
    Report tab 251, 252
Timesheet plugin
    about 252
    URL 252
Time Tracker plugin
    about 244
    URL 244
time tracking
    about 238
    activities, managing 238-240
    benefits 238
    spent time, checking 245

Time tracking block
    permission options 218
topics 144
trackers 222
Trackers page 222-224
troubleshooting 88-92
TurnKey Redmine appliance
    URL 48
    using 48

U

updates
    obtaining, via mail notifications 262-264
    obtaining, via news feeds 265
    obtaining, via Watch link 264
Use Gravatar user icons setting 56
user/group synchronization
    reference link 269

V

version links 190
Version page 126, 127
Versions tab 164-167
view files
    customizing 326

W

web server
    selecting 16-18
web service (WS) 73
What You See Is What You Get
        (WYSIWYG) editor 177
Wiki block
    permission options 219, 220
Wiki Extensions plugin
    about 138, 321
    URL 138
Wiki links 189
Wiki module 133-137
Wiki page
    creating 135
Wiki syntax
    about 180
    basics 180-185

www.ingramcontent.com/pod-product-compliance
Lightning Source LLC
Chambersburg PA
CBHW062051050326
40690CB00016B/3060

* 9 7 8 1 7 8 5 8 8 1 3 0 5 *